Cooking for Consciousness

Whole Food Recipes
for the Vegetarian Kitchen

Joy McClure and Kendall Layne

NUCLEUS Publications
3223 County Rd. 1670
Willow Springs, MO 65793

Cooking for Consciousness
Whole Food Recipes for the Vegetarian Kitchen
by Joy McClure and Kendall Layne

Illustrations and book design by Michael B. McClure

Revised Second Edition. First Edition published by Ananda Marga Publications.

Published by NUCLEUS Publications, 3223 County Rd. 1670, Willow Springs, MO 65793. (800) 762-6595. **Call or write for a free catalog.**

Library of Congress Cataloging in Publication Data

McClure, Joy and Kendall Layne
   Cooking for consciousness: whole food recipes for the vegetarian kitchen / Joy McClure and Kendall Layne.
      p. cm.
      Includes index.
      ISBN 0-945934-12-2 : $14.00
      1. Vegetarian cookery. 2. Cookery (Natural foods) I. Layne, Kendall.
   II. Title.
   TX837.M474 1993
   641.5'636--dc20   93-18069
                                                                CIP

DEDICATION

This book is dedicated to our children—Josh, Wynona and Tyler—and to all of the people around the world who are working in the spirit of divine love to bring peace to this planet and to help bring about a healthy human society.

ACKNOWLEDGEMENTS

We want to express our heartfelt appreciation of the many people who have already contributed in some way to the production of *Cooking for Consciousness*. Thanks also to the humble and anonymous medical doctor who pointed out errors in the revised edition's nutrition section and corrected them.

Joy wants to thank her family for their patience and humor as she went back through these recipes and brought them into the 90's. Her daughter, Nona, had many excellent suggestions, and helped with the testing. Son Josh mastered the computer program for the nutritional analysis and crunched all the data. Thanks, kids!

Lastly, but most important of all, our humble thanks to P.R. Sarkar and his hard-working helpers for guiding us on the path of meditation, helping us learn to love unconditionally, and inspiring us to let our energies be utilized in the creation of this book.

This book is the result of a team effort. You can help us to improve the book by sending us your feedback. Mail may be sent in care of the publisher.

Publisher's Acknowledgements

We would like to thank Joy McClure for all her hard work updating the recipes and preparing the information needed to expand and revise this edition of the book, and Kendall Layne for his editing and additions and his input into the look and feel of the new book.

We would especially like to thank all those whose hard work and dedication brought about the first edition—particularly our good friend Jody Wright, without whom this book would not have been published the first time around.

JOY'S PREFACE TO THE REVISED EDITION

Almost twenty years ago, before the age of microwaves, the original version of this cookbook was published. The idea for this cookbook began because I was always being asked for my recipes, so I started writing them down. At that time there were few cookbooks for vegetarians who wanted to eat natural foods.

The original version was written for our son, Josh, who was born the year it was written. Now Josh is in college! Kendall and I have gone our separate ways. He earned his law degree and moved to the suburbs. I moved to the Sierra Nevada foothills and returned to school for a Masters Degree in Social Work. Josh has been joined by two siblings: His father has another son, Tyler, and I have a daughter, Wynona.

As I reread the original cookbook, I realized that I thought I knew a lot. Now I realize I really know very little. As you may imagine, my life has changed in many ways: from raising a baby to teenagers; from part time work to more than full time, etc. Our family's tastes for food have changed as has the amount of time we have to prepare meals. These changes are reflected in this new version. Yet, even with all the changes in our lives, through the years I have remained a vegetarian stumbling along a spiritual path, and this cookbook still contains my favorite recipes!

Remember that no matter how healthy and pure our food, in order that it brings health to our bodies and souls, what matters most is how we feel when we prepare and eat it. Do this in love and peace. Our harmony here on Earth begins within.

Joy

KENDALL'S PREFACE TO THE REVISED EDITION

Here are some notes on the organization and contents of the book:

• The recipes are organized into sections according to the main ingredients (beverages, fruits, vegetables, etc.)

• A comprehensive index is located in the back of the book.

• Each section begins with a detailed Table of Contents to help make the finding of a favorite recipe as easy as possible.

• Sections on basic foods (fruits, vegetables, milk products, etc.) begin with mini-encyclopedias on the purchasing, storage, and preparation of foods in that category.

• All of the recipes in this book have been thoroughly tested. Many of the recipes include suggestions for substitutions or variations.

• The HERBS AND SPICES section includes herb blend recipes that are called for throughout the book.

• The KITCHEN WAYS section discusses various aspects of establishing and working in a natural foods kitchen.

• The CONVERSIONS AND EQUIVALENTS section contains tables of equivalent measures. The abbreviations used in the recipes are also explained.

All the good food in the world is not enough to make even a single person truly healthy and happy. Health and the sense of well-being which accompanies it are the result of attuning oneself to natural laws and living by the principles these laws make clear. This harmonizing of one's life is spiritual in nature. The goal of *Cooking for Consciousness* is to help us all to become more in tune with these natural precepts and begin to relate them to our eating habits.

Whether you are interested in meditation or not, this book is designed to help you eat well for good health.

In the pages that follow, you will find recipes for a wide assortment of dishes (some old favorites, and some new treats) which supply, in an appetizing and easily digestible form, all the nutrients known to be beneficial. When these nutrients are provided, together with adequate amounts of sunshine, fresh air, and pure water, the body can grow, do work, resist disease, repair itself, and carry on the multitude of activities necessary to provide a home for that mysterious thing we call consciousness. Physical health and emotional and mental well-being are the foundations of a satisfying and beautiful life. Spiritual growth and service to humanity are the culmination of that life, and the fullest expression of human potential. We offer this book in the hope that it will help each person establish the harmonious base of health and happiness from which selfless service can flow.

Bon appetit!

Kendall Layne

TABLE OF CONTENTS

INTRODUCTION

Preparing good tasting, nutritious natural food is easy and fun. All you need are a few basic skills, the right ingredients, and a little bit of time. In order to help you discover your own unique way of cooking, we have gathered some of the recipes and techniques which have evolved in our kitchens and compiled information about food, nutrition, herbs and many other topics.

Cooking for Consciousness is based on the practical experience of several natural food cooks. It is designed to introduce the beginning cook to the joy of natural food cookery as well as to provide the experienced cook with new and interesting approaches to the preparation of healthful, delicious foods.

An attempt has been made to present both the recipes and the general information in a form that encourages and assists exploration and experimentation. We have also provided information of general interest to those learning how to purchase, prepare, and enjoy natural foods. For working parents and otherwise busy cooks, we have included information on freezing and other methods of preparing foods ahead of time.

In the discussion of nutrition we have tried to limit ourselves to providing information that can be used by each individual in his or her personal decisions about food. However, the general focus and tone of the book does reflect the attitudes and beliefs of the authors. Pure and simple natural foods, love, and nutritionally sound methods of preparation are emphasized throughout the book.

The first edition of this book was published in 1976. Although much has changed in the world since then and natural foods can now be found nationwide at chain grocery stores, the food groups, basic nutrition information and preparation techniques remain about the same today. The first generation raised on this cookbook has entered college, but the authors and many others around the world still reach for this book when it's time to cook.

FOOD AND CONSCIOUSNESS

"There is in the living being a thirst for limitlessness."
—P.R. Sarkar

It is the inborn desire of all human beings to seek an identity beyond our limited selves, to try to find our place in the universe, and to want to experience the harmonious unity of creation. This search is basic to our humanity, and although worldly activities take up much of our time, they can never really satisfy our innermost desires.

The effects of food on the body are fairly well understood. Current scientific theories hold that the physical molecules of the food are utilized by the body to supply energy and the substances necessary for building, repairing, and regulating the various tissues and functions. Improper diet is known to have a negative effect on these processes.

However, the effects of food on the mind are just beginning to be acknowledged here in the West. Many people who have experimented with natural foods and vegetarianism have experienced themselves and the world around them in a different, more positive way as a result of the changes in their diet. Although these phenomena are considered surprising and difficult to explain to many Westerners, Eastern philosophy has a simple explanation for them which parallels some of the most far-reaching theorizing in Western science.

We have learned from Einstein's Theory of Relativity that the entire manifested universe is composed of vibrational energy. Matter can be understood as energy that is moving (or vibrating) slowly. Solids vibrate at the lowest (or slowest) frequencies, liquids and gases a little faster, and sound, light, thoughts and certain other energies vibrate at even higher frequencies. The higher frequencies can penetrate the lower frequencies. Light passes through water, sound travels through air, and in a similar way, the food we eat is permeated with its own subtle vibrations and those it has picked up from the people who have handled it. These subtle vibrations are incorporated into the mind and body of the person eating the food. Some people call this energy that emanates from food *prana* (a Sanskrit word meaning "vital energy"). Prana can be understood as an energy that is similar to electricity but vibrating at much higher frequencies and present in all forms of life. It is said that prana is the animating force of the universe—the divine essence that nourishes us when we breathe and when we eat. Certain foods are known to be good sources of the prana we need to insure our health and well being.

Over the last several thousand years, many spiritual teachers have based their eating habits on the knowledge that different foods have different vibrations or different amounts of prana. Certain foods affect consciousness in a positive way, sharpening and clearing the mind. These foods are called sentient (*sattvik* in Sanskrit) and are the basis of the yoga diet. Foods which stimulate the body and mind are termed mutative (*rajasik* in Sanskrit) and are eaten in moderation or not at all by those performing spiritual practices. Foods which are not normally beneficial to the mind or body are called static (*tamasik* in Sanskrit) and are not normally part of a yoga diet.

We have listed in the following chart some common foods according to the way they are classified by P.R. Sarkar, preceptor of Ananda Marga Yoga. This cookbook primarily includes sentient foods. Some mutative foods are included, since they may be deemed sentient in the context of illness or a particularly cold climate.

FOOD CLASSIFICATION

SENTIENT FOODS

fruits
most vegetables
most beans
grains
milk and milk products
moderate amounts of most herbs and spices

MUTATIVE FOODS

caffeine and foods containing it
other stimulants
medicines prescribed by a doctor
excessive hot spices

STATIC FOODS

meat and poultry
fish and shellfish
eggs
onions and garlic
mushrooms and other fungi
alcoholic beverages
drugs other than medicines
fermented food or that which is stale or
    spoiled

Note: Under certain conditions such as illness and/or extremes of climate, some mutative and static foods may have beneficial properties for the body.

For those following this diet, it is clear that what we eat has a definite effect on our minds, bodies and spiritual practices. Conversely, the spiritual practices we do also affect how food is absorbed and used by our bodies. Meditation and yoga postures can relax the body, reduce the heart rate, balance hormonal secretions, and help restore our bodies to their natural state of glowing health. By practicing yoga and eating sentient foods, we purify our bodies. As our bodies become more refined, we find that it is easier to calm and purify our minds through meditation.

Many years ago, under the direction of a teacher trained in India by an organization called Ananda Marga (Sanskrit for "the path of bliss"), the authors of this book began to follow the spiritual practices developed by P.R. Sarkar. Through meditation we have begun to experience for ourselves the Infinite Divinity or consciousness at the core of our own beings. Ananda Marga is not the only spiritual path to inner knowledge and peace. As the Buddha is reported to have said, "There are many paths up the mountain, but the view from the top is the same for all." We have found our way, and trust that you will find your way as well. Ananda Marga Yoga was the impetus for this cookbook and the focus of our lives. Through spiritual practices, we have begun to find an identity beyond our limited selves and to experience the harmonious unity of all creation. In the sense that the food we eat is one aspect of a spiritual path, we offer these recipes to you.

Books about Ananda Marga Yoga:

- *Some Still Want the Moon: A Woman's Introduction to Tantra Yoga*
  by Vimala McClure

- *Beyond the Superconscious Mind*
  by Ananda Mitra

- *The Ethics of Love: Using Yoga's Timeless Wisdom to Heal Yourself, Others and the Earth*
  by Vimala McClure

These and other titles are available from NUCLEUS Publications. They will send you a free catalog:

NUCLEUS Publications
3223 County Rd. 1670
Willow Springs MO 65793
800-762-6595

ABOUT THE NUTRITIONAL ANALYSIS

The nutritional analyses which are included in this book were computed using a MacDine® computer program on a Macintosh computer. Unfortunately, the MacDine® database does not have all the foods which are used in these recipes. Therefore, we occasionally had to substitute similar ingredients, such as chopped dry dates for date sugar or cracked wheat for wheatberries. Unless noted otherwise in the recipe ingredient list, analyses were computed using 2% milk, lowfat yogurt, salted butter, and safflower oil. If a recipe calls for a range of quantities for an ingredient such as 2 to 4 T oil, the nutritional analysis was done for the first amount listed.

Unless otherwise noted, the nutritional analysis has been done for one serving of the recipe.

Recipes have not had a nutritional analysis included if there were too many ingredients not in the MacDine® database or if the cooking process would significantly alter the nutritional content, such as in some canned foods.

The nutritional analyses were made with the most accurate information available to us, and although they are probably not 100% accurate, they are useful guidelines for us and we hope they will be for you.

ABOUT PREPARATION TIMES

Preparation time includes setting up and cleaning up in a reasonably well organized kitchen with few interruptions. Doubling recipes will usually add to preparation time. If there is a cooking period in the middle of the preparation, it is included in the preparation time. If it is baked or cooked (i.e., cookies, cakes, casseroles) after preparing, the baking or cooking time is not included in the preparation time. Of course, using already prepared foods (such as pre-grated cheese) or a food processor shortens the preparation time considerably.

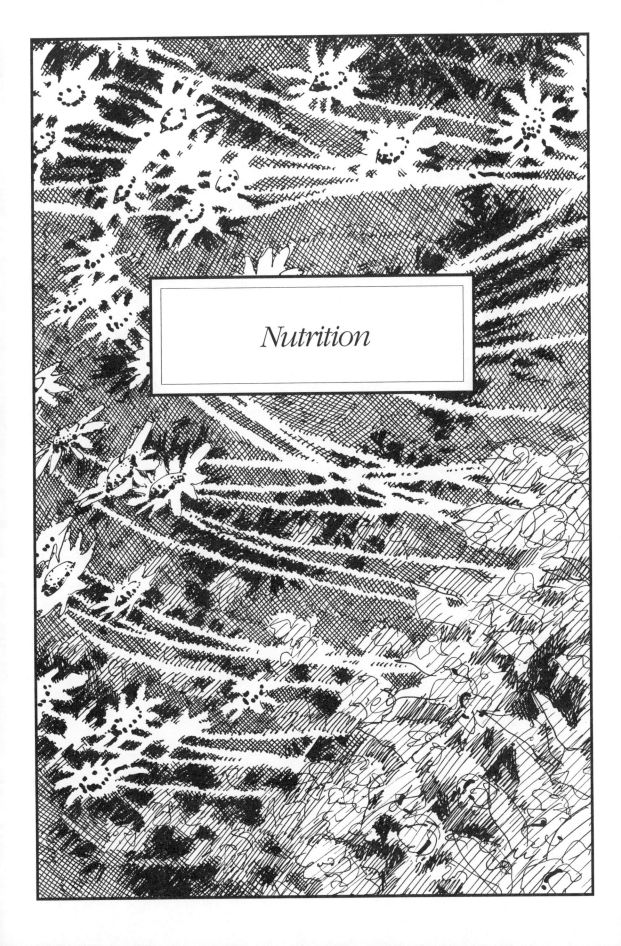

Nutrition

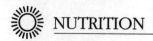
NUTRITION

We owe it to ourselves to provide our bodies with pure, healthful foods containing all the nutrients needed to maintain a state of glowing health. It is said that when the mind has been purified by meditation and the body has been purified by proper diet and practice of yoga postures, such perfect harmony can be established between mind and body that one knows intuitively what to eat, and the intellect is not needed to select the proper foods. For those (including ourselves) who still need to think about the foods they eat, we have collected some information about the needs of our bodies and how they can be met.

The research we have done has led us to three general conclusions:

1) We all need certain substances, called nutrients, to establish and maintain our health. When any of these substances are not provided in the necessary amounts or combinations in the diet, health is imperfect. Although the resultant physical and psychological manifestations may not always appear to be related to diet, it is increasingly clear that many illnesses can be linked to improper diet.

2) The typical American diet is not the best diet that can be imagined. Many beneficial substances are processed out of our foods, and many strange manufactured things, which might fairly be labelled garbage, are represented to the consumer as food.

3) The elimination of overprocessed, chemically treated foods from one's diet and eating primarily organically-grown natural foods can result in a noticeable improvement in health.

Health is more than just the ability to plod through the day and perform one's tasks: we understand the term to mean a sense of well-being and satisfaction with life, as well as the absence of disease. In order to enjoy good health, we need to supply our systems with all the necessary nutrients, and from this standpoint, all are equally important. However, we begin our discussion of nutrition in a conventional way—by talking about protein.

PROTEIN

Protein is often referred to as the "building material" of the body. This is an accurate and literal description. Most of our body tissues are formed from protein. Proteins are also very important in enzyme systems, antibodies, and disease fighting white blood cells. Vegetarians obtain protein primarily from milk products, soy and other beans, nuts, seeds, and grains. Proteins are constructed from smaller molecules known as amino acids. When protein is ingested, it is broken down into its constituent amino acids, which are then utilized individually or re-assembled into the various types of protein the body needs. There are about 22 amino acids, of which all but eight so-called "essential amino acids" (EAAs) can normally be synthesized in the body. If one of these eight amino acids is missing, the others cannot be utilized. It is therefore advisable to eat all eight essential amino acids at the same meal, as the body apparently will not store the leftovers. The essential amino acids must also be present in certain proportions to each other (eggs most closely approximate this proportion, and milk is next best). If the optimum portion of even one is not present, the excess of the other amino acids cannot be utilized. Foods or food combinations providing all the essential amino acids are said to contain complete protein. The more closely the composition of the protein resembles the optimum configuration of amino acids, the higher its biological value is said to be.

The Net Protein Utilization value (NPU) is arrived at by multiplying the biological value by the percentage of the protein which is digestible. Presumably, the digestibility of a protein is a function not only of its intrinsic properties, but also the circumstances under which it is eaten. There is significant variation in the efficiency of different people's digestive systems; even a given individual will sometimes be more or less able to digest a certain protein.

At this point, we want to lay to rest a common semantic misconception about the term "complete protein." Most proteins are complete, in that the 8 EAAs are all present. What varies is the percentage of the protein which is complete. It is a gross oversimplification to state, as many nutrition texts do, that complete proteins are of animal origin, and incomplete proteins are those of plant origin. Protein quality varies across a whole spectrum, from those with low biological and/or NPU values to those with high values on those scales. Any rational comparison of protein quality, given our present knowledge, should at least begin by referring to biological or NPU values.

The other thing to consider in determining whether a food is a good protein source is the percentage of the food which is protein. For example, brown rice, with an NPU of 60-70 (depending on which protein standard it is compared to, data from USDA Home Economics research Report No. 4, "Amino Acid Contents of Foods"), looks like a good protein source at first glance. However, since only 7.5% (Composition of Foods, and USDA Handbook #8) of the brown rice is protein, one would have to eat quite a bit of it in order to obtain even the minimum recommended amount of protein (almost a pound and a half of dry rice to obtain 30 grams of complete protein!). Soybeans, on the other hand, have a somewhat lower NPU of 55-62 but contain a much greater percentage of protein (34%). Less than half a pound (6-7 ounces) of dry soybeans will provide 30 grams of complete protein. Other legumes and grains on which data is available are less valuable protein sources

than soybeans or wheat, respectively. Nuts and seeds generally supply more complete protein per given serving size than grains and legumes; however, nuts are generally not eaten in as large a quantity as grains or legumes. See the NUTS AND SEEDS section for a chart (p. 216) showing the grams of complete protein in these foods.

The quantity of protein which an individual needs to ingest each day depends on that person's age, activity level, metabolic condition, and other factors. One internationally accepted technique for figuring average protein requirements suggests that average normal adults need around 30 grams per day of average quality protein. This amount might vary by 20 to 50% depending on circumstances. We suggest trying 30 grams a day, making adjustments if you feel that they are necessary.

CARBOHYDRATES

Carbohydrates are one of the main dietary sources of fuel. Because of their natural abundance (and therefore relatively low cost), they form the major part (excepting water) of most human diets. Carbohydrates are a dietary essential. A minimum intake of approximately 100 grams of carbohydrate per day is advisable. The carbohydrate plays a vital role in a crucial set of metabolic reactions which produces energy from fats, carbohydrates, and proteins. If insufficient carbohydrate is present in the diet, this set of reactions (called the Krebs cycle) gets discombobulated, and the fats are converted into ketone bodies. The ketone bodies accumulate, creating a condition known as ketosis, which can lead to death. This is why very low carbohydrate diets are dangerous unless closely supervised by a physician.

The term carbohydrates covers all the various sugars available in food, as well as starch. Both the simple sugars and the more complex starch molecules are made from carbon, hydrogen and oxygen. Carbohydrates are "built" in green plants by a process called photosynthesis. Carbon dioxide and water are combined in the presence of chlorophyll, utilizing the energy of the sun. When carbohydrates are digested, releasing CO_2, H_2O, and energy, it is the energy from the sun that is liberated for use in the body. Carbohydrates are classified on the basis of their molecular structure. The MONO (one) SACCHARIDES (sugars) are the basic unit.

GLUCOSE is the monosaccharide which is found in human blood. It is also referred to as dextrose because polarized light passed through the molecule rotates to the right. Some free glucose is found in grapes and in honey.

FRUCTOSE is also known as levulose, because it rotates polarized light to the left. Fruits, Jerusalem artichokes, and honey all contain fructose.

GALACTOSE has not been found alone in any foods yet. It occurs as part of a more complex sugar in milk.

These three monosaccharides are the most common and important basic sugars utilized by humans. Generally, they are ingested as part of larger molecules called DI (double) SACCHARIDES or POLY (multiple) SACCHARIDES. When two monosaccharides combine to form a disaccharide, one molecule of water is removed. Hence, during the digestion of disaccharides, some water is used to restore the molecules to their original form. (This process is called hydrolyzing.)

The three disaccharides involved in human nutrition are SUCROSE, LACTOSE, and MALTOSE. Sucrose is by far the most common, occurring in table sugar, fruits, and vegetables. Sucrose is formed from one molecule of glucose and one molecule of fructose. Lactose is formed from one molecule of glucose and one of galactose. Lactose is commonly called milk sugar, since milk is the only food in which it is found. Lactose which is not absorbed is converted to lactic acid in the intestine. Maltose, a double glucose molecule, occurs in germinating grains, as result of the breakdown of the starch molecules. This process helps make sprouted grains very easy to digest. Maltose is also the building block of starch molecules.

Glucose is absorbed into cells by active transport from the blood stream, and it provides "quick energy." The rate of transport of glucose into cells is regulated by insulin, a hormone secreted by the pancreas. The pancreas is stimulated to release insulin, which causes glucose to enter cells to be used for energy or stored as glycogen in the liver and muscles. In hypoglycemia, the insulin reaction is an "over-reaction," and the result is blood sugar levels below the approximately 60 mg./100 ml. of blood necessary to maintain normal metabolism. Hyperglycemia (diabetes) is the failure of the insulin reaction to hold blood sugar levels below approximately 100 mg./100 ml.

Glucose and galactose are absorbed at roughly equal rates. Fructose is absorbed by passive diffusion, at less than one-third the rate of glucose and galactose. Fructose is not regulated by insulin and does not stimulate the release of insulin. Also, fructose has over twice the sweetening power of glucose, and therefore satisfies a given level of "sweetness desire" with far fewer calories than glucose or galactose. Some people feel that this boils down to a logical reason to choose honey over refined sugar, because the proportion of fructose/glucose is higher in honey than it is in refined sugar. However, it's not that simple. Sucrose (table sugar) is absorbed at a rate in between that of glucose and fructose (the constituents of honey). The experience of many people is that white sugar gives a "rush and a letdown." Whether this is likely for biochemical reasons has not been completely established, as far as we know. There are many other arguments against the use of white sugar (and even some against the use of honey). Just to mention a few (and reveal our bias):

1) Refined sugar is sometimes filtered through charred beef bones. All sugar cane projects sold in California, and possibly other states, must by law be made with refined sugar. Brown sugar is refined sugar plus molasses.

2) Honey contains some trace minerals, vitamins and enzymes—sugar does not. Generally, sugar is an agribusiness product and honey is produced locally by bee keepers.

Recipes in this book call for honey, barley malt syrup (made from sprouted barley and sometimes corn), date particles or date sugar (more refined than date particles), and occasionally molasses. Molasses does contain trace minerals (unlike refined sugar), and although the method of its production is somewhat less acceptable than that of honey, molasses does impart a distinctive flavor which is desirable in some dishes.

POLYSACCHARIDES are long chains of mono-saccharide molecules. Their digestion is somewhat more complex than the digestion of simple sugars.

DEXTRIN is a slightly soluble intermediate-length carbohydrate molecule which is produced from starch during digestion or by dry heat (toasting bread, browning flour or whole grains, etc.). Dextrin is sweeter and easier to digest than the more complex starches from which it is made.

CELLULOSE, the most common polysaccharide on the planet, is not digestible by humans. It provides the fibrous bulk which is essential for proper elimination of solid waste.

VITAMINS

Vitamins are important substances which are necessary for the body's proper functioning. They are used in minute quantities and do not provide energy or serve as building units per se, but rather act in the regulation of metabolic processes. For example, they may function as co-enzymes or hormones, which catalyze and direct the chemical processes which underlie the functioning of our body.

VITAMIN C is contained in almost all raw, fresh fruits and vegetables, especially citrus fruits, bell peppers, fresh tomato juice, raw cabbage, broccoli, rosehips, sprouts and fresh strawberries. Ascorbic acid and sodium ascorbate (vitamin C) are highly soluble in water and easily destroyed by heat, oxygen and light.

The connective tissue which holds cells together and forms the ligaments, cartilage, and the walls of blood vessels cannot be formed without vitamin C. In children, teeth formed during a deficiency of vitamin C decay easily. Vitamin C concentrates in the lens of the eye and plays a role in vision which is not yet completely understood. Ascorbic acid apparently facilitates the absorption and utilization of other nutrients, particularly calcium, iron, and some B vitamins. It aids in the healing of wounds and may help keep blood cholesterol levels low. Perhaps the most important role of vitamin C is as a detoxifier in the blood stream—it participates in (and is destroyed by) reactions eliminating foreign substances from the blood. These foreign substances may be disease-producing agents, toxic wastes from improper digestion, or the end products of sugar metabolism (especially lactic acid), which cause fatigue.

An adequate supply of vitamin C may be obtained from a proper diet, but there are a growing number of people who advocate supplemental vitamin C (in tablet or powder form) as a regular part of the diet. Some people believe that natural vitamin C (derived from rosehips or similar sources) is somehow more valuable than synthetic ascorbic acid. There is no hard experimental evidence to support this belief. Bioflavinoids and other substances which are generally associated with naturally occurring vitamin C may have as-yet-unproven value. However, the percentage of vitamin C in rosehips is low enough that probably even "natural vitamin C" tablets contain synthetic ascorbic acid to supplement the rosehips. Usually, the most economical way to purchase ascorbic acid or sodium ascorbate is in crystalline granules. The granules can be dissolved in juice or other liquids. Also, since this form does not include buffers, there is less danger of adverse reactions from high doses. Currently, there is a controversy in scientific circles as to whether high doses of vitamin C can cause trouble in the body.

The B VITAMINS are closely related compounds that are often found together in foods. The best vegetarian sources are leafy green vegetables, whole grains, nutritional yeast, wheat germ, rice polish, and sprouts. Most Americans eat sparingly, if at all, of most of these foods, and thanks in part to modern methods of processing wheat and rice, vitamin B deficiency is perhaps more common than it should be. We have not taken the space to discuss the B vitamins separately, as they function together and are usually obtained together as well. The B complex is involved in dozens of vital body functions, including growth, energy metabolism, the formation of the sheath of nerve cells, proper kidney functioning, and the production of nucleic acids. The most common symptoms of deficiency include irritability, inefficiency, depression, mental sluggishness, fatigue, apprehension, confusion, worry, instability, moodiness, bad breath, canker sores and "trench mouth." If you are never inappropriately tired, or irritable, if your tongue is not swollen, is an even pink in color, and shows no grooves, fissure, indentations, etc., then you are probably getting enough B vitamins.

Pregnant women usually benefit from moderate B-6 supplementation (as well as more protein and all other nutrients). People who do not take milk products or eat eggs or flesh very definitely need to take supplemental B-12, as it occurs almost exclusively in animal products. Vitamin B-12 is known to be extremely important in the prevention of pernicious anemia, a disease which may reach a dangerous point before being noticed. If you decide to take vitamin B tablets, be aware that the B vitamins work "synergistically"; that is, increasing the supply of one generally increases the need for the others. Therefore, it is probably important to take all the B vitamins in the proper proportions if you take any.

Nutritional yeast contains a balance of B vitamins which comes close to the proportions found in the human body. It may be taken as a B vitamin supplement when needed to restore health. Many people find that mixing a tablespoon or two into orange juice or milk is the easiest way to take the yeast. There is at least one brand which actually disperses fairly well in the liquid and tastes reasonably good. Most B vitamins are water soluble and must be taken each day for effective supplementation. Some B vitamins are destroyed by heat, light, or oxygen, while others are relatively stable.

Even if you are not eating many B vitamins, your intestinal bacteria are (hopefully) synthesizing them for you. Eating cultured milk products such as yogurt, buttermilk, or kefir will help you maintain a population of these beneficial bacteria. If for some reason you must take antibiotics, afterwards you can eat yogurt to help re-establish the intestinal bacteria, or perhaps take a vitamin B supplement for a while.

VITAMIN A is made in the body from carotenoid compounds, which are found in (among other things) fresh and dried apricots, whole milk, sweet potatoes, carrots, broccoli, mangoes, and all green vegetables (the quantity increasing with the intensity of the yellow or green color). Vitamin A is involved in the formation of "visual purple", a substance which is broken down in the process of vision. A deficiency of vitamin A manifests in poor night vision (day vision has an additional mechanism not dependent on vitamin A). Test yourself by seeing how rapidly you recover normal vision after being blinded by oncoming headlights at night. Other symptoms of a deficiency are acne or roughness of skin (especially on elbows and knees). Whiteheads and blackheads may occur as a result of cells dying and clogging the pores. The same process takes place internally, and the mucous that covers and protects the internal organs may become clogged with dead cells, reducing one's resistance to infection.

From raw carrots, the body apparently absorbs only 1% of the carotene; from cooked carrots, about 20%; and from carrot juice, almost all of the carotene—provided the juice is drunk immediately after juicing, before the carotene is oxidized.

Vitamin A is fairly stable, except that it is easily oxidized. It is fat soluble rather than water soluble. Vitamin A is stored in the liver. In the average American diet, roughly one-fourth of the vitamin A is supplied by flesh and eggs. Presumably the increased consumption of dairy products, fruits and vegetables by vegetarians compensates for this reduction in vitamin A intake. There is evidence that the nitrates in chemical fertilizers destroy carotenoid compounds. Excessive vitamin A can be toxic. Symptoms of vitamin A toxicity (which generally manifest three to fifteen months after the beginning of high doses) include loss of hair, weight loss (in infants), cessation of menstruation, and rapid resorption of bone. Toxicity is produced only by preformed vitamin A derived from animal products (most supplements). Symptoms usually disappear soon after the high doses (50,000 I.U. or more a day) are discontinued.

VITAMIN D is involved in the absorption of calcium, and is therefore an important factor in bone formation and the maintenance of the blood calcium level.

Vitamin D can be formed on the skin during certain periods of clear days, when ultraviolet ray penetration is at its maximum level. Window glass, smoke, clothing and skin pigmentation all screen out ultraviolet light, thereby inhibiting vitamin D formation. Because it is difficult to obtain much vitamin D through natural irradiation, milk and other foods are commonly fortified with vitamin D. This has helped reduce the incidence of rickets.

VITAMIN E is found in the oils of grains, nuts, and seeds. Generally the vitamin E content of food is proportional to the amount of polyunsaturated fat. Vitamin E is stable to heat but oxidizes very rapidly. Its function includes the prevention of the oxidation of unsaturated fatty acids, vitamin A and certain hormones. If there is adequate vitamin E, it

concentrates in the pituitary gland, and is necessary for the proper functioning of that organ. Before the introduction of modern milling methods, we used to get about 150 mg of vitamin E per day. Now most Americans get 8 mg a day. Vitamin E may also help the liver detoxify harmful substances such as preservatives, bleaches used in flour, pesticide residues, nitrates and nitrites from fertilizers, etc.

VITAMIN K is important in blood clotting. It is produced by intestinal bacteria. Since newborn babies are not yet producing vitamin K, it is generally given by injection at birth in developed countries.

LIPIDS (fats and oils) are important in the diet for several reasons. First, they provide a lot of calories and energy, even when taken in small portions. This is especially important in cold climates and for people doing heavy physical work. Secondly, since the fats leave the stomach slowly, they contribute to a feeling of satisfaction after a meal, and prolong the interval before hunger is felt again. This is particularly important for people who are overweight, in controlling overeating. Fats aid in the assimilation of the fat-soluble vitamins A, D, E, and K. Most importantly, lipids provide linoleic acid, an essential fatty acid. The best sources of linoleic acid are unrefined vegetable oils, especially those derived from corn, soybeans, and safflower seed.

Lipids may be divided into two groups—those which contain mostly unsaturated fatty acids, and those which contain mostly fatty acids whose available bonding sites are saturated with hydrogen molecules. Saturated fats tend to be solid at room temperature, and unsaturated fats tend to be liquid at the room temperature. Unsaturated fatty acids are more soluble and more digestible than saturated fatty acids. In America, there is a high correlation between diets which contain a lot of saturated fat and high blood cholesterol levels, which increases the likelihood of atherosclerosis (hardening and narrowing of the arteries). If you don't feel like giving up butter, we suggest that you switch to BUTTER-OIL SPREAD (p.153), which contains many more nutrients than plain butter.

Natural vegetable oils, in addition to supplying vitamin E, are an excellent source of **ESSENTIAL FATTY ACIDS**. The symptoms of a deficiency of essential fatty acids include dry hair, dry scaly skin, and tendency to be overweight due to excessive retention of water. In fact, eating too little fat is a common cause of overweight, both because of water retention and because the body changes sugar to fat rapidly to try to supply the missing nutrients—this lowers the blood sugar and produces hunger. Fats are necessary for the proper functioning of the gall bladder, and this organ must function properly to absorb vitamins—so a fat deficiency can produce vitamin deficiencies.

Many nutritionists advise that some natural, unrefined, cold-pressed oil be eaten every day. The recommended tablespoon or two per day can easily be obtained by eating salad dressing or using BUTTER-OIL SPREAD (p.153) in place of butter.

CHOLESTEROL is a lipid that is present in all animal fats. Some cholesterol is needed for normal metabolism. However, excessive dietary cholesterol intake is commonly associated with excessive serum cholesterol levels, which are currently thought to be correlated with the incidence of certain types of vascular disease. Cholesterol is also produced by the liver, so dietary cholesterol is not the only determinant of serum cholesterol levels.

MINERALS

MINERALS perform many important functions in the body. They help maintain the internal pH balance, serve as catalysts in many different biochemical reactions, maintain water balance in various tissues, participate in the transmission of nerve impulses, and play a part in building certain tissues.

CALCIUM is needed to form the bones and connective tissues. Persons with low blood calcium levels may be irritable. Radical deficiencies can result in rickets, osteoporosis, or osteomalacia. Normally, the blood calcium level will be maintained at the expense of body tissues, so the whole body is affected in cases of deficiency.

Calcium is involved in many biological reactions, including muscle contraction and absorption of B-12. The person who does not eat milk products needs to be very careful to obtain enough calcium. Common vegetarian sources of calcium include milk products, almonds, collard and turnip greens, beans, sunflower seeds, dried figs and broccoli. Americans consume more calcium than the world average. Although there may be negative results from this habit, high calcium intake tends to limit absorption and storage of radioactive strontium 90, a deadly poison present in our world in minute quantities.

PHOSPHORUS is used in ATP and ADP, two chemicals which form the basis of energy storage and release in the human body, and in the metabolism of calcium. It is found in milk products, nutritional yeast, wheat bran and germ, rice bran and polish, legumes, nuts and seeds.

MAGNESIUM is needed in proportion to the amount of calcium eaten. A deficiency is thought to increase one's susceptibility to cardiovascular diseases. Good sources of magnesium include nuts, soybeans, whole grains and leafy vegetables.

POTASSIUM is concentrated inside the cells of the body. In conjunction with the sodium in the extra-cellular fluids, it is a major factor in maintaining the fluid balance in the body. Potassium and calcium are both involved in muscle relaxation. Potassium occurs in most foods, so usually deficiency is related to excessive salt intake: "Because of the antagonistic relationship between sodium and potassium an excessive intake of sodium may have the same effect as a suboptimal level of potassium." (*Introductory Nutrition,* by Helen Guthrie, 1967). In other words, the

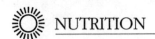

large amount of sodium chloride (table salt) which many people consume may directly contribute to increased muscle tension. Potassium is highly soluble, so take care to use all cooking water.

SULFUR is obtained from the amino acids cystine and methionine. Inorganic sulfur as sulfate is not useful to the body. Sulfur is present in certain body proteins (such as hair, skin, and nails) much more than in other tissues. It is involved in blood clotting, energy transfer, and detoxification of waste products.

MICRONUTRIENT or trace minerals are now thought to be fairly important in human nutrition. Unfortunately, traditional agricultural practices make no particular attempt to replenish the supply of trace minerals in the soil. As a result, our food now contains fewer trace minerals than it once did.

Of the micronutrient minerals, IRON is present in the largest quantities. Iron plays several roles in the blood. It is incorporated into the hemoglobin, which is responsible for transporting oxygen from the lungs to the various parts of the body and carrying carbon dioxide from the tissues back to the lungs for elimination. Prune juice, dried apricots, other dried fruit, legumes, green vegetables and molasses all provide reasonably large amounts of iron. Oats (and to a lesser extent, other whole grains) contain phytic acid, which combines with iron to make an insoluble compound which is useless to the body. Therefore, steady use of oats in the diet is not recommended for those especially needing iron. Iron is water soluble, so it is lost if the cooking water is not consumed. Iron deficiency anemia is a common problem among young children, adolescents and women. A constant supply of iron is needed to produce new hemoglobin cells. Menstruation causes the loss of iron, which is why women have a higher need for iron than adult men, and have a much higher incidence of anemia. Women and growing children should be very careful to obtain enough iron. Symptoms of

iron deficiency include tiredness, headaches, and the tendency to run out of breath easily. A simple blood test can be used to check for deficiency.

IODINE is crucial for the proper functioning of the thyroid gland. It is obtained from unrefined salt, iodized refined salt (which usually contains aluminum silicate to prevent lumping), seaweed, and to a lesser extent from dairy products and vegetables. Rutabagas, turnips, cabbage and nuts all contain substances which interfere with iodine utilization. A high calcium diet may also interfere with iodine absorption.

ZINC is related to insulin production or storage and is necessary for tissue respiration. Zinc is concentrated in the retina of the eye, but its role in vision is not clearly understood. Parsley, peas, whole wheat cereals, oatmeal, corn, peanut butter and milk all supply zinc.

SELENIUM can replace vitamin E in some processes and helps promote normal growth and fertility at low dietary levels. The bran and germ of cereal grains are relatively rich in selenium, if it was present in the soil in which the grain was grown.

MANGANESE is a catalyst to many enzymes and appears to be involved in bone development. Nuts, whole grain cereals and legumes are good sources of manganese.

COPPER is involved in prolonging the life of red blood cells and in maintaining healthy nerve fibers. Good sources include nuts, legumes and whole grains.

Now that you have read this very basic information on nutrients, you are probably beginning to realize that nutrition is a complicated science. If you want to learn more, we suggest you read one of the numerous books devoted exclusively to nutrition.

We have one very simple suggestion which we feel summarizes the nutritional information presented in this section. Eat a balanced diet which includes fresh fruits and vegetables (both yellow and green), high quality protein (from milk products, soy products, and nuts and seeds), essential fatty acids, and, if necessary to supplement caloric intake, additional carbohydrates (fruits supply some). If you have the time and energy to analyze your diet and tabulate exact amounts of specific nutrients, you can go about it by recording your food intake for a week or more, and then using a Table of Food Composition to figure out how much of each nutrient you are getting (or use the handy Nutritional Analysis included with most of the recipes in this book). Then compare these amounts to the Recommended Daily Allowances (see most popular nutrition books). This is really quite a chore but can point out deficiencies that can be remedied by a better diet or a short period of supplementation. In general, we do not recommend the use of pills except for short periods of time for those who really need it (pregnant and lactating women, those with definite deficiencies, etc.). Our feeling is that a wholesome, balanced diet of natural foods is the best possible foundation for proper nutrition.

Kitchen Ways

KITCHEN WAYS

This section covers the basics involved in setting up a natural foods kitchen, including the uses of utensils and other tools, storage, and some notes on the process of preparing foods and meals.

TOOLS

The more simple your life is, the fewer cooking tools you will need: perhaps only a sharp knife, bowl, spoon and maybe a pan. (If that is all you need then you probably aren't reading this book!) However, the path of the householder is strewn with attachments and the kitchen is no exception!

To set up a minimal kitchen from scratch, here is what you should obtain: (this list assumes that the kitchen has a sink, stove top and oven)

For Eating
(quantity needed depends on number of people to be fed)

- mugs or cups
- glasses
- eating bowls and plates
- settings of silverware

For Preparation

- 2 knives
  small paring knife
  larger knife for vegetables and bread
  or one medium size knife with a serrated edge
- a cutting board
- saucepans with tight fitting lids
  1 small pan for rice and soup, etc. (1-2 quart capacity)
  1 large pan for pasta, etc. (4-8 quart capacity)
- cast iron or other heavy frying pan (it's nice to have a lid too)
- pyrex or metal baking pan (8x12x2 inch or so)
- cookie sheet
- metal spatula
- serving & stirring spoon
- medium size bowl with lid (for salads etc.)
- hot pads or mitts

- can opener
Optional items: (What is needed from this list depends upon what is cooked.)
- toaster
- blender
- measuring cups and spoons
- rubber spatula
- grater
- steaming rack for the large pan
- colander
- soup ladle
- peeler
- bread knife (with a serrated edge)
- tea strainer
- wire whip
- glass jars for storing foods
- wooden spoons
- mixer
- crockpot
- microwave
- cloth and mesh shopping bags
- sharpening stone for knives
- rolling pin

For Cleaning

- natural fiber brush for scrubbing vegetables
- plastic mesh scrubby for cleaning pans
- sponge or dishcloth (even sponges can be washed to keep them clean)
- dish soap
- dish drainer

ABOUT COOKING UTENSILS

We have not found any convincing research on the effects of using cooking utensils made from various materials. We do have some information and opinions which we will pass along.

GLASS is very stable under the conditions normally encountered in the kitchen. Avoid rapid temperature changes and physical shocks to prevent breakage. Glass is ideal for bread and cake pans, casseroles and citrus juicers. If using glass in the oven, lower the temperature by 25 degrees, as it browns food more quickly than metal.

CAST IRON heats evenly and holds heat well, so it is excellent for frying pans and dutch ovens. It works well for dishes which need to be simmered a long time. Cast iron ware is seasoned in the following manner: First, wash the pan with soap and water; rinse well. Heat the new pan until it is very hot and then coat the inside with a vegetable oil. Remember to coat the sides too. After the pan cools, wipe out the excess oil with paper towels. If the pan is old and has meat grease in it or a "blotchy" old seasoning, the first step is to literally burn out the old seasoning by heating the pan until it stops smoking (fireplaces work well for this). Then season as if a new pan. To preserve the seasoning in a cast iron pan, avoid using anything except wooden utensils while cooking, and plastic mesh scrubbies when cleaning. Soap will remove the seasoning and is not usually needed for vegetarians. After rinsing the pan, wipe with a paper towel and dry over a low heat on the stove to prevent rusting. Avoid rapid changes in temperature: for example, don't put cold water in a very hot pan or it will crack. Also avoid physical shocks. Do not put cast iron in the dishwasher.

NOTE: Exclusive use of iron cookware, coupled with a phosphate-deficient diet, may result in an accumulation of iron in the liver, and possibly liver damage. Normal use of cast iron should not be a problem if you have a balanced diet.

ENAMELWARE is generally either very expensive or very short lived. The enamel coating on the cheap pans has a tendency to chip. To care for them, do not use metal utensils either in cooking or in cleaning. Avoid rapid temperature changes and physical shocks as these may cause the enamel to chip. Do not overheat. Do not use for cooking after the enamel has chipped or cracked.

PLATED (TINNED) STEEL BAKEWARE is the least expensive choice for cookie sheets and other baking pans. It will react to tomato products and other acids if they are left in the pan for a long period of time (such as a frozen lasagna casserole). Other than that, tinned steel is very sturdy, nonreactive and affordable.

STAINLESS STEEL is stable under normal kitchen conditions and is probably the best material for saucepans. It does not distribute heat well, so it is often combined with a copper, aluminum, or iron "core". These hybrid pans are easier to cook with than straight stainless steel, but are also more expensive. Stainless steel pans are the most rugged and are recommended for general use. They do not break, nor do they make food taste unpleasant; and they don't rust. Likewise, stainless steel knives don't rust, although good quality high-carbon steel is preferred by many chefs, in part because it is easier to keep sharp.

ALUMINUM pans are not popular with most natural food cooks. Many people believe that the aluminum salts which end up in the food are toxic and cause all sorts of health problems. Aluminum pans cause discoloration and a change in flavor in many foods, particularly acid foods such as those containing tomato or lemon. They are not recommended. (This warning does not apply to cookware with an aluminum layer sandwiched between two layers of stainless steel.)

NONSTICK FINISHES push our "plastic paranoia" buttons. We have no problems with sticking when using well-seasoned cast iron.

WOODEN UTENSILS feel and look good but need to be well maintained. Do not soak wooden bowls or utensils as they will probably crack and split if left too long in the soaking water. Wooden cutting boards do absorb flavors and the cuts on them can harbor lots of bacteria. It is recommended by home economists that wooden utensils be thoroughly cleansed in a bath of chlorine bleach (1 part bleach to 4 parts water) twice a year. This is particularly important for cutting boards, especially if your cutting board has been used for meat or if you cut a lot of cheeses.

FOOD

Kitchens without food are like bodies without souls: the main ingredient is missing. So let's begin by making a list of what foods are needed to begin to stock a kitchen. First think about what you like to eat and put those things on your list.

What grains do you like?
- rice (white, brown)
- wheat
- millet
- oats

Do you bake?
- flour (bread, pastry)
- baking soda, baking powder
- baking yeast
- honey, molasses

Do you eat bread?
- bagels, muffins
- rolls, buns
- tortillas
- crackers

What will you do for protein?
- tofu
- dairy products
- beans, nuts, seeds

How about fruits and vegetables?
- fresh
- frozen
- dried

What spices will you need?
- salt, pepper
- tamari, soy sauce
- herbs

What about beverages?
- milk
- juices
- teas

Condiments, etc.
- ketchup, mustard, mayonnaise
- oil (safflower, olive)
- jelly, jam
- nut butters (peanut, tahini)

These are the basics. Our son did this recently (on his own) and reported back to us that it had only cost him $40.00 to get started, and that it had included pot holders and pot cleaners! We were impressed.

Shop early in the morning, if you can, for the light and relatively warmer temperatures of the day hasten the loss of nutrients. Markets that do a lot of business generally have fresher food than smaller stores. Many rural communities have farm markets and roadside stands that buy directly from the growers and offer (at lower prices) food that is fresher and tastier than that in supermarkets.

FOOD STORAGE

Now you have the food you need to stock your kitchen. Let's think a little about how to store it.

First of all, a word about containers. Glass jars, plastic containers and metal coffee cans can be used to store almost anything. Wide mouth containers are easier to clean than narrow-mouth containers, and airtight lids keep food fresh longer. Labels can be made with ball point pen and masking tape or with a grease pencil directly on the container. Do not store acid foods (such as leftover tomato sauce, pineapple, etc.) in opened cans. The lead in the can may be leached by the acid, causing the food to darken and gain an unpleasant odor and taste. If left for an extended period of time, this can cause ptomaine poisoning.

Plastic wrap and aluminum foil are fairly difficult to reuse and not recyclable in some places. Leftovers can be stored in containers with lids or in bowls using small plates for lids.

For shopping use cloth and mesh shopping bags. If used, plastic bags can be washed, dried, and reused. To dry, suspend them over something so that air can reach the inside too. When they are no longer useable, they are recyclable.

FRESH VEGETABLES are best stored in tightly sealed plastic containers in the refrigerator. The idea is to keep the moisture content stable and to prevent oxidation and vitamin loss by excluding air and storing at low temperatures.

Potatoes and winter squash should not be refrigerated, but may be stored in a cool, dark, dry place where air can circulate around them. When refrigerated, the composition of the starch changes, which affects the vegetable's taste and texture. The exceptions to this are fresh red-skinned potatoes, which should be refrigerated and used within a short time after purchasing. Unripe tomatoes and eggplants can be stored until ripe in a single layer in a cool, dark dry place. Thereafter, refrigerate in plastic bags.

FRESH FRUIT, if it is ripe, will keep longer in airtight containers in the refrigerator. Unripe fruit can be stored in a bowl on the counter out of direct sunlight.

To ripen fruit faster, place it in a bag with an apple or banana. The gases given off by the banana or apple help the other fruit ripen.

DRIED FRUIT, BEANS, GRAINS AND FLOURS are all subject to infestation by insects. Storage in strong airtight containers will keep the bugs out and help reduce oxidation. Keep these containers in cool, dry dark places. Flours and cracked grains should be stored in the refrigerator if possible.

UNREFINED OILS should be kept refrigerated, or at least in a cool, dark place.

FRESH JUICES, DAIRY, TOFU and cooked foods need to be refrigerated in covered containers. Covering containers in the refrigerator keeps the flavors from blending, and helps prevent dehydration.

MOLASSES, HONEY AND OTHER SWEETENERS do not need to be refrigerated but should be stored in containers with tight fitting lids to discourage ants. Sunlight should be avoided.

HERBS AND SPICES should be stored in dark bottles away from sunlight and heat to retain their flavor.

Recycling and Composting

It is better not to use than to have to recycle, but that's not always possible. Whatever waste there is should be recycled if at all possible. Check with your local recycling center for what they will take. Even styrofoam packaging p-nuts are recycled and reused now!

Vegetable scraps and other food scraps can be fed to animals or composted. If you don't have a compost pile, compost can be buried. You might even get a volunteer plant in the spring. Even in cities there are compost piles. If you have no yard, check to see if there are community gardens that would take your compost.

Return and reuse what you can, making as little impact on Mother Earth as possible. That way we can all be here a little bit longer.

Thoughts About Keeping It All Together

• **Think ahead**. In order to maintain a peaceful atmosphere in the kitchen, it is important to prepare beforehand. Make sure the oven is turned on in time to heat up, the baked potatoes are started before the steamed vegetables so both are ready at the same time, the sink isn't full of dirty dishes when you need to wash some food, and you don't find you are missing some ingredient halfway through a complicated recipe.

• **Enjoy yourself**. If you feel tense or upset, sit quietly for a few minutes and establish a calm state of mind before beginning to cook. Food that is prepared and served in a calm, loving manner will nourish more than just the physical body.

• **Use your energy wisely**. Try getting everything that is needed for a recipe in one place before beginning to mix anything. This saves walking back and forth between the cupboard and the counter or finding out you don't have all the ingredients.

• **Be here now**. There's an old saying that "you can't cook in the living room." It took a few burned pans and cookies to convince us of the truth in this.

• **Keep it clean**. Wash your hands before beginning to cook, and frequently enough to avoid getting the outside of containers sticky or floury. Wash graters, blenders and other one-in-the-kitchen items right away, so they will be clean when they are needed next.

• **Keep it simple**. Especially when first learning to cook, don't overextend yourself by trying to cook a lot of fancy dishes at once. There are many recipes in this book which need only the addition of a salad, perhaps some bread and a beverage to make a complete meal.

• **Use the right tool for the job.** This simple guide can turn a chore into fun.

• **Be safe**. It is easy to cut yourself with a sharp knife or even a grater. Fires can be easily started with forgotten pans or dish towels on the stove. Stay alert.

• **Plan meals ahead.** Meals need to be nutritionally balanced, appealing (color, taste, and texture are all important), and varied enough to suit different situations and hold people's interest. It is also good to establish some kind of rhythmic schedule so that cooking and eating are part of the day's flow, rather than an interruption. People who work and don't have much time to cook during the week may wish to cook large quantities of one main dish recipe one day a week, and freeze it in meal-size portions. After a few weeks, with some planning, you'll be able to serve a great variety of meals with very little effort.

Notes to the Novice

• The top shelf of the oven is hotter, but food is more likely to burn on the bottom shelf, if it gets too close to the heat source.

• Aluminum foil can be used to line the bottom of the oven (but don't let it touch the heating element), and placed under burners to catch spills and drippings.

• Don't put a pan on a hot burner without putting food, water or oil in it first.

• Keep hair tied back so it stays out of the food and out of the fire.

• Food generally cooks faster with a lid. (Saves energy, too.)

• To reheat food it is usually necessary to add liquid and simmer in a covered pan. Stir well and frequently. Microwave ovens are also well suited to warming up most leftovers.

• Stirring distributes heat and keeps the food from burning or sticking. Stir so that the food is mixed up and down as well as around.

• Oil, turmeric, berry juice and many other goodies stain clothing. Wearing an apron helps keep your clothes clean.

Beverages

BEVERAGES

This section contains information on making fresh juices, smoothies, teas, and other beverages.

FRESH JUICES

There are several types of juicing machines. The most common is the pulp-ejector type. This machine shoots pulp out one direction and juice in another. Commercial juices are usually made with a triturator (grinder) and a hydraulic press, extracting more of the nutrients out of the juice, giving the juice a longer shelf life.

There are some general guidelines for preparing fresh juices. Make certain that the fruits and vegetables being juiced are very clean, very fresh and have no bad spots. If produce is old or wilted, the quality, yield, and flavor of the juice will suffer. Remove cores from apples and skin from fruit and vegetables if it is bitter.

Fresh raw juices are best when consumed within a few hours of being made. They do, however, freeze well. To freeze juices, fill plastic bottles to within 1 to 2 inches of the top and freeze upright. You may also freeze carrot juice in plastic glasses with tight fitting lids. These fit well into lunch boxes (keeping the lunch cold) and are defrosted but still cold by lunchtime.

For a beginning vegetable combination, try juicing 1 pound of carrots with 2 stalks of celery and a few leaves of chard or spinach. Feed the leafy vegetables through first so that the carrots can help push the other vegetables through.

For a beginning fruit combination, try juicing half grapes with half apples. Tart apples make a juice with more flavor than Red or Yellow Delicious. Grapes with seeds will often add a bitter taste to the juice. Excellent juices can be made from wine grapes. If you live where wine grapes are grown, these may be purchased directly from the growers or grown yourself!

FRUIT SMOOTHIES AND BEVERAGES

Basic Sweet Fruit Smoothie

Preparation time: 5-10 minutes
Yields: 2 servings

1 banana, peeled
1 large sweet fruit such as an apple, persimmon, papaya or 3/4 C berries
3/4 to 1 C apple or other fruit juice
2 to 3 pitted soft dates (optional)

Pour juice in a blender. While blending, add the fruits (cut into sections), one section at a time until drink is smooth. Drink as soon as it is made or store refrigerated in an airtight container.

Calories: 282.2
Fat (gm): .7
Protein (gm): 1.3
Cholesterol (mg): 6.0
Sodium (mg): 7.5

Hearty Fruit Smoothie

Preparation time: 5-10 minutes
Yields: 2 servings

2 bananas, peeled and cut into chunks
2 T honey
1 t vanilla
2 to 3 C apple juice
1/4 C raw wheat germ
2 ice cubes

Blend until smooth.

Calories: 339.7
Fat (gm): 1.7
Protein (gm): 5.3
Cholesterol (mg): 0
Sodium (mg): 20.2

Breakfast Smoothie

Preparation time: 5-10 minutes
Yields: 3-4 servings

*Our teenage son frequently has this for
breakfast and usually finishes it all himself!*

1/2 banana, peeled
1 plum
1 nectarine
1/3 C blueberries
2 to 3 T honey
1/4 C yogurt
1/4 C wheat germ
2 C apple juice
1 t vanilla
3 ice cubes

Place ingredients in blender, adding apple
juice first. Blend until smooth.

Calories: 227.8
Fat (gm): 1.3
Protein (gm): 4.8
Cholesterol (mg): .3
Sodium (mg): 28.8

Citrus Cooler

Preparation time: 5 minutes
Yields: 4 servings

1 quart orange juice
**1 pint box of strawberries, washed and
  stemmed**
1 banana (optional), peeled

Blend together and enjoy.

Calories:159.4
Fat (gm): .5
Protein (gm): 3.0
Cholesterol (mg): 0
Sodium (mg): 2.3

Hot Mulled Cider

Preparation time: 5 minutes
Yields: 4 servings

1 two inch long stick of cinnamon
1 whole nutmeg
3 to 4 whole cloves
3 to 4 whole allspice
1 quart apple juice or cider

Boil the juice with the spices for a minute
and then simmer for 15 minutes.

Calories: 138.5
Fat (gm): .7
Protein (gm): .2
Cholesterol (mg): 0
Sodium (mg): .8

VARIATIONS: Add 1/2 t dried orange or
lemon peel or a small slice of fresh peel or
1 t to 1 T fresh lemon juice. Use a different
kind of juice. Any kind of bottled juice will
work: cranberry mixes are excellent.

Hot Lemon Water

Preparation time: 5 minutes
Yields: 4 servings

2 lemons, peeled and diced
2 T honey
1/2 t cinnamon
2 to 3 cloves
5 C water

VARIATIONS: Substitute 1/3 C lemon juice
for the lemons. Substitute 1/2 t ginger for
the cinnamon and cloves. Add a pinch of
cayenne. This will help open your nasal
passages when congested with a cold, and
sooth a sore throat.

Sun Teas

Preparation time: 5 minutes
Brewing time: varies
Yields: 1 gallon

These are so refreshing on a hot day.

1 gallon water in a gallon jar
1 to 1$^1/_2$ C herbs
1 eight-inch square of cheese cloth or
  large strainer
Sunshine
1 C warmed or very liquid honey
  (optional)

Place herbs on cheese cloth and loosely tie corners together. Immerse in water in jar, leaving a corner over the edge so that it is easy to pull out. Place in the sun for several hours. The length of time it takes varies, depending upon the strength of the sun and heat, and the quantity and type of herbs used. When steeped, remove tea and if desired add honey. Stir well.

Here are a few of our favorite sun tea recipes to get you started:

HIBISCUS TEA: This is our favorite. It is a deep red with a lemony, fruit taste. Sweetened, small children cannot tell it from "Kool-Aid"®. Use 1$^1/_2$ C hibiscus flowers per gallon of water.

LEMON GRASS/MINT: Use about 3/4 C lemon grass and 1/2 C mint leaves to 1 gallon of water. Sweeten with 3/4 C honey.

HIBISCUS/LEMON GRASS: Use 3/4 C lemon grass and 3/4 C hibiscus to 1 gallon of water. Sweeten with 3/4 C honey.

HOT HERB TEAS

There are many herb teas available on the market today. Try them out and see which ones you like. Read the labels. Many prepared blends contain black or green tea and caffeine. Try herb tea with milk. In the winter you can make it in a coffee pot (the kind that has it ready when you wake up). Place the tea bags in the space for the coffee, or if you are using loose tea, use a coffee filter.

Warm water is usually necessary in order to extract the flavor from the herbs (however, there are herb teas which can brew in the refrigerator). The most common way to make tea is to boil water and add it to a cup or pot with herbs in it. Use 1 to 3 T herbs per C of water depending on how strong a flavor is desired. In the winter, the pot can be warmed by filling with boiling water which is then poured out before the herbs are placed in it. Then add boiling water and allow the herbs to steep for a few minutes. The longer the steeping period, the stronger the tea will be. Do not boil the water after the herbs have been added unless you are using whole spices. Strain the tea before serving and add honey, lemon or milk as desired.

NOTE: Flower teas (such as chamomile, hibiscus, etc.) brew fairly quickly, and may become bitter if overbrewed or brewed with water that is too hot.

Chamomile Milk

Preparation time: 5 minutes
Cooking time: 5 minutes
Yields: 1 serving

This is the tea that our children always requested when young.

**1 T chamomile flowers
1 C boiling hot water
1/4 C to 1/3 C milk
1 t honey**

Pour boiling water over chamomile. Let steep until golden. Strain and add honey and milk to taste.

Calories: 32.2
Fat (gm): 1.1
Protein (gm): 2.2
Cholesterol (mg): 4.5
Sodium (mg): 35.5

VARIATION: Serve without milk or honey. Use other herbs with or in place of the chamomile.

Yogi Tea

Preparation time: 5-10 minutes
Cooking time: 20-30 minutes
Yields: 1 serving

**4 whole cardamom seed pods, seeded
6 whole peppercorns
1 slice fresh ginger root
3 whole cloves
1/2 stick cinnamon (1$^{1}/_{2}$ inches long)
1$^{1}/_{2}$ to 2 C water**

Combine the above and bring to a boil. Simmer for 20 to 30 minutes. Strain and serve hot (or cold) with milk and/or honey.

Calories: 5.7
Fat (gm): 0
Protein (gm): .1
Cholesterol (mg): 0
Sodium (mg): 11.5

NUT AND SOY MILKS

Nutmilks can be used in almost any recipe calling for milk for people who choose not to consume dairy products.

NutMilk

Preparation time: 10-20 minutes
Yields: 1 quart

**1 quart water
1 T honey
1 C cashews or blanched almonds**

Combine in blender and liquify until smooth. This may need to be strained.

Calories: 233.6
Fat (gm):16.3
Protein (gm): 5.0
Cholesterol (mg): 0
Sodium (mg): 12.6

Soymilk

Preparation time: sort beans (10-15 minutes); soak (overnight); grind and drain (30-45 minutes)
Cooking time: about 20 minutes
Bottling and cleanup: 20-30 minutes
Yields: 3 quarts

**1 C soybeans
spring water
1/2 T vanilla
2 T honey
1/2 t salt
1 T lecithin (optional)**

EQUIPMENT NEEDED:

large pan (8 to 10 quart capacity)
blender
large bowl
candy thermometer
clean muslin

Sort soybeans, and soak overnight in a very large bowl full of water in the refrigerator (soybeans ferment very easily). In the morning, drain and rinse. Blend the beans until smooth, 1 C at a time with 2 C water, until all the beans are liquified.

Place a 2 to 2$^{1}/_{2}$ foot square of clean muslin over a large bowl and pour the liquified soybeans into it. Gather up the edges and squeeze the milk out of the pulp (don't get any pulp in the milk!).

Measure the soymilk from the bowl into the large pan. Add water to make 3 quarts (12 C). Heat to a rolling boil, stirring very frequently as it tends to stick and boil over quickly. Boil 6 minutes. Add vanilla, honey, salt and lecithin. Stir until dissolved.

Bottle in clean mason jars, cool and refrigerate. Soymilk may be used in any recipe calling for milk. Yogurt and kefir can also be made from soymilk.

Per C:
Calories: 36.0
Fat (gm): 1.1
Protein (gm): 2.1
Cholesterol (mg): 0
Sodium (mg): 90.2

CHILLED MILK BEVERAGES

Orange Jubilee

Preparation time: 5-10 minutes
Yields: 1 serving

1 C orange juice
1/2 C powdered milk
1$^{1}/_{2}$ T honey
1/8 t vanilla
1/2 C ice chips

Whip in a blender until frothy. Serve immediately.

Calories: 319.2
Fat (gm): .4
Protein (gm): 13.2
Cholesterol (mg): 6.0
Sodium (mg): 165.2

Carob Cooler

Preparation time: 5-10 minutes
Yields: 3 servings

5 to 6 regular sized ice cubes
1 C cold milk
4 to 6 T carob powder
1/4 C powdered milk
1/2 t vanilla
1 to 2 T honey

Blend together in a blender.

Calories: 173
Fat (gm): 4.1
Protein (gm): 6.3
Cholesterol (mg): 16.3
Sodium (mg): 82.1

VARIATION: Substitute 2 T CAROB SYRUP (p. 205) for the carob powder, powdered milk, vanilla and honey. Add 1/4 t cinnamon.

Ginger Buttermilk

Preparation time: 5-10 minutes
Yields: 1 serving

1 C chilled buttermilk or yogurt
1/4 C orange juice
1 t lemon juice
2 T honey
pinch ground ginger

Blend until well mixed. Serve chilled.

Calories: 258.4
Fat (gm): 2.0
Protein (gm): 9.3
Cholesterol (mg): 9.0
Sodium (mg): 260.8

Krishna Drink

Preparation time: 5-10 minutes
Yields: 2 servings

1 C yogurt
1 C buttermilk or milk
1 small banana, peeled
6 dates, pitted

Combine ingredients in a blender until smooth. Serve chilled.

Calories: 246.1
Fat (gm): 3.4
Protein (gm): 10.7
Cholesterol (mg): 12.6
Sodium (mg): 216.1

Date Milkshake

Preparation time: 5-10 minutes
Yields: 1 serving

1 C milk
1/2 C ice cream
2 T date sugar

Blend together in a blender until smooth.

Calories: 317.1
Fat (gm): 11.1
Protein (gm): 11.6
Cholesterol (mg): 48.0
Sodium (mg): 180.6

Carob Milkshake

Preparation time: 5-10 minutes

1 C milk
1/2 C ice cream
2 T CAROB SYRUP (p. 205)

Blend together in a blender until smooth.

Calories: 384.7
Fat (gm): 11.7
Protein (gm): 12.9
Cholesterol (mg): 50.2
Sodium (mg): 197.6

WARM MILK BEVERAGES

These beverages can be warmed on top of the stove or in a microwave. Either way, be careful to not scald the milk. These beverages can also be made with nutmilk, but the flavor will be slightly different.

Hot Date Milk

Preparation time: 5 minutes
Yields: 1 serving

1 C milk
2 T date sugar or 3 dates, pitted and minced
1/4 t cinnamon

Simmer date sugar and cinnamon in milk until milk is steaming and date sugar is softened and mostly dissolved.

Calories: 182.1
Fat (gm): 4.5
Protein (gm): 9.1
Cholesterol (mg): 18.0
Sodium (mg): 122.7

Hot Ginger Milk

Preparation time: 5 minutes
Yields: 1 serving

1 C milk
1/4 t or less ground ginger powder
1 T honey

Combine ingredients and warm.

Calories: 155.0
Fat (gm): 4.4
Protein (gm): 8.8
Cholesterol (mg): 18.0
Sodium (mg): 122.7

Spiced Hot Milk

Preparation time: 7-10 minutes
Yields: 2 servings

When our son was younger and couldn't sleep, he would ask for a cup of this and soon be in dreamland.

2 C milk
2 T honey
pinch saffron, crushed
12 pistachios, shelled
6 cashews
6 blanched almonds
2 t raisins
pinch ground nutmeg

Gently warm the above ingredients. Pour milk into 2 mugs and spoon in the nuts and raisins.

Calories: 264.4
Fat (gm): 9.4
Protein (gm): 10.7
Cholesterol (mg): 18.0
Sodium (mg): 124.8

Golden Milk

Preparation time: 7-10 minutes
Yields: 3 servings

3 C milk
3 T honey
1 t turmeric
1/4 t American saffron, crumbled
1/2 t nutmeg
2 T cashews (optional)
1 T raisins (optional)

Combine ingredients and heat until just warm. Pour into mugs and spoon in the nuts and raisins if used.

Calories: 190.8
Fat (gm): 4.6
Protein (gm): 8.8
Cholesterol (mg): 18.0
Sodium (mg): 123.4

Hot Carob Milk

Preparation time: 5 minutes
Yields: 1 serving

1 C milk
1 to 2 T CAROB SYRUP (p. 205)
1/4 t cinnamon (optional)

Mix syrup into milk, heat and serve.

Calories: 185.3
Fat (gm): 4.7
Protein (gm): 9.6
Cholesterol (mg): 19.1
Sodium (mg): 130.8

Fruit

FRUIT

FRUIT

ABOUT FRESH FRUITS

Fresh ripe fruits are simply delicious, and the easily digestible sugars they contain are among the best sources of "quick energy." The flavor and nutritive value of fruit varies widely, depending upon the type of fruit, where and how it was grown, and how ripe it is. Most raw fruits are good sources of vitamins and minerals, but not good sources of protein.

Fruits are like delicate flowers; if they are picked too early, they won't ever develop their full beauty. When fruits are picked too green, they will ripen after a fashion, but the sugar content will rarely reach the level that it would were the fruit allowed to ripen naturally on the plant. Some fruits, such as pears and avocados, do better if their final ripening occurs after harvest.

Fruits are very perishable. Buy only what will be used before it spoils. Most fruits bruise easily. It pays to follow the adage, "Love 'em, smell 'em, look at 'em, but easy on the squeezin'." Most "store bought" fruit will need to finish ripening at home. Really ripe fruit usually can't survive the amount of handling it could get at a market, so usually the fruit that is sold is not quite ripe.

When purchasing fruits, look for those which are heavy for their size and have a rich color. Avoid fruit which is hard as a rock, has brown spots, or is overly soft. Out of season fruits are more expensive and usually of lower quality than in-season fruit. Organically grown fruit is often smaller than chemically fertilized fruit but makes up for its size with a better, sweeter flavor. Generally speaking, the best places to buy fruit are farmers' markets, roadside stands or markets which specialize in selling high quality produce with little or no chemicals used in production.

In order to help you enjoy a wide variety of fruit, the recipes in this section are prefaced with information on the purchasing and preparation of the most common fruits arranged in alphabetical order. First, a few words about different classes of fruit.

FRUIT CLASSIFICATION

In this book, fruits are classified according to their predominant characteristics. Within reason, fruits in a given class may be substituted for each other in many recipes.

ACID FRUITS tend to contain more citrus, oxalic, and ascorbic acids than other fruits. They all have a distinct sharp or tart taste, which may disappear as the fruit becomes perfectly ripe. Acid fruits include cranberries, currants, gooseberries, grapes, grapefruits, lemons, limes, mandarin oranges, oranges, pineapples, tangelos, tangerines, and temple oranges.

DRIED FRUIT can be made from most sub-acid and sweet fruits, as well as some acid fruits like grapes and pineapples. Dried fruits are discussed just before the fruit recipes, following the alphabetical discussions of fresh fruits.

MELONS form a class of their own due to the extremely high percentage of water they contain, and because they are most often served alone. Melons are subjected to more unproductive thumping, smelling, hefting and going-over than any other food that comes to mind. Choosing a good tasting melon need not be difficult if you know what to look for. Tips on selecting particular melons follow in the discussions of cantaloupes, casabas, crenshaws, honeydews, muskmelons, persians, and watermelons.

SUB-ACID FRUITS and SWEET FRUITS include apples, apricots, bananas, berries, cherries, figs, kiwis, mangoes, nectarines, papayas, peaches, pear apples, pears, persimmons, plums, pomegranates, raisins, and other dried fruits.

FRESH FRUITS

APPLES are some of the most popular fruits in the U.S. They can be used in many ways, are available throughout the year, and are relatively inexpensive. They become ripe in the late summer or fall and are at the peak of their flavor and texture at that time. When buying apples, keep in mind what you want to do with them. Eating apples should be fully ripe but still crisp (the skin should not give at all when gently pushed). Cooking apples needn't be completely ripe, but will need more sweetener if they are green. Supermarket apples are frequently waxed. The wax can be removed by washing in hot water and soap or peeling. Apples are best peeled if eaten cooked as the peel gets an unpleasant texture when cooked. If sauce is to be put through a food mill, the peel can be left on when cooked as it is removed by the food mill processing. The peel will sometimes cause the sauce to become pink.

CORTLANDS are tart, red-skinned apples, good for eating fresh or making applesauce.

DELICIOUS apples are the most commonly found apples in supermarkets, and their crisp, sweet juicy flesh makes them the most popular apples for eating fresh. They have a high sugar content and are best for eating fresh. They are rather bland when cooked. Delicious apples can be identified by the five bumps on the blossom end. When ripe they should not have green right under the skin. Golden or Yellow Delicious have a somewhat more delicate flavor than the Red Delicious and do a little better in storage and as cooking apples.

GRANNY SMITH apples, which are grown "down under" in Australia, are picked during the Northern Hemisphere's spring, when there are no fresh domestic apples available. Those grown on the West Coast ripen in the fall. All have bright green skins.

GRAVENSTEINS are the earliest ripening apples in most places on the West Coast. They turn from green to yellow to red as they ripen. They are not the best eating apples but because they are the first, their freshness is appreciated. They are excellent cooking apples.

JONATHANS are small tender, tart apples with a bright red skin which may be flecked with green. They are good for eating or cooking.

MCINTOSH apples are two-toned green and red apples with a rich spicy taste. They are good for eating and cooking and store fairly well.

NORTHERN SPYS are large, firm textured apples with waxy, bright skins. They have a pleasant, spicy taste which makes them popular for eating fresh.

PIPPINS are larger round, slightly flattened, green skinned apples with a tart flavor and crunchy texture. They are usually used for cooking, but are good raw too. They often are still tasty in the spring when most apples have lost their flavor.

RHODE ISLAND GREENINGS are primarily used for cooking and baking.

ROME BEAUTIES are big and round with green stripes or specks in their predominantly red skin. Their firm texture and mild flavor make them ideal for cooking or baking. A little tart, but also good raw. They store very well.

STAYMANS are large and have a rich red colored skin. Related to WINESAPS, they are semi-firm and have a tart, spicy wine flavor. They store well.

YORK IMPERIAL apples are lopsided and have a red and green skin. Firm and tart, they are good cooked or baked.

WINESAPS are typically small and somewhat rounded with a deep red skin. The fruit is firm and tart. These are good all purpose apples which may be eaten fresh, cooked, baked or juiced.

APRICOTS are small, beautiful orange fruits. They are a good source of vitamin A and iron, especially when dried. They are slightly more tart and drier than peaches, and they are less messy to pack in a lunch or eat as a snack. They are delicious in salads, compotes, pies, smoothies and preserves. Especially when eating organically grown fruit, split the fruit open and check for worms before eating.

AVOCADOS, although technically a fruit (the definition of which is "a ripened ovary containing seed"), are included in the vegetable section since they are usually used as a vegetable.

BANANAS are an excellent source of potassium. Bananas which are imported into the U.S. are usually picked green and then ripened in rooms filled with a gas which they produce naturally in small amounts. Changes in the color of the skin reflect the ripening process of bananas. As the fruit goes from green to yellow, the starches are converted into sugars. How ripe the fruit is when "good" is definitely a matter of personal preference and also depends on the variety of banana in question. The fruit bruises easily, with the bruises showing as black areas on the skin. Bananas turn black when refrigerated, but a short refrigeration does not hurt the quality of the fruit. If ripe, they can be peeled and frozen for banana bread or smoothies, but they cannot be defrosted and eaten as is. Bananas provide a thick, rich texture to smoothies, fruit salads and baked goods. Bananas can be ripened at home in a paper or plastic bag in a warm place out of the sun. The fruit is at its best when it is white or yellow-white and uniformly soft. A hard center is a sign of under-ripeness.

BERRIES (raspberries, blueberries, blackberries, loganberries, ollalaberries, etc.) mold very quickly once they are picked, so it is advisable to buy them very fresh, store them refrigerated or frozen and/or use them right away. Ripe berries are usually soft and a uniform deep color. Blueberries should be firm, not soft. Discard any moldy berries before the mold spreads.

CHERRIES are small round fruits which herald the beginning of the summer fresh fruit season. There are many varieties. Usually the ones first available on the market are not as large or as sweet as the later varieties. Cherries come in different colors. The dark ones (Bings, Tartarians, and Black Lamberts) are best for eating fresh but when canned, develop a tough skin. Dark skinned cherries turn from bright red to a deep blackish purple and become slightly soft as they ripen. The light colored varieties (Royal Annes, Napoleons, and Rainier) are better for canning. Sour cherries are used only for cooking.

CRANBERRIES are not eaten raw. Cooked, they are found in everything from pudding to sauces and breads. They are available dried but may have been sugared. The dried ones are a tangy and chewy addition to a fruit salad.

CURRANTS are little sour fruits usually used dried or in jellies. Dried, they are like sweet baby raisins and may be substituted for raisins in any recipe.

DATES are available dried, and (in the fall) fresh. Because of their high sugar content, they ferment easily and should be kept refrigerated. They are sweet treats and an interesting addition to fruit salads. Split the fruit open and check the inside for worms before using. The Deglet Noor variety is the most common, but the Medjool is tastier. Deglets are available fresh or dry. The fresh ones are chewy; the dry ones ("bread dates") are great backpacking food. Unlike fresh dates, dried dates do not ferment and do not require refrigeration. These are the dates from which date sugar and date pieces are made.

FIGS, in the U.S. commercial market, are mainly grown in California. Calimyrna figs are a white or light yellow color and are the sweetest figs, fresh or dried. Black Mission figs are usually the variety found fresh and are most commonly dried. They are a black color and are smaller and less juicy than the Calimyrna. Kadota figs are used for canning and cooking as their flavor, texture and color hold up best when canned. Other popular varieties include the Brown Turkey, Brunswick, and Celeste. Figs are easy to dry (Directions are given in the CANNING AND PRESERVING section, p. 225). If purchased to eat fresh, pick those with the darkest color that are filled out and plump, not withered. They mold easily and need to be eaten soon after picking or purchasing. If the skin of the fresh ones makes your mouth itch, break the skin open and turn the fig inside out before eating it. (This may sound strange, but it was shown to us by a fruit distributor who ate a lot of figs, and it works.)

GOOSEBERRIES are green, waxy berries which are not usually eaten raw or found in groceries except canned. They make an excellent pie, but require a lot of sweetening.

GRAPES are available in many varieties. When ripe, they should still be slightly firm and have a well developed round or slightly elongated shape. Taste one to see if the flavor is developed or if they were picked too green to be sweet. Thompson Seedless, Muscat, Perlette and other green grapes actually turn slightly yellow-brown and translucent when they are ripe. Concord, Cardinal, Emperor and other red-purple grapes are ripest when the color is very deep and dark. The most readily available grapes are the Thompson Seedless. Early in the season, the small green Perlette grapes are available, while later in the summer you can get the larger varieties. Grapes grown in South America are ripe at the opposite time of year, so fresh grapes are available almost all year. A favorite of ours is the Red Flame. If cooking with grapes, most cooks prefer the Concord for its flavor and intense color. For eating raw, most people prefer the seedless varieties. Many varieties grown for wine are also excellent raw or juiced.

GRAPEFRUITS are citrus fruits high in Vitamin C. Grapefruits are best from December through February. They come in pink and white varieties. Ruby Red grapefruits (identifiable by the red blush that shows through a small section of skin)

usually have a sweeter flavor and definitely a prettier color than the white varieties. Grapefruits' bitter taste comes from the natural quinine in the membranes. To pick juicy ripe grapefruit, pick the ones that are heaviest for their size and slightly soft.

KIWIS are little brown fuzzy fruits with green flesh and tiny edible black seeds. They are ripe when slightly soft. Kiwis have a lemony taste and are excellent in fruit salads. They also can be eaten peeled or sliced in half and spooned out.

LEMONS are citrus fruits most often used for their juice. Lemon juice added to a dish right before serving will heighten and accent the flavors of the dish. Lemon juice can also be used in place of vinegar in salad dressings. Meyers lemons are sweet and are excellent in baking, sauces, fruit jells and marmalade. To increase the amount of juice in a lemon, just before using roll the fruit on a counter top, pressing hard enough to depress the fruit but not hard enough to burst the skin. Small to medium sized fruits are preferred for their thin skin; choose ones that are heavy for their size.

LIMES are similar in size and shape to lemons but their skin is green and their juice more sharp and delicately flavored. They may be used like lemons.

MANDARIN ORANGES include TANGELOS, TANGERINES, TEMPLE ORANGES and TANGORS. All are all small orange-like citrus fruits, each with a distinctive taste. They are usually only available in the winter months. Tangelos are a cross between a grapefruit and a tangerine and have a tangy taste. Mandarin oranges are usually the sweetest of these. All of them peel easily and are good in children's lunches, but most do have seeds.

MANGOES are tangy tropical treats rich in Vitamins A and C. The fruit is usually yellow with tinges of red. It is slightly soft when ripe (but not mushy) and has a fragrant aroma. The skin should be peeled and the fruit cut from the large, flat pit. Mexican mangoes are huge compared to the more commonly marketed Hawaiian varieties.

MELONS

CASABAS, unlike most melons, have a flatter bottom end on which they are usually sitting when sold. When ripe, this end should be slightly soft and the melon should have a pleasant melon odor. The skin turns slightly golden and the flesh gets whiter (less green) and translucent as it ripens from the center out. They are excellent served with lemon.

CRENSHAWS have a fairly smooth, hard yellow-green skin. They have an elongated shape with rather pointed ends. As with the Casaba, their skin begins to turn yellow as the melon ripens and the blossom end should be slightly soft and aromatic. The flesh is a translucent pale salmon color and is excellent served with lemon.

HONEYDEWS are available with a white to green flesh or with an orange flesh. The white fleshed ones are good served with lemons. The melons should be reasonably round, with a smooth skin that tends toward yellow when ripe. The orange fleshed honeydews have an orange glow through the skin. Mature melons have a waxy feel. Scar lines on the surface are not blemishes, but rather the result of an excess of sugar (they are called sugar scars) and indicate a sweet melon. When ripe, they will be just a little soft at the blossom end with a sweet fragrance

MUSKMELONS (cantaloupes, persian melons, etc.) are ripe when the netting on the skin begins to stand out a little from the skin. They have a sweet smell. The stem end should be a smooth, evenly shaped hollow. The melon should be firm, without soft spots, not soft and mushy. Look for medium to large oval shaped melons with a yellow gold (not green) skin.

WATERMELONS should have a slightly dull skin and well rounded ends. The bottom side will turn yellow or tan as the melon ripens. Thumping is not always reliable, but a dull thud is indicative of an underripe melon and a resounding sound is a sign that the melon is ripe. If cut, look for a deep red color and dark colored seeds. White seeds indicate an immature melon. Melons that are past their prime will be dry and mealy or stringy. A watermelon makes a fun and colorful salad bowl. Cut off the top third of the melon the long way. Remove the flesh of the melon and gently scrape the insides. Then notch the edge as for "jack-o-lantern" teeth, and fill with fruit salad.

NECTARINES are not hybrid fruits, although they resemble both peaches and plums. They may be freestone or cling, which explains why some slip from their pit and others are hard to separate from it. They have smooth skins which turn reddish gold as the fruit ripens. The fruit is ripe when it is uniformly slightly soft (not as soft as a peach gets) and the skin is yellow (not green) in between the red areas, and can easily be pulled off the fruit. The flesh is slightly tart yet sweet. They do not need to be peeled and are a delightful addition to fruit salads, and are also good in jams, pies and canned.

ORANGES are citrus fruits with a high vitamin C content. The two varieties most frequently found commercially are Valencias and Navels (so called because of the depression left when the "baby orange" sometimes found inside is removed). Ripe Valencias may sometimes have a green tinge due to "re-greening" on the tree. Pick firm but not hard fruit that is heavy for its size. When juicing oranges, they may be rolled hard enough to depress them but not hard enough to break the skin, until soft before cutting in half.

PAPAYAS become more yellow or even red and develop a distinct fragrance as they ripen. When ripe, they will be slightly soft but not mushy. To prepare, peel and remove the black seeds. They can be eaten plain by cutting in half, scooping out the seeds and then spooning out the flesh. They are good with a squeeze of lemon.

PEACHES are round, fuzzy fruits with a golden color and sometimes tinges of red. Fruit with green skin is not yet ripe. They should be slightly soft with a peach fragrance when ripe. Although some people eat them with the skin, most people prefer to eat them peeled. When ripe, the skin peels easily. When peeling a large number, it is easiest to blanch them (see p. 236). It is easier to can the freestone varieties than the cling peaches as the fruit slips away from the pit. There are numerous modern varieties, but the old fashioned Elberta and Rio Oso Gem varieties can be much juicier and more flavorful.

PEARS should be firm but not hard when ripe. They ripen quickly and are mealy when overripe. If picking pears, they should be picked when green and allowed to ripen off the tree, as they become mealy when allowed to ripen on the tree. There are several varieties and colors available.

BARTLETT pears are the most common, with a pleasant texture and mild flavor. They ripen earliest (in the summer) but do not store well. They should be a clear yellow or red color, with perhaps a tinge of green when ripe.

BOSC pears are a winter variety, smaller than Bartlett, with a long tapering neck. They have a yellow or reddish skin with a marked tendency to russet (turn rough and brown). Russeting is normal and does not adversely affect the quality of the fruit.

COMICE pears have the most delicate and "melt-in-your-mouth" flavor. They bruise very easily and do not store well. They are usually available from late fall to Christmas time. The skin (which does not taste very good) turns greenish yellow or red when the fruit is ripe.

D'ANJOU pears are mid-season fruits which store well. They are a creamy yellow to yellow-green when ripe, and may russet.

PEAR APPLES OR ASIAN PEARS resemble a cross between a Bartlett pear and a Golden Delicious apple, but they are true pears. They are available in the late summer and early fall. They should be chosen when very firm, so they will have a crisp juicy bite with more of the delicate flavor of a pear. They add the flavor of pear to a fruit salad, but hold up better than U.S. and European varieties.

WINTER NELLIS pears are small and often heavily russetted. They store well, maintaining a good flavor and texture.

PERSIMMONS have an awful reputation for puckering mouths; however, if they are ripe, they don't cause puckering at all. Because they are far too delicate to ship when ripe, one must wait—sometimes for weeks—for the fruit to get ripe. They ripen most evenly in the cold and can be frozen when almost ripe, then defrosted and eaten raw. For the common Hachiya variety with the pointed ends, wait until the skin gets translucent and the fruit is extremely soft. The smaller, flatter, tomato shaped Fuyu persimmon loses its astringency before it gets ripe, and can be eaten when firm or crispy. Persimmons are good raw, in fruit salads or as an ingredient in frozen fruit ice creams or baking. They are available in the very late fall or early winter.

PINEAPPLES which are ripe will give slightly when pushed at the stem end and the inner leaves will detach with a gentle pull. Normally, the skin is greenish brown when unripe, yellow when almost ready to eat, and tinged with red and orange when fully ripe. The "pineapple smell" will get stronger and stronger as the fruit ripens and the little bumps will stand out more. Avoid those with mold on the bottom or a fermented odor, as the fruit has passed its prime.

To prepare for eating, cut off the leaves and a small part of the top. Quarter the pineapple from end to end. With a small paring knife cut off the skin, cutting off the "eyes" but not the flesh. These quarter "boats" can be scraped with a soup spoon to remove all the flesh and juice or can be used as fruit salad bowls. Remove the tough center core and cut the pineapple in spears or chunks. Alternatively, the fruit can be sliced into circular sections and then peeled and cored with a paring knife.

PLUMS come in green, yellow, red, purple and blue skins with tastes ranging from tangy to sweet and skins that are bitter or sweet. Most fresh plums are Japanese or domestic varieties. The pits of most are difficult to remove. Plums are slightly soft but not mushy when ripe and are a colorful addition to fruit salads. They also make a tasty unusual pie.

PRUNE PLUMS (European plums) are a type of plum grown almost exclusively for drying. However, some varieties such as the Italian prune are excellent raw also. The dark blue fruit is smaller and oval in shape with a greenish brown sweet flesh.

POMEGRANATES are bumpily rounded and covered with a dark red skin which dries out and gets tough and leathery as the fruit ripens. Eat them when they begin to shrivel up and the shape of the seeds becomes visible through the skin. The jelly like stuff around the seeds is good to eat, the pith is not. Cut the fruit in half and remove seeds or try this technique: Thoroughly mash the insides of the pomegranate by rolling it around, being careful to not break the skin. Then carefully puncture the skin in one place and suck out the juice. Be careful, the juice stains and may spurt out of the pomegranate.

RAISINS are dried grapes, usually a seedless variety. The most common are the Thompson seedless and the Black Monukka (large, very black and sweet raisins). Golden raisins, made from Sultana grapes, are seedless, and are used in Indian and Middle Eastern cuisine.

RHUBARB is not a fruit, it is a stalk vegetable, but it is being included here because most people eat it as a fruit. Do not eat the leaves: they are poisonous! The stalks, however, are delicious when simmered with honey and eaten as a sauce or used in pie. Rhubarb is also delicious combined with apples or other fruits such as berries. If possible, pick thin red stalks as they will be tender and impart a red tint to the sauce. If the stalks are thick, they may be peeled as celery so that the sauce does not

have coarse fibers in it. The light pink hothouse variety is less tart and not as stringy. To prepare, wash, and cut in 1/2 inch pieces. Use about 2/3 C of honey and 1/4 C of water for every pound of rhubarb and simmer in a heavy pan until rhubarb is soft. Pies may be spiced with cinnamon.

About Dried Fruits

Many fruits are available dried. Almost any fruit can be dried at home or made into FRUIT LEATHERS (p.237). Dried fruit keeps very well if it is kept cool, dry and in bug-proof containers. Storage is discussed more completely in the section on KITCHEN WAYS (p. 21). The drying process itself is discussed in the section on CANNING AND PRESERVING (p. 237). It is possible to eat dried fruit as is or reconstituted by soaking or cooking it in water or fruit juice. Try soaking dried apricots overnight in orange juice. The orange juice absorbs some of the apricot flavor and the apricots become plump and soft. Dried fruit is the perfect food for backpacking or taking along in a sack lunch. As a candy substitute, dried fruit is great, but just like candy, it sticks to the teeth and encourages decay if not removed by brushing the teeth.

Most commercial dried fruit has been treated with sulfur and some form of chemical preservative or fumigant. Naturally-dried fruit is often drier than the soft, chewy commercial product, which reduces the need for chemical preservatives. The lower moisture content makes the fruit tougher, but soaking easily softens it. In the absence of sulfur, there is a tendency for the fruit to darken and discolor, but this doesn't affect the nutritional value or taste. Naturally-dried fruit may ferment in hot, moist conditions, so buy it from someplace where it is stored in a cool location. It's a good idea to wash the fruit to remove dust and possible insect eggs. When purchasing large amounts of dried fruit (i.e. from a buying club or co-op) remember that the best quality fruit is available soon after the season of that particular fruit.

FRUIT SALADS

Fruit salads can be served with any meal as a salad or as a dessert. You will find salads containing both fruits and vegetables in the SALADS section (p. 59). Some salad dressings in the SALADS section may also be used on fruit salads.

The salads that follow include fruit available during different seasons. Experiment, using what you have available locally. Cut the fruit into small bite-sized pieces but do not mince. You want to be able to identify the fruit and also have the flavors blend.

Include contrasting colors and textures. Fruit salads will keep 24 to 36 hours if your fruit is fresh, you don't use bananas, and it is kept refrigerated in a tightly closed container. Serving sizes are approximate, depending upon when and to whom you are serving these salads. On summer days you can make a fruit salad for breakfast which can also be eaten for lunch or for snacks throughout the day.

Spring Sweet Fruit Salad

Preparation time: 15 minutes
Yields: 4-6 servings

**2 medium apples, cut into bite-sized
   pieces
2 firm bananas, peeled and sliced
1/4 C raisins or currants or dried
   cranberries
1/4 C date pieces
1/4 C minced apricots or prunes
1/2 C shredded coconut
1 basket strawberries, sliced or quartered
2 T honey
1/4 C apple juice**

Combine the above ingredients except the honey and apple juice. Mix the apple juice and honey and pour over salad.

Calories: 416.6
Fat (gm): 17.5
Protein (gm): 3.2
Cholesterol (mg): 0
Sodium (mg): 15.3

VARIATIONS: Omit honey and apple juice or substitute dried figs or other minced dried fruit for the dried fruit in the recipe. Add an avocado for a more substantial salad. Add or substitute other sweet fruits in season such as pears, other berries, peaches, etc.

Tropical Delight

Preparation time: 20 minutes
Yields: 4 servings

**2 C pineapple, peeled and cut into
   bite-sized pieces
1 grapefruit, peeled and cut into
   bite-sized pieces
2 oranges, peeled and cut into bite-sized
   pieces
1/4 to 1/2 C date pieces
1 avocado, peeled and cut into bite-sized
   pieces
1^1/$_2$ T honey**

Combine ingredients and stir vigorously to mix juices. This makes a creamy dressing.

Calories: 228.4
Fat (gm): 7.3
Protein (gm): 2.0
Cholesterol (mg): 0
Sodium (mg): 6.9

Summer Salad

Preparation time: 20-25 minutes
Yields: 6 servings

1 C seedless grapes (halved if large) or
    blueberries
3 plums, cut into bite-sized pieces
4 large apricots or 2 kiwis, peeled and cut
    into bite-sized pieces
2 nectarines or 2 peaches, peeled and cut
    into bite-sized pieces
2 small bananas, peeled and sliced
1 large crisp apple, cut into bite-sized
    pieces
1 large slice dried pineapple (minced) or
    6 dried apricots (minced)

Wash fruit, prepare as directed in list of
ingredients and mix in a bowl. Serves 6.

With dried apricots:
Calories: 118.5
Fat (gm): .6
Protein (gm): 1.3
Cholesterol (mg): 0
Sodium (mg): 1.0

Apple-less Salad

Preparation time: 15-20 minutes
Yields: 6 servings

2 C melon balls or bite-sized pieces
2 firm bananas, peeled and sliced
3 plums, cut into bite-sized pieces
4 apricots, cut into bite-sized pieces
2 peaches (peeled), or nectarines
    (peeled), cut into bite-sized pieces
1 C sliced strawberries or blackberries or
    blueberries

Wash fruit and cut into bite-sized pieces. Mix
and serve.

Calories: 103.2
Fat (gm): .5
Protein (gm): 1.6
Cholesterol (mg): 0
Sodium (mg): 5.6

Winter Fruit Salad

Preparation time: 10-15 minutes
Yields: 4 servings

2 firm bananas, sliced
3 small to medium apples, cut into
    bite-sized pieces
1/4 C cashews
1/4 C minced dried apricots, raisins or
    date pieces or other dried fruit

Mix ingredients and top with BANANA
HONEY DRESSING (p. 46), or a T of honey.
If apples are old or slightly overripe, a
squeeze of lemon juice perks up the flavor
and helps keep the salad from discoloring.

Calories: 186.8
Fat (gm): 4.4
Protein (gm): 2.2
Cholesterol (mg): 0
Sodium (mg): 3.3

VARIATION: Add 1 C sliced canned peaches
or other canned fruit.

Banana Orange Salad

Preparation time: 10 minutes
Yields: 2 servings

1 large orange
1 large banana
1 T honey

Peel and cut the orange into bite-sized
pieces. Add the honey. Mash a few pieces of
the orange to draw out the juices. Peel and
slice the banana and fold into the orange and
honey mixture.

Calories: 116.0
Fat (gm): .2
Protein (gm): 1.0
Cholesterol (mg): 0
Sodium (mg): 1.0

Indian Fruit Salad

Preparation time: 20 minutes
Yields: 6 servings

1 large pear, cut into bite-sized pieces
1 C fresh seedless grapes, cut in half
1 apple, cut into bite-sized pieces
1 banana, sliced
1 C berries (raspberries, blueberries or
   blackberries)
1/2 C cashew pieces
1/3 C cream
1/2 t vanilla
seeds of 2 cardamom pods or 1/4 to 1/2 t
   ground cardamom
1 pinch saffron
2 T honey

Mix ingredients and serve.

Calories: 195.4
Fat (gm): 8.7
Protein (gm): 2.6
Cholesterol (mg): 11.4
Sodium (mg): 7.9

FRUIT DRESSINGS
(See also LEMON HONEY DRESSING, p. 65)

Banana Honey Dressing

Preparation time: 10 minutes
Yields: 3/4 C

1 large banana
2 T cashews or walnuts
1 T honey
1 t lemon juice

Mix in a blender until smooth.

Per Tablespoon:
Calories: 23.3
Fat (gm): .7
Protein (gm): .3
Cholesterol (mg): 0
Sodium (mg): .5

Spicy Fruit Dressing

Preparation time: 10 minutes
Yields: about 1³/₄ C

*This dressing almost has the consistency of
mayonnaise.*

1/2 C honey
1/4 t salt
1 C oil
1 T mustard powder
1¹/₂ T poppy seeds
1/2 C lemon juice

Blend ingredients together.

Per Tablespoon:
Calories: 92.0
Fat (gm): 7.5
Protein (gm): .2
Cholesterol (mg): 0
Sodium (mg): 20.3

Fruity Fruit Salad Dressing

Preparation time: 10 minutes
Yields: 1¹/₄ C

1 large banana, peeled
1 peach, peeled and pit removed
1 t lemon juice (optional)
1 t honey (optional)

Liquify fruits in blender. If desired, add the
lemon and the honey. The lemon will keep
the banana from turning brown. Serve over a
fruit salad.

Per Tablespoon:
Calories: 7.1
Fat (gm): Trace
Protein (gm): Trace
Cholesterol (mg): 0
Sodium (mg): .1

VARIATION: Add blueberries—yum!

NOTE: This dressing is good on "dry" salads,
but it does not keep even for a few hours
and should be eaten immediately.

Avocado Yogurt Dressing

Preparation time: 10-15 minutes
Yields: 6-8 servings

1 avocado, peeled and pit removed
1/4 C dried coconut
1/2 C yogurt
2 T honey

Blend together until smooth.

Per serving:
Calories: 147.6
Fat (gm): 10.6
Protein (gm): 2.0
Cholesterol (mg): 1.4
Sodium (mg): 21.9

FRUIT JELLS

Remember the colorful jells filled with delicious fruit that you probably enjoyed as a child (not to mention as an adult)? Here are some healthful versions for vegetarians. They are made with agar, a clear seaweed product that works as gelatin does (gelatin is a non-vegetarian product).

Most agar jells will seep liquid after 24 hours or so. This does not affect the jell and can be drained. For those of you who have worked with gelatin and know that you cannot use fresh pineapple in a gelatin jell, that does not apply to agar jells. Agar will jell raw pineapple.

Agar comes in at least 3 different forms. If you do not have agar flakes, you can substitute granulated agar or kantan bars. Agar can also be substituted for gelatin. If your agar doesn't turn out the consistency you like, adjust the amount used next time.

- 1 T agar flakes = 1 T gelatin
- 1 T agar flakes = $1^1/_2$ t granulated agar (If you are using granulated agar in these recipes, you need to use 1/2 as much as you would agar flakes.)
- 1 bar of kantan (about 1/4 oz.) will jell $1^1/_3$ C liquid

Agar jells can be used for salads, snacks and desserts. Layer different flavors and colors in parfait glasses and top with whipped cream for an elegant dessert. Jell in a small plastic container with a tight lid or small thermos for a child's (or adult's) lunch. All of the following recipes jell well and can be made in molds to be served shimmering on a plate. Have fun!

Basic Fruit Jell

Preparation time: 20-25 minutes
Chill time: 2-3 hours
Yields: 3 servings

$1^1/_2$ C fruit juice
2 to 4 T honey
1/4 C lemon juice
1 T agar flakes or $1^1/_2$ t granulated agar
1 C fruit, cut in bite-sized pieces

Cut the fruit before starting as the jell sets very rapidly. Stir the agar into half of the fruit juice and let sit for 1 to 2 minutes. Add the honey. Bring to a boil and boil for 2 minutes, stirring constantly. It will foam so you need a pan about 4 times as deep as the liquid. Remove from the heat and add the rest of the liquid. Cool to room temperature and gently stir in the fruit. Refrigerate until set.

Using orange juice and peaches:
Calories: 162.2
Fat (gm): .1
Protein (gm): 1.7
Cholesterol (mg): 0
Sodium (mg): 2.8

Orange Agar Jell

Preparation time: 20-25 minutes
Chill time: 2-3 hours
Yields: 4 servings

3¼ C orange juice
2 to 4 T honey (optional)
2 T agar flakes or 1 T granulated agar
2 to 3 C fruit

Cut the fruit before starting as the jell sets
very rapidly. Stir the agar into half of the
fruit juice and let sit for 1 to 2 minutes. Add
the honey. Bring to a boil and boil for 2
minutes, stirring constantly. It will foam so
you need a pan about 4 times as deep as the
liquid is. Remove from the heat and add the
rest of the liquid. Cool to room temperature
and gently stir in the fruit. Refrigerate until
set.

Calories: 164.9
Fat (gm): .2
Protein (gm): 2.7
Cholesterol (mg): 0
Sodium (mg): 2.7

Berry Orange Jell

Preparation time: 20-25 minutes
Chill time: 2-3 hours
Yields: 6 servings

2 T agar flakes or 1 T granulated agar
1½ C cold water
1¾ C orange juice
2 C raspberries

Stir the agar into the water and let sit for 1 to
2 minutes. Bring to a boil and boil for 2
minutes, stirring constantly. It will foam so
you need a pan about 4 times as deep as the
liquid. Remove from the heat and add the
orange juice. Cool to room temperature and
gently stir in the fruit. Refrigerate until set.

Calories: 78.9
Fat (gm): .4
Protein (gm): 1.5
Cholesterol (mg): 0
Sodium (mg): 3.8

Pear Apple Cinnamon Jell

Preparation time: 20-25 minutes
Chill time: 2-3 hours
Yields: 6 servings

2 T agar flakes or 1 T granulated agar
3½ C apple juice
3 C canned pears
1/2 t cinnamon

Cut the fruit before starting as the jell sets
very rapidly. Stir the agar into half of the
juice and let sit for 1 to 2 minutes. Add the
honey and cinnamon. Bring to a boil and
boil for 2 minutes, stirring constantly. It will
foam so you need a pan about 4 times as
deep as the liquid. Remove from the heat
and add the rest of the liquid. Cool to room
temperature and gently stir in the fruit.
Refrigerate until set.

Calories: 129.5
Fat (gm): .1
Protein (gm): .4
Cholesterol (mg): 0
Sodium (mg): 8.8

Banana Lemon Jell

Preparation time: 20-25 minutes
Chill time: 2-3 hours
Yields: 6 servings

3 C water
5 T lemon juice
3 T honey
2 T agar flakes or 1 T granulated agar
2 bananas, pureed smooth
2 C fruit, cut into bite-sized pieces

Cut the fruit before starting as the jell sets
very rapidly. Stir the agar into half of the
water and let sit for 1 to 2 minutes. Add the
honey. Bring to a boil and boil for 2 minutes,
stirring constantly. It will foam so you need
a pan about 4 times as deep as the liquid.
Remove from the heat and add the rest of the
liquid. Cool to room temperature and gently
stir in the fruit. Refrigerate until set.

Using plums:
Calories: 100.0
Fat (gm): .4
Protein (gm): .8
Cholesterol (mg): 0
Sodium (mg): 6.8

Grape Pineapple Jell

Preparation time: 20-25 minutes
Chill time: 2-3 hours
Yields: 4 servings

$1\frac{1}{2}$ T agar flakes or 3/4 T granulated agar
$2\frac{3}{4}$ C grape juice
$1\frac{1}{2}$ C fresh pineapple cut into bite-sized
  pieces

Cut the fruit before starting as the jell sets
very rapidly. Stir the agar into half of the
fruit juice and let sit for 1 to 2 minutes. Add
the honey. Bring to a boil and boil for 2
minutes, stirring constantly. It will foam so
you need a pan about 4 times as deep as the
liquid is. Remove from the heat and add the
rest of the liquid. Cool to room temperature
and gently stir in the fruit. Refrigerate until
set.

Calories: 135.2
Fat (gm): .1
Protein (gm): 1.1
Cholesterol (mg): 0
Sodium (mg): 5.0

Downright Delicious

Preparation time: 20-25 minutes
Chill time: 2-3 hours
Yields: 8 servings

3 T agar flakes or $4\frac{1}{2}$ t granulated agar
$2\frac{1}{2}$ C water
3/4 C honey
$1\frac{1}{2}$ C orange juice
1/2 C lemon juice
$1\frac{1}{2}$ C cantaloupe balls
$1\frac{1}{2}$ C blackberries

Prepare the fruit before starting as the jell
sets very rapidly. Stir the agar into water and
let sit for 1 to 2 minutes. Add the honey.

Bring to a boil and boil for 2 minutes, stirring
constantly. It will foam so you need a pan
about 4 times as deep as the liquid. Remove
from the heat and add the rest of the liquid.
Cool to room temperature and gently stir in
the fruit. Refrigerate until set.

Calories: 145.8
Fat (gm): .1
Protein (gm): .8
Cholesterol (mg): 0
Sodium (mg): 9.8

Ambrosia

Preparation time: 25-30 minutes
Chill time: 2-3 hours
Yields: 8 servings

*This lives up to its name and is one of our
favorites.*

2 T agar flakes or 1 T granulated agar
1 C cold water
1/3 C honey
1 C fruit juice
1 C thick yogurt
1 C pineapple cut into bite-sized pieces
  (canned unsweetened will work)
1 C grapes, cut in half
1 C oranges, fresh peeled and cut into
  bite-sized pieces or unsweetened
  canned mandarins
1 C coconut
1/2 C cashews
1 t dried lemon or orange rind

Cut the fruit before starting as the jell sets
very rapidly. Stir the agar into the water and
let sit for 1 to 2 minutes. Add the honey.
Bring to a boil and boil for 2 minutes, stirring
constantly. It will foam so you need a pan
about 4 times as deep as the liquid. Remove
from the heat and add the rest of the liquid.
Cool to room temperature and gently stir in
all the other ingredients. Refrigerate until set.

Calories: 345.4
Fat (gm): 21.7
Protein (gm): 4.6
Cholesterol (mg): 2.0
Sodium (mg): 36.4

FROZEN FRUIT DISHES

Banana Ice Cream

Preparation time: 5-10 minutes (freeze
    bananas overnight)
Yields: 6 servings

4 bananas

Freeze bananas in their skins until hard.
Remove from the freezer and cut into 1 to 2
inch pieces. Slice the skin and peel it off
(they may need to thaw a little). Or, peel the
bananas before freezing and freeze in a
plastic bag. Put the pieces in small amounts
into a blender and blend until smooth, or
thaw a little and squish with a fork. Eat
immediately or refreeze in a covered
container. Top with CAROB SYRUP (p. 205),
fruit, nuts, or use in a parfait.

Calories: 70.0
Fat (gm): 0
Protein (gm): .7
Cholesterol (mg): 0
Sodium (mg): .7

Nanapeachi (Fruit Ice Cream)

Preparation time: 5-10 minutes
Yields: 8 servings

5 ripe bananas, frozen
4 medium peaches, pits removed

Let frozen bananas thaw slightly. Peel,
chunk and puree peaches. Peel and slice the
bananas, adding them to the peaches in a
blender. Blend until mixture is a fairly
uniform consistency like ice cream. Eat as is
or return to the freezer for a while to harden
slightly.

Calories: 84.1
Fat (gm): 0
Protein (gm): .9
Cholesterol (mg): 0
Sodium (mg): .6

Zinnamaroon

Preparation time: 5-10 minutes
Yields: 6 servings

5 frozen bananas
1 pint box of blackberries
1/4 to 1/2 t cinnamon
1 or 2 nectarines, chopped
1/3 C date pieces

Peel and blend bananas. Fold in cleaned
berries, cinnamon, dates and chopped
nectarines.

Calories: 156.3
Fat (gm): 0
Protein (gm): 1.6
Cholesterol (mg): 0
Sodium (mg): 1.2

VARIATIONS: Use applesauce in place of the
bananas. Add coconut. Substitute other dried
fruit for dates.

Banana Popsicles

Preparation time: 5-10 minutes
Yields: 2 servings

1 banana
1 t honey
2 T cashews
2 popsicle sticks

Cut firm peeled bananas in half crosswise.
Insert popsicle stick. Coat bananas with
warmed honey. Roll in chopped cashews.
Freeze unwrapped until solid, then store in
freezer containers or plastic bags.

Calories: 112.2
Fat (gm): 0
Protein (gm): 1.8
Cholesterol (mg): 0
Sodium (mg): 1.9

VARIATION: Dip in CAROB SAUCE (p. 205)
instead of honey.

Basic Frozen Fruit Parfait

Preparation time: 10-15 minutes
Yields: 6 servings

**1/2 recipe ZINNAMAROON or
NANAPEACHI, or 2$^1/_2$ C pureed frozen
bananas
2 C blackberries, persimmons, papaya or
peaches**

Layer in glasses, creating stripes. Top with a
sprinkling of whole berries. May be topped
with whipped cream or yogurt and honey.
These are quite festive.

Calories: 102.8
Fat (gm): .4
Protein (gm): 1.1
Cholesterol (mg): 0
Sodium (mg): .6

Banapple Parfait

Preparation time: 10-15 minutes
Yields: 4 servings

**2 frozen bananas, peeled and pureed
2 C very hot apple sauce
1/2 C chopped walnuts (optional)**

Layer ingredients in parfait glasses or swirl in
dessert dishes. Serve immediately as the
contrast between the hot and cold
ingredients is a delightful experience which
is lost when the dessert is allowed to sit.

VARIATIONS: Add CAROB SYRUP (p. 205),
or slices of fresh fruit.

Calories: 175.6
Fat (gm): 8.3
Protein (gm): .5
Cholesterol (mg): 0
Sodium (mg): 2.8

FRUIT SAUCES, COMPOTES, PUDDINGS, ETC.

Raw Applesauce

Preparation time: 20 minutes
Yields: 4 servings

**6 medium apples
1/2 C apple juice
1$^1/_2$ t lemon juice**

Wash, core, and chop apples, leaving skins
on. Put in the blender a few pieces at a
time, adding enough apple juice to make
blending easy. Scrape sides of blender
frequently and gradually add the rest of the
chopped apples. For best nutrition, color
and flavor, raw applesauce should be
prepared immediately before serving. It can
also be added to cakes and breads, giving
them a moist, rich texture.

Calories: 137.1
Fat (gm): 0
Protein (gm): .4
Cholesterol (mg): 0
Sodium (mg): 3.5

VARIATION: Add other fruit such as bananas,
berries, nectarines, peaches, or pears.

Applesauce

Preparation time: 20 minutes
Cooking time: 30-60 minutes
Yields: 4 servings

8 apples
1/2 C honey
1 t cinnamon

Core and chop the apples. Peel if skins are the slightest bit bitter. Using the heaviest gauge pan you have (cast iron is best), cook apples on the lowest heat possible. Cover tightly. If only a light gauge pan is available, or quick cooking is desired, add a small amount of water or apple juice. Simmer very slowly until juice is beginning to come out of the apples and they are beginning to soften. Add honey and cinnamon to taste. The amounts given are approximate because the amounts needed depend upon the size, age and variety of apples used. Cook until desired consistency; apples should be soft. If smooth applesauce is desired, put it through a food mill, blend, or process in a food processor. If apples are bland or mealy, add 2 to 4 T lemon juice to perk up the flavor. Serve warm or cold.

Calories: 275.5
Fat (gm): 0
Protein (gm): .5
Cholesterol (mg): 0
Sodium (mg): 2.2

VARIATIONS: Add raisins, chopped dates or other fruit.

Fig Apple Compote

Preparation time: 20 minutes
Cooking time: 30-45 minutes
Yields: 4 servings

1 C fresh figs, stemmed and cut in
  quarters
1 medium apple, cut into chunks
1 small pear, cut into chunks
1/4 C dried apricots, finely chopped
2 T raisins
pinch powdered ginger
pinch cinnamon

Simmer fruit and spices over a medium low heat, stirring frequently until apples are soft and the figs and pears have cooked down into a sauce. Serve hot or cold with millet or yogurt.

Calories: 171.1
Fat (gm): 0
Protein (gm): 1.2
Cholesterol (mg): 0
Sodium (mg): 4.5

VARIATIONS: Add 1/2 t dried lemon peel or 3 T lemon juice. Substitute 1 t CURRY POWDER (p. 223) for the other spices. Substitute berries for the figs, peaches or plums for the pears, prunes for the dried apricots, or dates for the raisins.

FIG APPLE PIE OR TURNOVER FILLING:
Thicken by adding 2 T arrowroot dissolved in 2 T water. Add to the above mixture after cooking into a sauce but before filling the pie shell.

Holiday Ginger Fruit

Preparation time: 20 minutes
Cooking time: 30 minutes
Yields: 8 servings

1/2 C pitted prunes
1/2 C dried apricots
1/2 C dried cranberries or raisins
1 C ginger ale (there are several varieties without sugar)
1/2 C orange juice
1/3 C honey
1/2 t minced peeled ginger root or 1/4 t ground ginger
1 cinnamon stick
3/4 C pineapple, cut into bite-sized pieces
1/2 C peach slices

Heat the dried fruit, ginger ale, orange juice, honey, and spices in a large saucepan until boiling. Reduce heat to low, cover and simmer until fruit is tender (about 20 minutes). While cooking, prepare peaches and pineapple. If using canned fruit, drain it well. Stir into the dried fruit mixture. Serve warm or chilled. This can be served over yogurt or with cream.

Calories: 167.8
Fat (gm): 0
Protein (gm): 1.1
Cholesterol (mg): 0
Sodium (mg): 7.7

Winter Breakfast

Preparation time: 20 minutes
Cooking time: 30-45 minutes
Yields: 4 servings

3 C chopped cooking apples
1/4 C water
1/4 C chopped dates
1/4 C minced mixed dried fruit or raisins
1/4 t cinnamon
1 medium banana, sliced

Combine all of the above ingredients except banana and cinnamon. Cook slowly in a covered kettle until apples are mushy. At this point, add bananas and cinnamon. Cover,

turn off heat, and let bananas steam until slightly soft.

Calories: 129.8
Fat (gm): .3
Protein (gm): .9
Cholesterol (mg): 0
Sodium (mg): 7.2

Curried Fruit

Preparation time: 20 minutes
Yields: 4 servings

This is excellent served over yogurt or plain. It can be made without the butter but the taste suffers. This is from Joy's mother's recipe. She used a whole cup of butter! It can be made in the winter from canned unsweetened fruit. (If fruit is sweetened, omit or reduce the honey).

1 C pears, peeled and cut in half
1 C pineapple chunks
1 C peaches, peeled and quartered
1/2 to 1 C honey
2-3 t CURRY POWDER (p. 223)
1/4 C butter

Melt the butter with the honey and curry powder. Spread mixture on fruit in a flat baking pan. Bake at 300° for an hour, basting occasionally. Serve hot. Excellent with yogurt.

Calories: 303.5
Fat (gm): 11.7
Protein (gm): .9
Cholesterol (mg): 33.0
Sodium (mg): 126.4

VARIATION: Use bananas, apples, cashews, and dates.

 FRUIT

Tapioca Fruit Pudding

Preparation time: 20 minutes (includes
   cooking)
Yields: 6 servings

*Joy's daughter refers to this as "Tadpole Egg
Pudding" because of the shape of the tapioca
as it cooks. It is one of her favorites.*

1¹/₂ C water
1/3 C granulated tapioca (refer to "About
   Tapioca" in the DESSERTS section
   p.193)
1/4 C honey
1/4 t salt
1/2 C pineapple or other juice
1¹/₂ T lemon juice
1/2 C crushed pineapple
2 C fruit, cut in bite-sized pieces
   (nectarines, peaches, grapes, berries)

Mix tapioca, water, honey and salt in a heavy
saucepan. Heat over medium heat, stirring
frequently, 5 to 10 minutes until tapioca is
clear. Remove from heat and cool slightly.
Stir in the pineapple and lemon juices and
fold in the fruit. Chill.

Calories: 120.3
Fat (gm): .2
Protein (gm): .5
Cholesterol (mg): 0
Sodium (mg): 92.7

Honey Stewed Prunes

Preparation time: 30-40 minutes (includes
   cooking)
Yields: 5 servings

1 orange
20 large pitted prunes
1/3 C honey
1 T arrowroot
2 C water

Juice the orange and cut the peel into fine
strips. In a saucepan, combine prunes,
water, orange peel and honey. Bring to a
boil, cover and simmer 20 minutes until
prunes are soft. Using a slotted spoon,

remove prunes to a serving dish. Combine
arrowroot and orange juice. Add to syrup in
saucepan. Bring to a boil and cook, stirring
until thick and smooth. Pour over prunes.
May be served warm or cold. Good served
with yogurt, cottage cheese or cream cheese.

Calories: 161.4
Fat (gm): 0
Protein (gm): .9
Cholesterol (mg): 0
Sodium (mg): 5.1

Ginger Poached Pears

Preparation time: 20 minutes (includes
   cooking)
Yields: 4 servings

1/2 C honey
juice and grated rind of 1 lemon and 1
   orange
1/2 to 1 t ginger
4 pears, peeled and cored

Bring the first three ingredients to boil. Add
pears and simmer for 5 minutes, basting with
the liquid mixture frequently. Good served
with yogurt, cottage cheese or cream cheese.

Calories: 239.0
Fat (gm): 0
Protein (gm): .6
Cholesterol (mg): 0
Sodium (mg): 3.4

Summer Fruit Soup

Preparation time: 20 minutes
Yields: 4 servings

2 C peeled peach slices
1 C plum slices
2 C water
1/4 C honey
2 T arrowroot
1 T lemon juice
1/2 t vanilla
1½ C berries
1½ C nectarines

Puree peach and plum slices in a blender.
Combine water and arrowroot in a saucepan,
stirring well to prevent lumping. Mix in
pureed fruit and honey. Bring to a boil,
stirring to prevent lumping. Remove from
heat, add lemon and vanilla. Stir well, cover,
and chill. Just before serving, add additional
fruit.

Calories: 179.0
Fat (gm): 0
Protein (gm): 1.6
Cholesterol (mg): 0
Sodium (mg): 5.8

BAKED FRUIT DISHES

(See also DESSERTS (p. 179) for PEACH
COBBLER, APPLE CRISP, STRAWBERRY
SHORTCAKE, and FRUIT PIES)

Baked Apples

Preparation time: 10-15 minutes
Cooking time: 40-60 minutes
Yields:

1 apple for each person

For each apple:
1 T raisins or chopped dates
1 t walnuts or cashews
1/8 t cinnamon
1/2 T honey

Wash and core apples. Fill the cavity with
raisins, nuts, and honey. Sprinkle with

cinnamon. Bake at 350° for 40 to 60 minutes
(depending on the size of the apple), until
apple is soft. If apples begin to dry out, baste
with apple juice or water and cover.

Calories: 160.3
Fat (gm): 0
Protein (gm): .8
Cholesterol (mg): 0
Sodium (mg): 3.1

Baked Banana Apples

Preparation time: 15 minutes
Cooking time: 1 hour
Yields: 6 servings

2 medium bananas
1 T lemon juice
1/4 C honey
1/4 t nutmeg
6 medium baking apples

Wash and core apples and place in a shallow
baking dish. Peel and mash bananas and
mix with lemon juice, honey and nutmeg.
Fill apples with banana mixture. Bake at
375° for 1 hour or until tender.

Calories: 160.3
Fat (gm): 0
Protein (gm): .6
Cholesterol (mg): 0
Sodium (mg): 2.5

 FRUIT

Baked Bananas

Preparation time: 10 minutes
Cooking time: 10 minutes
Yields: 2 servings

2 medium bananas
2 T lemon juice
2 T honey

Peel bananas and halve lengthwise.
Combine lemon juice and honey and spread
over bananas, coating them thoroughly. Bake
at 400° for 10 minutes or until bananas are
golden.

Calories: 173.0
Fat (gm): 0
Protein (gm): 1.0
Cholesterol (mg): 0
Sodium (mg): 5.0

VARIATIONS: Use molasses instead of honey.
Add 1 T butter to basting mixture. Add 1 t
dried orange rind or 1/2 t ginger. Add 1/4 C
coconut shreds to basting mixture.

Baked Curried Bananas

Preparation time: 15 minutes
Cooking time: about 15 minutes
Yields: 4 servings

4 large bananas
1/4 C butter
1 t CURRY POWDER (p. 223)
1 T honey

Cut bananas in half crosswise and then
lengthwise. Melt butter in shallow baking
dish in preheated 350° oven. Stir in curry
powder and honey. Dip banana pieces in
mixture, turning to cover well. Bake about
15 minutes.

Calories: 230.8
Fat (gm): 11.7
Protein (gm): 1.1
Cholesterol (mg): 33.0
Sodium (mg): 124.5

Baked Peaches

Preparation time: 15-20 minutes
Cooking time: 30 minutes
Yields: 6 servings

1/3 C honey
1/4 C lemon juice
1/2 C water
6 to 8 medium peaches

Mix the first 3 ingredients. Peel peaches, cut
in half and pit. Arrange them in a 2 quart
casserole. Pour honey mixture over peaches.
Cover and bake at 350° for 1/2 hour or until
tender. Serve warm or cold. May be served
with cream or yogurt.

Calories: 102.4
Fat (gm): 0
Protein (gm): .5
Cholesterol (mg): 0
Sodium (mg): 3.5

Honey Baked Pears

Preparation time: 10 minutes
Cooking time: about 30 minutes
Yields: 4 servings

3 T lemon juice (1 lemon)
1/2 C honey
1 t cinnamon
2 t oil
4 large pears, halved and cored

Mix first four ingredients and pour over pear
halves in shallow, slightly oiled baking pan.
Bake until soft at 350°. Serve hot. May be
served with yogurt or cream.

Calories: 252.5
Fat (gm): 2.3
Protein (gm): .5
Cholesterol (mg): 0
Sodium (mg): 3.2

OTHER COOKED FRUIT RECIPES

Fried Bananas

Preparation time: 10 minutes
Cooking time: 10 minutes
Yields: 4 servings

3 bananas
1/4 C flour
1/4 t mace
1 to 2 T milk, apple juice or water
1/4 C honey
1/4 t cinnamon
1/4 t dried lemon peel
2 T oil

Add flour to honey. Add seasonings. Add enough liquid a little bit at a time to make a thick batter. Cut peeled bananas in half crosswise and then lengthwise. Coat in batter and saute in the oil until batter browns.

Calories: 231.5
Fat (gm): 6.8
Protein (gm): 1.9
Cholesterol (mg): .3
Sodium (mg): 4.0

VARIATIONS: Substitute 1/4 t to 1/2 t turmeric for all the above spices.

Broiled Grapefruit

Preparation time: 5 minutes
Cooking time: 3-8 minutes
Yields: 2 servings

1 grapefruit
$1^1/_2$ T honey
1 T butter

Wash and dry grapefruit and cut in half crosswise. With a sharp knife, cut around the sections, separating the soft fruit from the membranes. Spread the top with honey and dot with butter. Broil until the honey begins to caramelize. Serve hot for breakfast.

Calories: 141.8
Fat (gm): 5.8
Protein (gm): .8
Cholesterol (mg): 16.5
Sodium (mg): 62.2

Salads

 SALADS

SALADS

If you are looking for a FRUIT SALAD or FRUIT SALAD DRESSINGS, please refer to the FRUITS section (p. 35). This section contains vegetable salads, those salads which have both fruits and vegetables in them, and additional salad dressings.

Waldorf Salad

Preparation time: 10 minutes
Yields: 4 servings

2 red apples, cored and diced, but not peeled
1 large stalk celery, minced
1 T honey
1 t lemon juice
1/2 C chopped pecans or walnuts
2 T TOFU MAYONNAISE (p. 153) or YOGURT (p. 213) (omit lemon juice if using yogurt)

Blend mayonnaise, honey and lemon juice. Add to celery and diced apple. Mix well and top with nuts.

Calories: 187.5
Fat (gm): 11.8
Protein (gm): 1.2
Cholesterol (mg): 0
Sodium (mg): 34.2

Basic Vegetable Salad

Preparation time: 15-20 minutes
Yields: 6 servings

This salad will keep well for 48 hours if kept tightly sealed and refrigerated. Practically speaking, that means that it can be made on the weekend and last for 2 work nights with just a little addition of something different each night. Adding any other vegetables included under the variations will cut down on the storage time. This salad is also good in sandwiches in place of plain lettuce.

1 head red leaf lettuce, thoroughly washed and torn into bite-sized pieces
1 large carrot, peeled and grated
1 beet, peeled and grated
1 C alfalfa sprouts
1 stalk celery, minced
1 medium zucchini, thinly sliced or grated

Combine ingredients and toss. Serve as is, topped with sunflower seeds, or with any of the dressings included in this section.

Calories: 18.5
Fat (gm): trace
Protein (gm): .7
Cholesterol (mg): 0
Sodium (mg): 18.4

VARIATIONS: Add a tomato or two, thinly sliced. Omit beets. Substitute another type of lettuce. Substitute grated Jerusalem artichokes for the carrots or beets. Substitute cucumbers or other summer squash for the zucchini. Add another type of sprout or broccoli or cauliflower florets. Avocados, peppers, fresh raw sweet corn and any other fresh vegetables can be added when they are available.

Buffet Salad Bar

Preparation time: 45-60 minutes

This salad is great for guests or an informal family meal. On a serving table, place the following:

- BASIC VEGETABLE SALAD (p.61)
- Bowls of tomatoes, broccoli and cauliflower flowerettes
- Bowls of chilled, cooked vegetables such as corn or asparagus.
- Bowls of drained, cooked kidney or garbanzo beans
- Bowls of GOMASIO (p. 223), sunflower seeds, artichoke hearts, nuts, pitted olives, grated cheeses
- Containers of a couple of different dressings
- GUACAMOLE (p. 154)

This can be served with bread or dessert or as a meal unto itself.

Solid Salad

Preparation time: 25 minutes
Yields: 2 servings

1 large carrot, peeled and grated
1/2 pound green beans, cooked and cut
1 C bean sprouts
1/2 C alfalfa sprouts
1 stalk celery, minced
2 T olive oil
1 T lemon juice
1 t SALAD HERBS (p. 222)
GOMASIO (p. 223) (optional)

Toss together.

Calories: 219.8
Fat (gm): 13
Protein (gm): 4.8
Cholesterol (mg): 0
Sodium (mg): 42.3

VARIATIONS: Nuts and seeds can be added if desired. This can be made with other vegetables: try raw peas, steamed asparagus, raw or steamed corn, raw broccoli or cauliflower florets.

Sadhu Salad

Preparation time: 30 minutes
Yields: 6 servings

8 leaves of swiss chard or 1 bunch of spinach, torn in bite-sized pieces
4 small tender zucchini, thinly sliced
1 to 2 C cut green beans, steamed and cooled
3 medium carrots, scrubbed or peeled and grated
florets from 2 stalks broccoli
3/4 C RUSSIAN DRESSING (p. 65)

Toss with dressing.

Calories: 165.6
Fat (gm): 12.7
Protein (gm): 1.9
Cholesterol (mg): 0
Sodium (mg): 651.6

Hearty Salad

Preparation time: 30 minutes
Yields: 3-6 servings

1$^1/_2$ C lentil sprouts
1 large carrot, peeled, quartered and thinly sliced
florets of 2 medium stalks of broccoli
1/2 medium head of red leaf or butter lettuce
Optional: steamed peas, tomatoes, romano cheese, sunflower seeds

Lightly steam the broccoli, carrots and sprouts. Cool. Tear the lettuce into bite-sized pieces. Layer the lettuce on plates and top with a mound of the cooked vegetables. Garnish with any of the optional ingredients.

Calories: 64.5
Fat (gm): .2
Protein (gm): 3.0
Cholesterol (mg): 0
Sodium (mg): 19.0

Carrot Jell

Preparation time: 20-25 minutes
Chill time: 2-3 hours
Yields: 6 servings

2 C finely grated carrots (scrubbed or
    peeled)
3 C water
1/3 C lemon juice
3 T honey
2 T agar flakes or 1 T granulated agar

Grate the carrots first as this sets quickly.
Dissolve the agar in 2 C of the water in a 2
quart saucepan. Add the honey and heat,
stirring occasionally, until boiling. Boil 2
minutes. (It will tend to boil over.) Remove
from heat and add the rest of the water. Cool
until it is cool enough so that it won't cook
the carrots. Add the lemon juice and carrots.
Pour into a 4 to 5 C mold.

Calories: 51.1
Fat (gm): 0
Protein (gm): .2
Cholesterol (mg): 0
Sodium (mg): 19.3

VARIATION: Add 1 to 2 C pineapple chunks.

Coleslaw

Preparation time: 15-20 minutes
Yields: 4 servings

2 C finely shredded cabbage (red
    provides a nice color)
1 carrot, peeled and grated
1 stalk celery, finely minced
1/3 C TOFU MAYONNAISE (p. 153), sour
    cream or YOGURT (p. 213)
2 T lemon juice
1 T honey

Combine ingredients well and chill.

Calories: 98.7
Fat (gm): 5.7
Protein (gm): 1.9
Cholesterol (mg): 0
Sodium (mg): 31.8

Italian Salad

Preparation time: 30-40 minutes
Yields: 6 servings

1 bunch broccoli, raw or lightly steamed
    and cut into bite-sized florets
1 head cauliflower, raw or lightly
    steamed and cut into bite-sized
    florets
3 medium carrots, scrubbed or peeled
    and sliced thin
3 stalks celery, minced
1/2 C sunflower seeds
1 C black olives, halved and pitted
2 C artichoke hearts, quartered (optional)
$1^{1}/_{2}$ T lemon juice
1/2 t crushed fennel seeds
1/2 C chopped parsley
1/4 t salt
1 t oregano
1/2 to 1 C feta cheese, crumbled
    (optional)

Combine ingredients and toss. Serve on a
bed of lettuce.

Calories: 207.4
Fat (gm): 13.3
Protein (gm): 5.0
Cholesterol (mg): 0
Sodium (mg): 467.0

Potato Salad

Preparation time: 90 minutes (includes
   cooling time for potatoes)
Yields: 6 servings

**4 medium potatoes, cut into cubes,
   steamed and cooled (leave skins on)**
1 stalk celery, minced
1 carrot, peeled and grated
1/2 t dill weed
1/2 t salt
1/2 t dry mustard
1/3 C TOFU MAYONNAISE (p. 153)

Combine all ingredients and serve.

VARIATION: add minced dill pickles and
minced olives; use new red potatoes (6 to 8
small ones).

Calories: 128.1
Fat (gm): 3.8
Protein (gm): 2.4
Cholesterol (mg): 0
Sodium (mg): 199.2

Broccoli Corn Salad

Preparation time: 30 minutes-2 hours
   (depending on whether broccoli and corn
   are steamed and chilled)
Yields: 6 servings

Florets of one bunch of broccoli
3 ears of sweet corn
**3 small carrots, scrubbed or peeled and
   grated**
4 leaves of chard or 8 of spinach
4 leaves of romaine lettuce
8 leaves of red leaf lettuce
1 C alfalfa sprouts

Wash the broccoli. Husk the corn and slice
off the kernels. If desired the corn and
broccoli florets may be lightly steamed and
chilled or used hot. Wash the greens and tear
into bite-sized pieces. Toss the greens,
sprouts, and grated carrots. Place on plates
and top with the corn and broccoli. If you
have steamed the corn and broccoli and are

using them hot, serve immediately so that the
hot vegetables do not wilt the greens.

Calories: 61.4
Fat (gm): .3
Protein (gm): 1.8
Cholesterol (mg): 0
Sodium (mg): 68.2

VEGETABLE SALAD DRESSINGS

Refer to the FRUITS section (p. 35) for FRUIT
SALAD DRESSINGS. Some dressings for
FRUIT SALAD may be equally tasty with
VEGETABLE SALADS.

Basic Vegetable Salad Dressing

Preparation time: 10 minutes
Yields: 3/4 C

1/4 C lemon juice or vinegar (or more)
1/2 C oil (or less)
**1 t SALAD HERBS (p. 222) or 1/4 t dill
   weed, oregano, basil or pepper**
1/4 t salt to taste

Combine ingredients in a jar that can be
shaken without leaking. The flavor of the
herbs will be enhanced by steeping in the oil
and lemon overnight. Shake well
immediately before use.

Per Tablespoon:
Calories: 81.0
Fat (gm): 8.4
Protein (gm): 0
Cholesterol (mg): 0
Sodium (mg): 178.7

Lemon Honey Dressing

Preparation time: 10 minutes
Yields: 1 C

This is good with both fruit and vegetable salads.

1/2 C lemon juice
1/2 C honey
1/2 t salt

Mix all ingredients together.

Per Tablespoon:
Calories: 34.0
Fat (gm): 0
Protein (gm): trace
Cholesterol (mg): 0
Sodium (mg): 68.6

Alfalfa Sprout Dressing

Preparation time: 20 minutes
Yields: 3/4 - 1 C

Besides using this on salads, this is great on sandwiches and used as a dip.

1 C alfalfa sprouts
1/2 C mashed avocado
1 lemon (juice and pulp) or 3 T lemon
  juice
1/4 t salt
1/2 t savory
1 t oregano
1 t basil
1 t thyme

Blend together. This is thick and may need to be thinned with a bit of oil.

VARIATION: Substitute SALAD HERBS (p. 222) or a commercial blend of Italian herbs for the herbs listed.

Per Tablespoon:
Calories: 18.9
Fat (gm): 1.3
Protein (gm): .3
Cholesterol (mg): 0
Sodium (mg): 45.8

Tapasvini's Squeeze Bottle Dressing

Preparation time: 20 minutes
Yields: 1 C

This tastes good on cooked vegetables or green salads. It is thick and smooth so can be stored and served in a squeeze bottle. Kids love it!

1/4 C lemon juice
1/2 t salt
3 T honey
4 ounces tofu
2 T sesame seeds
2 T water

Combine all ingredients in blender and blend until sesame seeds are ground. This will keep for a couple of days in the refrigerator.

Per Tablespoon:
Calories: 24.4
Fat (gm): .8
Protein (gm): .7
Cholesterol (mg): 0
Sodium (mg): 68.5

Russian Dressing

Preparation time: 10 minutes
Yields: 1 C

1/2 C oil
2 T lemon juice
1/2 C tomatoes or puree
2 t salt
1/4 t SALAD HERBS (p. 222)
1/2 t paprika

Blend well in a jar which won't leak when shaken.

Per Tablespoon:
Calories: 61.7
Fat (gm): 6.3
Protein (gm): trace
Cholesterol (mg): 0
Sodium (mg): 267.4

Vegetables

VEGETABLES

ABOUT VEGETABLES

A vegetable is the edible root, stalk, leaf or flower of a plant. Corn (which is a grain) and the "fruits of the blossom" (tomatoes, beans, eggplants and squash) are usually called vegetables, although technically they belong in other food groups. The word vegetable comes from a word which means "animating; hence, full of life"—an apt description of this group of foods. Plants, as part of their life process, manufacture vitamins, proteins, and carbohydrates. When we eat plant life, our bodies extract those nutrients, as well as benefitting from the cellulose or "bulk", a fibrous material which conditions the intestines and facilitates elimination.

To help choose vegetables from the marketplace, we offer here a guide to the indicators of freshness and quality and hints on how and when to buy. First, some general comments.

When shopping for vegetables, it is wise to carefully check behind and beneath the stack in the produce case. Often the freshest food is put there in the hope that people will buy the more accessible older food first. Generally vegetables that are no longer crisp are less nutritious and flavorful than they were when fresh. Small vegetables are often better tasting than the larger chemically fertilized vegetables. Good normal coloring and shape are important in determining the flavor and age. Avoid vegetables with blemishes. If possible, buy root vegetables with the tops still attached as they will be the freshest. (Take along some string bags or small cloth bags you have made from fabric scraps so that you don't need to use plastic bags.) Following are brief descriptions of vegetables you will encounter in most markets. It is not an all-inclusive list. There are many vegetables available today that are not included here. Buy them, taste them and use them in recipes for vegetables which seem similar to them. For example, in the last couple of years we have seen a green cauliflower that is considered a broccoli. It is excellent in recipes calling for either broccoli or cauliflower. Experiment and enjoy!

After getting the vegetables home, cut the tops off your root vegetables as the tops continue to draw the moisture and nutrients from the root until removed.

Package in containers which will keep the vegetables crisp and fresh and then refrigerate your vegetables. The exceptions to this are potatoes, whole winter squash, yams, sweet potatoes (and onions, if you use them). These vegetables need to be stored in a cool, dry, dark place where air can circulate around them.

Before using, thoroughly wash your vegetables, including each lettuce leaf and every root. Scrub your root vegetables with a scrub brush reserved for vegetables. Peel root vegetables if you desire. Many natural food experts say that vegetables should be scrubbed but not peeled. Others say that unless the food is organic, it should be peeled because the skin concentrates the chemical poisons found in the soil.

Classification of Vegetables

Fresh ROOT VEGETABLES are hard and firm: carrots, for example, will snap in half when bent sharply. Yellowed or limp leaves on root vegetables indicate that the food is getting old. Often, especially with beets, produce workers cut off any yellowed greens; check near the root for places where the stalks have been cut. Usually, root vegetables sold in plastic bags with the greens completely trimmed away are very old and undesirable. (Carrots and parsnips are exceptions.)

Peeling root vegetables results in the loss of much of the vitamin content; scrubbing with a stiff brush under running water does an adequate job of cleaning and is also less time consuming. Note that root vegetables can accumulate many times the concentration of DDT (and other poisons) that is present in the surrounding soil, and that very little is known about the cumulative effect of these toxins on the human body. For this and other reasons, you may wish to obtain organically grown vegetables, or grow your own. On the whole, root vegetables tend to be somewhat starchy, and they may take longer to cook than other vegetables. Most roots can be added to soups and stews, and some, particularly potatoes and parsnips, will help to thicken the broth.

The most commonly eaten root vegetables are beets, carrots, celeriac, garlic, girasole, jicama, onions, parsnips, potatoes, radishes, rutabagas, salsify, turnips, yams and sweet potatoes. All (except radishes) are good in soups and stews.

In addition to the obvious—celery—STALK VEGETABLES include asparagus, kohlrabi, and rhubarb (see FRUITS section).

All LEAFY VEGETABLES can be used like lettuce in salads. Some—romaine, spinach, kale, endive and mustard greens, to name a few—can be stronger tasting or more bitter than others, and it may be advisable to use them in combination with the milder greens—red leaf, butter, and Australian lettuces, for example. It is widely believed that healthy green vegetables are a darker green than their supposedly less nutritious brothers and sisters. As far as we know, the validity of this theory has not yet won the approval of the scientific establishment, but organic gardeners report that nitrogen-deficient vegetables are identifiable by their lighter color. The amounts of other nutrients may also be associated with the coloring; streaks of red or brown in a leaf may indicate deficiencies of some kind in the soil. (Of course, they may also just be signs of decay that has set in after the vegetable was harvested.) Small amounts of "rusting" at the edge of the leaves is nothing to worry about, but it does indicate less than perfect quality.

Leafy vegetables last only a short time after they are harvested, shipped, displayed and sold. Careful handling is very important. Lettuce that is packed too tightly in crates bruises and spoils. Greens need to be kept very cold to preserve their crispness and often they are sprayed with water during storage to prevent dehydration. (This may result in a loss of water-soluble vitamins.) Traditionally, discolored greens are trimmed before and during the period of their display at the market. It's fairly easy to judge the freshness of leafy vegetables and their crispness. Tired, wilted greens are not such a great buy at any price. The life force is leaving them rapidly, and taste and nutritional value are also deteriorating.

To preserve freshness, store lettuce and other greens in clean, airtight plastic bags in a cold refrigerator. Whether to wash them before storing or right before eating is a matter of personal choice: we wash vegetables at the last minute, in order to preserve them as closely to their natural state as possible for the longest period of time. Other people prefer to wash the vegetables before storing them, on the theory that they keep better that way, or just to simplify and speed up preparing meals at a later time. In any event, wash them well, either under running water or by rinsing one leaf at a time in a bowl of water. Gritty salads are very unappetizing.

Wild greens such as dandelion, sorrel, cress, and miner's lettuce grow in almost every part of the world. Like other greens, they can be used in salads or steamed very briefly (two to five minutes). Wild greens tend to be slightly bitter. Most greens contain significant amounts of vitamin A and the B complex.

Greens shrink an incredible amount during cooking; be sure to buy enough. Beware of overcooking: greens take only a few minutes to cook, even at low heat.

Some vegetables are technically FLOWER BUDS. Globe artichokes, broccoli, brussels sprouts, and cauliflower are the most common of these.

Sometimes called "fruits of the vine", SUCCULENT VEGETABLES include avocados, tomatoes, peppers, eggplant, squash, beans, and other foods which are technically fruits, but are used as vegetables.

Fresh Vegetables

ARTICHOKES (GLOBE) are the flowerbuds of a thistle plant. Fresh, well developed artichokes will have a fat stem and a flat or rounded (not conical) top. When they are fresh, the leaves are packed tightly together. As they get older, the leaves open up and the shape of the choke becomes more pointed. If you suspect worms, soak them for an hour in lightly salted water. The salt will cause the worms to come out. The size does not affect the flavor but it does affect the cooking time. They may be steamed whole or in halves. If no steaming rack is available, open up the leaves and place stem up in an inch of simmering water; cover and steam until tender. They are done when the stem end can be easily pierced with a fork. To eat, pull off the leaves from the outside in. Hold the pointed end of the leaf and scrape the soft lower part of the leaf across your teeth. When you reach the center of the choke, remove the feathery leaves by shaving them off with a spoon, and eat the heart. Most people agree that the heart of the choke (the part just above the stem) is the tastiest part. The stem is not as tasty but can be eaten. The leaves can be individually dipped in melted butter or a sauce (LEMON HERB BUTTER (p.177), or TOFU MAYONNAISE, (p. 153). Alternatively, remove the center feathery leaves and fill with the dipping sauce. Artichokes are also delicious chilled and make a wonderful addition to a packed lunch.

ASPARAGUS is a stalk vegetable. The young tender shoots are quite a delicacy either slivered (raw or cooked) into a salad or steamed. The entire stalk is very nearly as tasty as the tips; it just requires more cooking to reach the same state of tenderness. Choose stalks that are crisp, have tightly closed tips and smoothly rounded spears. The stalks are most tender if they do not exceed 1/2 inch. When preparing asparagus, bend the stalk near the cut end. When it snaps, discard the tough lower portion.

AVOCADOS are technically a fruit. They ripen best when they are picked after they have matured but before they are ready to eat. Overall softness is the best way to judge the ideal state of ripeness. The avocado should be barely soft but not mushy or it may very well be rancid. The two most common types of avocados available commercially are the Hass variety (with its thick, dark knobby skin), which is in season from spring through late fall; and the thin skinned, lighter green Fuerte type, which are the most popular winter avocados. Hass avocados hold their flavor and texture for a longer period of time after ripening and are not as perishable as Fuerte avocados. They also have a much higher oil content. Be wary of letting Fuerte and other thin skinned avocados become too ripe, as they don't last well at all once they are ready to eat. Bacon and Zutano avocados tend to be watery, as will any avocado frozen on the tree. Florida avocados all tend to be larger and less rich than the California types.

When the fruit is ripe, it can easily be peeled by cutting just through the peel and then removing the strips of skin. Not quite ripe fruit will be difficult to peel in this manner. To prepare avocados that are going to be mashed or eaten "in the shell": cut in half from stem to blossom end, remove the pit and crosshatch the avocado with cuts just to the skin about 1/4 inch wide and then at 90 degrees. Then the avocado can be easily mashed or removed.

BEANS can be divided into two groups: those with edible pods (which are usually eaten whole) and those with inedible pods (which are shelled before eating). Edible pod or snap beans are also known as string beans. However, thanks to modern agriculture, beans are now available with no strings attached. If they do have strings, they may be removed by breaking a little bit from the stem end and pulling, sort of like unzipping a zipper. Buy fresh beans which are still crisp (snapping when you break them); whether they are green, yellow, or purple, look for beans with good color. Reddish brown flecks, shriveling, and limpness are signs of age. Steaming the beans whole preserves the most nutrients, but they can be cut and cooked with other vegetables. The classic gourmet touch is to sliver them from one end to the other (julienne cut) and serve with BUTTERED ALMOND SAUCE (p. 177).

Inedible pod beans (for example limas and fava beans) need to be shelled before cooking. Then they can be steamed or used in casseroles.

BEETS of all sizes, if they are firm and have crisp green tops, are a tasty addition to any meal. If the greens have been removed, they are probably old and will lose texture and flavor. Remove the greens and keep them separate. Grated raw, beets are excellent in salads. Sliced or quartered and steamed, they can be served with a little lemon juice or a sauce.

BEET GREENS are often chopped and lightly steamed in their own juices or braised in a small amount of oil and water. They are a tasty addition to CURRIED VEGETABLES (p. 95).

BROCCOLI is a green flowerbud vegetable which is sometimes tinged with purple. Avoid selecting broccoli which is tinged with yellow, which is limp or with flowerbuds no longer closely packed. Peel the stalks to remove the tough fibers and steam them with the tops. Discard the stem if it is hollow. Raw or steamed and chilled broccoli is fantastic in salads. Steamed broccoli with lemon juice or cheese sauce is also excellent.

BRUSSELS SPROUTS are buds which grow on a tall stem. They look and taste like little cabbages and are a member of the same family. Small, firm, dark green sprouts make the best eating. Soak in salt water for an hour if they are organic and you see evidence of worms. Trim the individual stalks of each bud and remove any yellowed leaves. Steam lightly, perhaps sprinkling them with a tiny bit of tarragon. This is a good vegetable to serve by itself with lemon and butter or LEMON HERB BUTTER (p. 177).

CABBAGE is considered a leafy vegetable. It stores as well as or better than any other vegetable. It is a crunchy, flavorful addition to a salad (particularly the red variety), but will cause a salad to turn bitter if stored more than 24 hours. Cabbage is best not overcooked. It is excellent steamed, stir fried or sauted with herbs.

There are many varieties of cabbage: white (or green), red (or purple), savoy (with wrinkly leaves) , bok choy and Napa. Bok choy (or pak choi) has dark green leaves and large celery-like stalks. Napa cabbage is lighter in color and the leaves form a firm head.

CAULIFLOWER is a delicacy that can be eaten raw, steamed or baked in casseroles. Choose firm, tightly packed heads with a snow white color. As it ages, the head gets softer, separates, and turns a creamy color. The stalk is as good as the florets but needs to be cooked slightly longer. Like all of the cabbage family, it is flavorful served in a cream or cheese sauce. It is also good in steamed vegetable combinations, curried vegetables and salads.

CARROTS are some of the sweetest roots and can be used grated in salads, eaten as a raw vegetable or cooked in numerous ways. Carrots should be so crisp that they do not bend but snap. Small, tender carrots have a milder taste than the large "easy to cut or shred" version. Carrots with splits or cracks may be bitter; rubbery ones are flat tasting. Soft moldy places are undesirable. Green areas at the top of the root are due to the presence of chlorophyll and do not affect the taste. Carrots can be cubed, julienne sliced, sliced or made into sticks. For more flavor, try cutting them very thin on the diagonal. Frequently the outer skin of a carrot is bitter, so you may want to thinly peel them.

CELERIAC is the root of a certain variety of the celery plant. It is good in soups, steamed or baked like potatoes. Celeriacs up to 3 to 4 inches in diameter are preferable to the larger roots which may be woody or hollow. Celeriac needs to be peeled. Parboiling makes peeling easier.

CELERY is a versatile stalk vegetable widely used as an appetizer or snack (plain, stuffed or with dips), and in salads, stews and just about every other kind of dish that exists. The whole plant is edible from the leaves (used in salads, soups or dried as an herb) to the root (see CELERIAC). The base of the stalk is just as good as the rest, although it is usually lighter in color. Crisp, dark green heads that haven't been trimmed are the best buy. To release more flavor in cooking, mince or thinly slice on the diagonal.

CHARD is a leafy vegetable which is a variety of the common beet. Both green and red varieties are available. They taste the same, so you might like to use the red for the color it imparts. The young tender leaves are surprisingly good as salad greens. The smaller leaves are most tender, but many times quite large leaves can be used with excellent results. The leaves have a tendency to get bitter when over mature. It may be cooked in the same ways as other greens.

CHICORY is a leafy vegetable also known as French endive. Chicory, endive and escarole are all very closely related and are excellent in salads. Some varieties of chicory have an especially large root which can be washed, sliced 1/4 inch thick and roasted until it is dark brown and brittle throughout (about 4 hours at 300°). The roasted roots may be ground and used like coffee. (They have a similar taste but no caffeine).

The French or Belgian endive sold in stores has small whitish green torpedo shaped heads. Its light color is the result of being grown in almost total darkness.

COLLARDS are a variety of KALE. (Refer to KALE (p. 74), and/or LEAFY VEGETABLES, (p. 70.)

CORN is technically a grain but is included in this section also because people eat sweet corn as a vegetable. Fresh corn is very perishable. Homegrown corn is so sweet and tender that it is good raw; however, most corn on the market has lost so much of its sugar already that it needs to be cooked to perk up the flavor (the right amount of cooking turns the starches into sugars). When shopping for corn, look for ears which have a healthy green husk and a lightly colored tassel. Pale husks and/or dark, shrivelled tassels are signs of old age. Pull down the husk a little to see that the kernels come all the way to the end of the ear, are small and tender (not puckered), and are medium yellow in color. White ones are immature (unless it's white corn) while sun yellow ones are over mature.

Corn can be briefly steamed or baked, in or out of the husk. To bake husked corn, wrap tightly in aluminum foil and bake for approximately 20 minutes at 350°. It can be brushed with butter if desired. Don't overcook. If cutting the kernels off the cob of either raw or cooked corn, scrape the cob to get the corn germ, which is stuck way down in the bottom of each corn socket. Corn combines well with almost all other vegetables. Its bright yellow color and sweet flavor add a nice touch to most dishes.

CUCUMBERS are crunchy additions to salads or hors d'oeuvre trays. To be crisp, they need to be very dark and firm, with no soft spots. Commercial cucumbers are frequently waxed and if so, may need to be peeled. Lemon cucumbers look like knobby tennis or golf balls with a sweet and somewhat lemony taste.

DANDELION GREENS add a snappy touch to spring salads. At other times of the year, they are best steamed for a few minutes. The root can be used like chicory for a coffee substitute (see CHICORY).

DOCK is a leafy vegetable that grows in numerous places around the world. The narrow leafed varieties, such as yellow dock, are great in salads. The broad leafed varieties are rather strong and need to be cooked. They can be added to stir fried vegetable mixtures or they may be steamed.

ENDIVE (Refer to CHICORY.)

EGGPLANTS (AUBERGINES) are a great addition to sauces and casseroles. They are not good raw. Choose lightweight eggplants which have a dark, dull colored skin and are free from serious skin defects. Ripe eggplants do not need to be peeled. The color and texture of their peel adds zest to dishes. Unripe eggplants are heavy for their size, are green right under the skin, and may have a bitter taste. This bitter taste can be minimized by peeling the eggplant, slicing into 1/2 inch slices, lightly salting the slices and laying them out on paper towels for 15 minutes to leach out the bitter juices.

ESCAROLE resembles leaf lettuce more than its curly cousin, endive. It is an excellent addition to salads.

GARLIC is a stimulating spice which is valued by some for its cleansing properties. Though useful in treating illnesses, it is not usually recommended for those who meditate in the Yoga tradition. See ONIONS in this section and in FOOD AND CONSCIOUSNESS (p. 1) for more information.

GIRASOLE is the root of a sunflower plant native to Canada. It is also called the JERUSALEM ARTICHOKE, due to the historic mispronunciation of the Italian name. This tuber has a crisp, nut-like flavor when added to salads (grated) and is also good cooked. Choose as you would any other root; avoid soft spots and overall flabbiness. Clean well with scrub brush—if necessary, break off the knobs to get at the dirt. It does not require peeling.

GREENS (Refer to LEAFY VEGETABLES, p. 70.)

JICAMA is a root which is frequently used like potatoes in Mexico. Raw, it has a crisp, juicy, refreshing texture. It can be grated or

cubed and added to salads, or eaten raw like apple slices. It can be cooked and used like potatoes but may not as be as good as when used raw. The roots are usually large and last well wrapped and refrigerated. Peel before using. Discard if moldy.

KALE is the leafy vegetable from which modern cabbages probably originated. There are many varieties colored green, blue, purple and variegated. Kale does well in soups; it will help thicken them and can be used in place of spinach in any of the soups in this cookbook. It can also be used as other greens.

KOHLRABI looks like a root vegetable but in fact is a stalk vegetable growing above the soil. It is a member of the cabbage family and looks like a green turnip that decided to grow stems and leaves out of a number of places instead of just the top. Golf ball to tennis ball sized ones are generally more tender. The big ones get a very thick, tough skin. Peel and steam (don't forget to include the leaves) or dice and cook in a cream sauce. They may be sliced and broiled for a potato chip type snack.

LEAFY VEGETABLES (See p. 70.)

LETTUCE is the sweetest salad green. Choose tender, lively-looking greens with good coloring. Each kind of lettuce has its own distinctive character. Romaine is crunchy with a strong and sometimes bitter flavor. Red leaf is sweeter and softer as well as being beautifully colored. Butter lettuce is smooth and melts in the mouth. Australian and Oak leaf have interestingly shaped leaves and a taste similar to endive and escarole but sweeter. Iceberg is great as "lettuce cups" on which to serve fruit or molded salads. It is not as perishable but is less nutritious than the other lettuces.

MUSTARD GREENS are a rather pungent leafy vegetable. (Refer to LEAFY VEGETABLES, p. 70.)

NASTURTIUM FLOWERS are not really a vegetable, but they are a colorful and tangy addition to any salad. Grow some in your garden and add them and their seeds to raw vegetable dishes or as a garnish.

OKRAS are greenish colored pods popular in Creole-style cooking. The smaller ones ($1^1/_2$ to 2 inches) are the most tender. Try adding them to cooked black eyed peas and tomato. Add some *gumbo file* (a spice combination based on sassafras, which adds flavor and thickening) for a Creole treat.

ONIONS are stimulating root vegetables, similar to garlic. They create heat in the body and many yoga teachers say that onions, garlic and similar foods have a negative effect on the mind and recommend that they not be eaten by those who meditate regularly. For this reason, onions, garlic, chives, leeks, scallions and other members of the onion family have been omitted from the recipes in this book. Most dishes which traditionally call for onions can be made even tastier without them; onions and garlic tend to overwhelm the other seasonings. Bell peppers and spices are good substitutes for those who desire a mild "bite" in a particular dish. Sauted celery or diced/shredded cabbage adds the texture, appearance and bulk that onions have if you are substituting for them in a recipe.

PARSLEY is most often used as an herb but its high vitamin content and pleasant perky taste have made it popular as a salad green too. Good in soups, steamed vegetables, sandwiches and salads.

PARSNIPS are root vegetables which look somewhat like wrinkled white carrots. If they aren't old, they are very sweet. Look for firm roots, preferably less than one inch in diameter at the top. They have a tough and sometimes bitter skin which can be peeled or rubbed off after they have been steamed. Try them steamed and mashed like potatoes, or in casseroles or in steamed vegetable combinations. Parsnips can be sliced lengthwise, dredged in flour, sprinkled with oil and baked until tender. They make an excellent addition to soup stock. They can also be used like kohlrabi, carrots or turnips.

PEAS, like beans, come either with or without an edible pod. The edible pod varieties (called sugar or snow peas) are picked before the peas get very large. When buying them, pick firm, crisp peas without blemishes. They mold easily so they must be used soon after purchasing. Remove the string from the pods by breaking off the stem end and pulling down the string like you would unzip a zipper. Steam or stir fry the whole pods briefly. They get overcooked in casseroles. When using shelled peas, count on using a lot more than you think you need, as there are not many peas in each pod. Remove from pod before cooking.

PEPPERS come in many different sizes and degrees of "hotness." Many commercial peppers, especially the larger ones, are waxed. The wax is very difficult to remove but can be removed by scrubbing, peeling or roasting the pepper.

BELL peppers are the most mild peppers. The green bell pepper is an unripe version of the sweeter red bell. Bell peppers also come in orange, yellow, a cream color, and a purple color. Raw yellow and red bell peppers are sweet and make tasty finger food.

ANAHEIM peppers are long, skinny and dark green. They are mildly hot peppers, traditionally used for Chili Rellenos.

JALAPENO peppers are very dark green and generally only an inch or two long. They are very hot. Yellow wax peppers are usually not quite as hot as jalapenos.

POTATOES are root vegetables which come in many varieties and sizes, including white, red, and russet (or brown). The russet potatoes are best for baking and keep well. The white and red potatoes are better for potato salad and for steaming. They do not keep well. If small (1 to $1^1/_2$ inches in diameter), they should be refrigerated. Tiny red potatoes are heavenly when steamed with just a little butter.

Potatoes (other than small, new potatoes) store best in a cool, dry, dark place. This fools them into thinking that they're still underground, and minimizes the chance of them getting soft and sprouting. They're still edible after they've sprouted, but their flavor and texture suffer. (The sprouts are poisonous and should be cut out.) Potatoes need not be peeled; a scrubbing will do. Potatoes may be baked at any temperature between 325° and 450°, so they can easily be coordinated with other baked dishes. It is advisable to pierce the skin a few times before baking to prevent the tubers from exploding. The skins may be oiled prior to baking to make them softer. Potatoes are done when they can be easily squashed (use a hot pad) or easily pierced with a fork. They'll cook faster with a large (16 penny) ungalvanized nail stuck in the center (do not attempt this with a microwave oven!). At 350°, allow about 1 hour for medium sized potatoes. In a microwave, allow 5 to 20 minutes on high for each potato. The time will vary with the size and power of the microwave, the size and age of the potato.

When steaming potatoes, allow lots of water as they take a long time to cook and the cooking water boils off. Cooking times will vary depending upon the size of the potato pieces and the quantity.

Mashed potatoes become "gluey" when made from white or red potatoes because of the delicacy of the starch molecules (as opposed to the russets, which develop a stronger "skin" on the starch molecules). Additionally, it is best to not use a food processor to make mashed potatoes. The agitation frequently causes the starch molecules (even in russets) to disintegrate, causing the glue-like texture.

RADISHES are root vegetables. They, like onions, garlic and hot peppers, contain what are known as "volatile oils." They impart a slightly hot or tangy flavor and are often used to jazz up a green salad. They are also good on the hors d'oeuvres tray. The white radishes are much hotter than the average red ones.

RUTABAGAS are root vegetables belonging to the turnip family. They have yellow insides, and although they have a much stronger flavor, they can be used in the same ways as turnips. Those three inches or less in diameter are best. These are generally used in soups and stews. Try steaming and seasoning with caraway seed, nutmeg or basil.

SALSIFY is a root known as the "vegetable oyster". It has a delightful flavor and can be used as the basis for a delicious vegetable burger. Simply peel, grate and mix with carrots or other vegetables; form into patties, and fry. May also be cooked like parsnips.

SPINACH is as available as lettuce in most places. Wash the leaves very thoroughly as it has a tendency to be sandy. Try chopped steamed spinach in VEGETABLES PAKORA (p. 97) or mixed with mashed potatoes.

SQUASH (SUMMER) have soft skins, do not contain much starch and are about 95% water. When purchasing them look for smaller, firm ones with no blemishes. When small and tender, they are quite good raw, as a snack or in salads. They can be steamed or sauteed. Oversized squash are good stuffed. All varieties of summer squash can be used interchangeably. The most common varieties follow.

ZUCCHINI (COCOZELLE or ITALIAN MARROW) is the most popular variety of summer squash. Select very dark green firm ones. Any that are larger than about 6 inches will not have as much flavor. They can be grated into salads, breaded and sauted or used to give body to soups and stews.

SCALLOP SQUASH (PATTY PAN or GREEN BUSH) have a nice shape and lend themselves well to breading (try cornmeal) or dipping in a batter and sauteing.

YELLOW (STRAIGHT or CROOKNECK) squash have a slightly bumpy skin. Choose those which are small and lighter in color. They add a nice color to vegetable dishes and have a sweeter taste than the other summer squash.

SQUASH (WINTER) have hard skins and a high carbohydrate content. They store incredibly well without refrigeration if they are kept cool and dry. When they're ripe, they're very sweet. Generally those that are of average size, shape and color are the best buys, as they are less likely to be pithy or bland. The skin should be hard, not just firm. Softening of the skin often indicates internal decay. When buying cut pieces of squash at the market, beware of blemishes on the skin, a shrivelled inside or mold on the skin or interior. The seeds, which are usually removed before cooking, can be roasted. Refer to NUTS AND SEEDS (p. 215).

Winter squash are most often cooked in one of the following ways. They are done when a fork pierces them easily.
- After cutting into pieces, bake in a covered casserole with a little bit of water.
- Cut and steam.
- Cut and bake uncovered (this will be very dry).
- Bake whole. After cooking cut open and remove seeds.

Cut pieces may be basted with honey, maple syrup, butter, orange juice or water. Acorn and Butternut squash halves may be filled with nuts or dried fruits, or the squash can be pureed after cooking.

There are many popular varieties of winter squash. The different varieties can be substituted for each other in almost any recipe. For example, pumpkin pie can be made with any winter squash.

ACORN squash have the shape of an acorn and are dark green (or golden orange). They are usually slit in half from the stem to the blossom end and baked. Each half serves 1 to 2 people.

BANANA squash have a pale beige to orange colored skin and are usually so large that they are sold in cut up portions. This is the squash that is most frequently seen in cut pieces in supermarkets.

BUTTERNUT squash have a caramel colored skin and a buttery taste. They are usually baked in halves with one half serving 1 to 3 people, depending upon the size of the squash.

GOLDEN NUGGET squash look like miniature pumpkins and have an excellent flavor. They can be steamed and then stuffed or used as soup bowls for a cream or other soup.

HUBBARD squash have a very dark green, incredibly hard skin. They are usually very large and sold in cut pieces. Recently a smaller version of the Hubbard has been available which is excellent stuffed.

PUMPKINS are included here because they are a winter squash and because they are excellent stuffed or used in any of the recipes calling for winter squash. When buying a pumpkin, look for a sugar pumpkin. They are smaller, darker, and frequently have lines of scarring caused by the high sugar content. The tiny miniature pumpkins are beautiful stuffed or filled with soup.

TURK'S TURBAN squash are classified as ornamental in some seed catalogs. Although they are not as sweet or flavorful as some other types of squash, they are so beautiful you may wish to stuff them for a holiday meal.

SPAGHETTI squash are different from the other types listed here. They are full of strands which can be used to replace spaghetti, hence their name. To prepare, bake or steam whole. When tender, crack open and scoop out and discard the seeds. Then scoop out the strands. Sauce and toss as for spaghetti.

SWEET POTATOES are similar to yams, but they are somewhat lighter in color, stringier and not as sweet. They can be prepared like potatoes, either baked or steamed. They may be substituted for yams, and pureed they make a delicious pie (substitute for an equal amountof pumpkin in the PUMPKIN PIE recipe, p. 199).

SWISS CHARD (Refer to CHARD.)

TOMATOES are really acid fruits, but are usually treated as a vegetable, so they are included here. Vine ripened tomatoes are the sweetest, but those that are picked mature but unripe will ripen to a reasonable state if stored out of direct sunlight at room temperature. Avoid overly soft tomatoes or those with bruised or soft spots. An easy way to create a sauce is to add some tomatoes to whatever you are cooking.

TURNIPS are small root vegetables. The smaller ones (no larger than $1^1/_2$ inches in diameter) are sweeter and more tender. Peeled and quartered, they can be eaten raw. Turnips can be steamed, baked or prepared as for hash browns with or without the potatoes. They also can be stuffed.

TURNIP GREENS are similar to beet greens except for coloring. They can be used in place of chard or spinach.

WATERCRESS is a leafy vegetable that, with its small, round leaves, little white flowers and biting flavor, is an appealing addition to salads.

YAMS are the sweetest root vegetables. They may be baked in their skins or peeled, steamed and mashed. Little ones that have been baked in their skins are delicious the next day cold. The skin can be peeled off as they are eaten. They are like little candy bars in their own wrappers and are excellent in lunches. If baked, cook the yams until beads of sugar pop out on the skins and the yam sags in its skin. They can also be made into pie (substitute an equal amount for the pumpkin in PUMPKIN PIE, p. 199), or used in casseroles. Purple velvet yams have a red-violet layer just under the skin, and are some of the best-tasting yams.

SPROUTS

Sprouted seeds, grains and beans are alive and contain valuable enzymes as well as being an excellent source of energy. Many sprouts, especially alfalfa, have a high mineral content and almost all are rich in vitamins. Sprouts often contain more nutrients than the parent seeds. They can easily be grown at home in a matter of days, are inexpensive, and taste good too.

For best results, it is important to use good quality seeds and beans. Use the current year's crop for sprouting and make certain that the seed is unhulled (except for sunflower seeds).

We have experimented with various methods of sprouting and have found that there is one way which is significantly more reliable and somewhat less trouble than the others.

The materials needed are inexpensive to obtain: a wide mouthed Mason jar and ring and a piece of plastic screening, nylon stocking or cheesecloth slightly larger than the jar opening.

Place the appropriate amount of washed seeds, grains or sorted grains (see chart, p. 79, for amounts) in the jar with about 3 times as much water as seeds. Place the screening over the jar opening and secure it with the ring or rubber band. Let the seeds soak overnight unless otherwise noted and then pour off the soaking water. (The soaking water can be saved for soup stock.) Rinse the sprouts by adding more than enough water to cover, gently shaking the jar, and pouring off the water. Repeat until the water is clear. Keep them damp, rinsing from one to three times a day, depending upon the weather and the type of sprouts. Keep them in a well ventilated place (tilted so that the excess water can drain) and out of the direct sun until they reach the desired length. This usually takes from one to seven days depending on the weather and type of seeds.

QUICK REFERENCE CHART FOR SPROUTING

Amt. of seed for 1 qt. jar	Type of seed	No. of days	Best length (in inches)
3 T	Alfalfa	3-4	1-2
1 C	Garbanzo beans	3	1
3/4 C	Lentils	3	1/2-1
1/2 C	Mung beans	2-3	2-3
1 C	Soybeans	3	1/2-3/4
1 C	Wheat	2	1/4-1/2

The sprouts can be exposed to filtered sun for a few hours at the end of their growing period. This will radically increase the chlorophyll content. The sprouts are now ready to eat, or they may be stored for a few days in an airtight container in the refrigerator. Most sprouts are excellent raw in salads. Some sprouts are easier to digest after they have been lightly steamed. All sprouts are excellent cooked with whole grains, added to bread dough or incorporated into loaves and casseroles. We have included suggestions for using the different kinds of sprouts in the following pages. Sprouts can be substituted for many vegetables in the recipes in different sections. Be creative—the best dishes are often improvisations on a recipe.

To help reduce mold problems, make certain to wash the sprout jar thoroughly with soap and hot water between batches.

Sprouted beans can be substituted for unsprouted beans in most recipes and require less cooking. They also add a nutritious gourmet touch to your favorite recipes.

We have successfully sprouted combinations of seeds, combinations of grains, and combinations of beans, but have not gotten very good results when we combined the different groups.

If your sprouts don't sprout, check that they are getting enough water, and are properly soaked and rinsed at the appropriate intervals. Make certain that the seed is fresh, untreated and unhulled. The temperature should be moderate (not too hot or cold) and they need to be out of direct sun.

ALFALFA sprouts can be made with a minimum of effort. They are the most popular type of sprout. Start with 2 to 3 tablespoons of seed per quart jar and soak them overnight in a small amount of water—1/2 to 3/4 inch in the bottom of the jar is fine. Follow the basic procedure outlined above. Rinse enough to keep them moist—once a day is enough, unless you live in a hot, dry climate. Be sure to drain the sprouts and keep them in a cool, well ventilated place way from sunlight. Let them grow about an inch and a half long—this usually takes 3 to 6 days. Alfalfa sprouts are good in or on almost anything. Try them raw in salads, sandwiches, and juice combinations or as a garnish for steamed vegetables, soups or casseroles.

RED CLOVER is similar to alfalfa and is sprouted in the same way, but unlike alfalfa, red clover has a bite. Although the taste and texture of the two differ slightly, they can be used interchangeably.

CRESS, ENDIVE, RADISH, MUSTARD, FENNEL and **FENUGREEK** seeds are also sprouted like alfalfa. These sprouts are somewhat bitter, sharp or pungent. They may be added in small quantities to salads, mixed with other sprouts or used to flavor vegetable dishes.

HULLED SUNFLOWER SEEDS which are not broken may be coaxed into sprouts; the taste is worth the effort. They need careful washing as they are delicate. Remove any which begin to mold. They are a nice addition to salads or baked goods such as cookies and breads. Unhulled sunflower seeds need to be soaked about 24 hours in lukewarm water. Then, proceed as for alfalfa. Remove hulls before eating. They are very sweet and nutritious.

WHEAT can be soaked for 3 to 5 hours and then sprouted in another 24 hours. If the sprouts are allowed to get longer than 3/8 inch, they start losing flavor and have an unpleasant texture. For a quart of sprouts, wash and remove the chaff from 3/4 to 1 C wheatberries. If you have a choice, sprout hard wheat, not soft wheat, as it has more protein and is easier to sprout. Soak, drain, and then water twice during the growing period. They can be mixed half and half with alfalfa sprouts and topped with RUSSIAN DRESSING (p. 65) for a quick salad. Wheat sprouts are excellent in breads (see recipe for SPROUT BREAD, p. 135).

RYE sprouts are grown like wheat sprouts are but can grow slightly longer before getting "hairy".

CORN is sprouted like wheat but must be soaked overnight.

OATS, RICE, BARLEY, MILLET and **BULGUR** bought at a food store will not sprout. Except for bulgur, which has been steamed, all of these grains have been milled, losing their outer hull.

BEANS take longer to sprout than other seeds and they tend to mold if they aren't babied along. It is important to carefully sort out all hulls, funny looking or broken beans and rocks before attempting to sprout any kind of bean. Thoroughly wash 1/2 C beans and soak overnight in a jar full of water. The next day, rinse until the water is clear. Thereafter, rinse 3 to 4 times daily until the water is clear, being very careful not to break off any of the delicate sprouts. Remove any broken or moldy beans. With a lot of attention, an equal amount of luck, and moderate weather, they'll be ready to eat in 3 to 5 days.

LENTILS are easier to sprout than most other beans. They are great when lightly steamed and added to a salad, or steamed in combination with other vegetables, such as carrots, cauliflower and squash.

SOY and **MUNG** beans are very similar. Both are difficult to sprout, but well worth the effort. The long sprouts in the produce section of the supermarket are commercially grown mung sprouts. Ours are tasty but much shorter. They also can be grown in moist dirt in a box with a lid.

WHOLE PEAS and **GARBANZO BEANS** will sprout and are excellent added to steamed vegetables.

LIMAS, KIDNEYS, PINTOS, GREAT WHITE NORTHERN and **BLACK BEANS** have not been worth the effort it has taken to coax them into sprouts.

COOKED VEGETABLES

There are many methods of cooking vegetables. Many people grew up with boiling as the primary way vegetables were cooked. Boiling is not included in this cookbook because most of the nutrients are lost in the cooking water. In this introductory section to the recipes, we describe several methods for cooking which keep more of the nutrients in the vegetables.

Steaming Vegetables

Steaming retains more of the nutrients in the vegetables than boiling because the vegetables are not immersed in the water. There are three basic methods of steaming vegetables. The most common method is using a steamer basket (or placing vegetables on a rack) over hot water, in a pan with a tight fitting lid. A variation of steaming can also be done in "waterless cookware," which has a vapor seal lid. With this cookware, a little bit of water is used over medium heat. They must be watched carefully so that the vegetables don't burn. Vegetables can also be cooked in a pressure cooker, which saves the nutrients much like steaming. However, with a pressure cooker one must be extremely precise about cooking times to avoid overcooked vegetables.

Stir Frying

Stir frying is done in an uncovered pan without water. A round-bottomed wok is preferable because the stirred vegetables have no corners in which to get stuck. The next best pan is a cast iron skillet or dutch oven. The main idea of stir frying is to stir the vegetables continuously to avoid overcooking them. To do this the vegetables need to be cut the same size. Slow cooking vegetables need to be put in first and quick cooking ones later. Sesame oil is the best oil to use (peanut oil is good also) because it has a higher flash point (the point at which it bursts into flame) than other oils and will not burn or smoke as readily at the high temperature needed for stir frying.

After preparing the vegetables, heat the wok. Make a small ring of oil around the upper edge of the pan so it can drip down to the center, coating the sides as it goes down. (It is easiest to dispense the oil evenly if it is in a small squeeze bottle.) Add herbs and spices (if any), then add vegetables and stir until hot but still crisp. If desired, 1 T water may be added to starchy vegetables; or sliced tomatoes can be placed on top of the other vegetables.

An easy sauce can be made for stir fried vegetables by putting several very thinly cut slices of peeled ginger root in with the vegetables. Stir fry the vegetables, and then when they are almost cooked, pour in a mixture of 1 T arrowroot dissolved in 1 C water. Stir until clear and bubbly. Season to taste with tamari (soy sauce).

Sauteing

Sauteing is similar to stir frying but takes less attention because it is done at a lower temperature. The oil seals in the juices, holds the flavors and helps develop a crust on the vegetables. Heat $1^1/_2$ to 2 T oil and/or butter in a large frying pan with any herbs and spices being used. When the oil is hot (but not smoking), add the vegetables and stir. Reduce the heat to medium or low and continue cooking, stirring occasionally. Cover if desired. When crispy tender, remove from heat.

If you are using several kinds of vegetables, they can be cut into different sized pieces according to their cooking time; they may all be cooked together (with hard vegetables such as carrots cut thin and quick-cooking vegetables such as cabbage cut larger). Or the vegetables can be added one type at a time, in order of the length of time required for cooking, leaving some time between each addition (for example, first carrots, then broccoli, then celery). Or different vegetables can be cooked completely separately and removed while others are cooked and then added back in.

Different fats give different flavors. Olive oil imparts a rich flavor; safflower and canola a light flavor. Butter also imparts a rich flavor but (besides not being as healthful), it burns easily when not mixed with oil. An alternative to butter is ghee or clarified butter, which doesn't burn as fast (see p. 213).

Braising

Braising involves the use of oil (to seal in the juices and flavor of the vegetables) and water (to slowly steam them until cooked). Heat oil and herbs or spices in a dutch oven, a heavy pan or wok (use about 1 t oil per cup of vegetables). Add cut vegetables and quickly stir them around in the hot oil. When they are well coated, cook another minute or so. Then add a few tablespoons water or vegetable liquid and cover. (The amount of water will vary, depending on pan surface, amount of vegetables and steaming time.) Continue cooking at a low heat until done. Watch the level of the water. With practice, the water will all be gone at the same time the vegetables are ready to be served.

Deep Fried Vegetables

Deep frying is not nearly as healthy as other methods of cooking vegetables. However, it does result in a unique texture and flavor. It is best to use sesame or peanut oil, both of which can be heated to a higher temperature without breaking down. Do not use soy or corn oil as both tend to foam and boil over. Use a heavy gauge pan with edges about 3 inches higher than the level of the oil. Add about 2 inches of oil to the bottom of the pan. Use a well marked cooking thermometer to accurately determine the temperature of your oil. Fry at 375°. Do not let the oil go above 400°. A lower temperature than 375° will allow the food to absorb more oil. Oil can be reused two or three times, but never more. The quality of the oil will lessen each time. After using the oil, it must be cooled and strained through a strainer or cheese cloth. Cooking cubes of potato just before frying foods in used oil will clean out any odors from the oil. Again,

remember that this is not a healthy way to cook but in small amounts will not be detrimental to your health. Also, the oil used for deep frying reaches a very high temperature and can easily cause burns. Be very careful with the handle of the pan, turning it so that it cannot be knocked over. Carefully ease the foods into the hot oil so that it doesn't spatter. It is not advisable to allow young children to help with cooking with hot oil because it can easily cause severe burns.

VEGETABLE RECIPES

STEAMED VEGETABLE RECIPES

Here are a few suggestions for combinations of vegetables to steam. There are many more combinations than these. Often what you steam together depends upon what you have available. Choose combinations which have a variety of colors and textures. Put the vegetables that take longer to cook (such as carrots, potatoes and other root vegetables) on the bottom. Add the vegetables which take only a few minutes at the end of the steaming when the root vegetables are almost done (for example, peas, leafy greens and tomatoes). Steam vegetables until tender, not completely soft.

COMBINATION #1: For each serving use 1 carrot, 1 small beet, 1 small stalk broccoli, and a few florets of cauliflower. Clean vegetables. Beets, carrots, and broccoli stems may be peeled if tough. Slice carrots, beets, and broccoli stem very thin and place on the bottom of the steaming rack. Add broccoli and cauliflower on top.

COMBINATION #2: Use string beans on the bottom, corn kernels in the middle, adding sliced zucchini when beans are almost done.

COMBINATION # 3: Use new potatoes, peas and carrots. Scrub but do not peel the potatoes. Cube them and place on the bottom of the steamer rack. Next place carrot slices, and add peas when potatoes and carrots are almost done.

COMBINATION # 4: For each serving use the kernels of 1 ear of corn, 1 medium stalk of broccoli, 1/2 C whole cherry tomatoes. Peel stalk of broccoli and cut into thin slices. Put on the bottom of steamer rack. When almost tender, add broccoli florets, then corn kernels. At the very end, add cherry tomatoes and steam 1-2 minutes longer.

Suggestions for Leftover Steamed Vegetables

Leftover vegetables can be:
• Used whole or pureed in soups
• Added cold to salads
• Pureed for sandwich fillings or baby food (may be mixed with avocado)
• Mixed with cooked grain, topped with grated cheese or CHEESE SAUCE (p. 175) and bread crumbs and baked until hot
• Used for filling in PARATHAS (p. 120) or BO-PE (p. 159)
• Mashed and added to bread, biscuits, or burgers

STOVE TOP COOKED VEGETABLES

Ratatouille

Preparation time: 60-75 minutes (includes cooking)
Yields: 4 servings (as a main dish) or 8 servings (as a side dish)

1 ripe eggplant (5 C of 1 inch cubes)
1 red bell pepper cut into 1 inch squares
3 medium zucchinis (4 C of 1/2 inch slices)
2 T olive oil
$1^1/_2$ t salt
1 T basil
1 t honey
1/2 to 1 C water
2 C tomatoes cut into wedges

In a dutch oven or heavy frying pan, heat olive oil and add bell pepper and eggplant. Cook for 5 to 10 minutes, stirring frequently. Add the zucchini, seasonings and 1/2 C water. Bring to a boil, reduce heat to medium low and simmer for 30 to 40 minutes, stirring occasionally, until vegetables are tender. Add tomato wedges and heat through. Serve hot. Good with rice or toast for a light main dish.

As a main dish:
Calories:161.4
Fat (gm): 6.5
Protein (gm): 2.1
Cholesterol (mg):0
Sodium (mg): 823.1

Browned Almond Cauliflower

Preparation time: 20-30 minutes (includes cooking)
Yields: 5 servings

1/3 C slivered almonds (preferably blanched)
1/3 C butter
1 medium head cauliflower, steamed

Melt butter and add almonds. Cook until butter is lightly browned and almonds are crisp (check crispness of almonds by eating one: undone ones will be tough). Pour almond butter over hot cauliflower and serve.

Calories: 173.1
Fat (gm): 17.2
Protein (gm): 1.8
Cholesterol (mg): 34.8
Sodium (mg): 131.1

Honey Orange Parsnips

Preparation time: 30 minutes
Yields: 4 servings

1 pound parsnips
2 T butter or oil
1 T honey
1 t grated orange rind
2 T orange juice

Peel parsnips and cut into 1/4 inch diagonal slices. Steam until tender. Place in a saucepan, add remaining ingredients and simmer a few minutes.

Calories: 171.4
Fat (gm): 6.5
Protein (gm): 1.2
Cholesterol (mg): 0
Sodium (mg): 12.0

Sweet 'n Sour Beets

Preparation time: 50 minutes (includes cooking)
Yields: 5 servings

6 to 8 large beets
1 T arrowroot
1/3 to 1/2 C lemon juice
a few whole cloves
3/4 C honey
1 T butter

Scrub or peel, slice and steam beets. Stir arrowroot into lemon juice until arrowroot is dissolved. Add honey and cloves. Bring to a boil and boil for 5 minutes. Add butter. Stir until melted. Pour over beets and let stand for 20 minutes. Reheat and serve.

Calories: 210.4
Fat (gm): 2.3
Protein (gm): .5
Cholesterol (mg): 6.6
Sodium (mg): 61.4

Gingered Carrots

Preparation time: 20-30 minutes (includes cooking)
Yields: 4 servings

6 medium carrots
1/2 t honey
a pinch of ginger powder (1/8 t)
2 T lemon juice
2 t dried parsley
2 T butter

Scrub or peel carrots and cut into thin slices diagonally. Steam until just barely tender. Mix other ingredients and toss with steamed carrots.

Calories: 105.9
Fat (gm): 5.8
Protein (gm): .8
Cholesterol (mg): 16.5
Sodium (mg): 99.6

Minted Carrots

Preparation time: 20-30 minutes (includes cooking)
Yields: 4 servings

1 pound carrots
2 T butter or oil
2 T honey
1 t lemon juice
1 T fresh mint leaves, minced

Scrub or peel and slice carrots. Steam until just tender. Melt butter and add remaining ingredients including carrots.

Calories: 135.7
Fat (gm): 5.8
Protein (gm): .8
Cholesterol (mg): 16.5
Sodium (mg): 165.4

Caraway Beets and Peas

Preparation time: 60-75 minutes (includes
  cooking)
Yields: 4 servings

1 pound fresh beets
**3/4 C shelled peas (fresh are best but
  frozen work)**
2 T butter
1/2 t caraway seed
1 T lemon juice
1/2 C cultured sour cream or thick yogurt

Cut off beet tops above crown; don't remove
tap roots. Scrub thoroughly and steam whole
30 to 40 minutes until tender. Rub off or
lightly peel skins; cut off tops and roots and
slice beets. This method of cooking beets
preserves more of the flavor and the color.
Heat butter and add peas. Steam on low heat
until barely tender. Add all other ingredients
except sour cream. Heat thoroughly. Serve
topped with sour cream.

Calories: 203.4
Fat (gm): 11.0
Protein (gm): 3.7
Cholesterol (mg): 26.5
Sodium (mg): 207.5

Lemon Chilled Broccoli

Preparation time: 90 minutes (includes
  cooking)
Yields: 4 servings

2 T lemon juice
2 T olive oil
1/8 t salt
1 T dried parsley
1 t minced bell pepper
2 C steamed broccoli florets

Combine all ingredients except broccoli. Pour
mixture over broccoli. Chill for 1 hour.

Calories: 84.9
Fat (gm): 6.4
Protein (gm): 1.5
Cholesterol (mg): 0
Sodium (mg): 45.7

Creole Stir Fry

Preparation time: 15 minutes (includes
  cooking)
Yields: 4 servings

2 C whole tiny okra (about 1/2 pound)
2 C sliced zucchini (3 six inch zucchinis)
2 C corn kernels
2 T oil

Heat oil to sizzling in a wok or cast iron pan.
Toss in okra and stir fry for a minute or so.
Add zucchini and corn and continue stir
frying 3 to 4 more minutes until vegetables
are crispy tender.

Calories: 170.6
Fat (gm): 6.7
Protein (gm): 3.1
Cholesterol (mg): 0
Sodium (mg): 9.5

VARIATION: Stir fry 1 pound of tofu and
then add the rest of the vegetables as
directed in the recipe.

Crunchy Cooked Salad

Preparation time: 20-25 minutes (includes
   cooking)
Yields: 2 servings

1 carrot, sliced
1/2 bell pepper, diced
1/2 C lentil sprouts
several broccoli florets
1 summer squash (patty pan, zucchini or
   crookneck)
salt
thyme
parsley
oregano
marjoram
summer savory
1 t lemon juice

Saute vegetables together, adding the salt
and pinches of each of the herbs. Remove
the vegetables from the heat while they are
still slightly crunchy. Add the lemon juice.
Cool and serve at room temperature or
chilled. Can also be served hot with a grain.

Calories: 57.5
Fat (gm): .1
Protein (gm): 2.3
Cholesterol (mg): 0
Sodium (mg): 286.6

Carrot-Cabbage Saute

Preparation time: 20-25 minutes (includes
   cooking)
Yields: 4-6 servings

3 T butter or oil
1 small head cabbage (about 1^1/$_4$
   pound), finely shredded
3 large carrots, scrubbed or peeled and
   coarsely grated (about 3 C)
1/2 t dill weed
1/2 t tarragon
2 t lemon juice
1/2 t salt to taste

Melt butter or heat oil on high heat in a wok
or a cast iron skillet. When hot (but not
burning or smoking), add cabbage and

carrots. Stir and lower heat to medium. Saute,
stirring frequently, until halfway tender
(about 4 minutes). Add dill, tarragon, and
salt, tossing to mix. Continue sauteing until
crispy tender, about 4 more minutes. Toss
with lemon and serve.

Using oil:
Calories: 160.1
Fat (gm): 9.5
Protein (gm): 1.5
Cholesterol (mg): 0
Sodium (mg): 319.7

Country Fried Winter Squash

Preparation time: 45-60 minutes (includes
   cooking)
Yields: 3-4 servings (as a side dish)

1^1/$_2$ pound winter squash (a medium
   sized butternut or acorn squash or a
   piece of a hubbard or banana squash),
   peeled and thinly sliced
1 stalk celery, minced
1 medium bell pepper, minced
2 T BUTTER OIL SPREAD (p. 153) or
   butter
1/2 t salt

Heat butter in a heavy skillet. Add squash,
bell peppers, and celery. Sprinkle with salt.
Turn to coat with butter. Cover and cook
over medium heat, turning 2 to 3 times until
lightly browned and tender (about 15
minutes).

Calories: 166.8
Fat (gm): 8.6
Protein (gm): 1.9
Cholesterol (mg): 22.0
Sodium (mg): 451.9

Zucchini Parmesan

Preparation time: 30 minutes (includes
    cooking)
Yields: 4 servings

*"I'm amazed Mom, you actually made
zucchini taste good!" Need anything else be
said?*

2 T olive oil
4 C medium zucchini, thinly sliced
1 bell pepper, minced
1/2 C celery, minced
2 T parsley, minced
1/2 t salt
1/2 t oregano
1/4 t rosemary
**4 C tomatoes, finely chopped (or 1^1/$_2$ C
    tomato puree)**
1/2 C grated parmesan cheese

Heat oil in a large heavy skillet. Add all
ingredients except tomatoes and cheese.
Saute over medium heat, stirring frequently,
until vegetables are tender (about 20
minutes). Stir in tomatoes and continue to
saute until tomatoes are thoroughly heated
(about 5 minutes); pour into a serving dish
and sprinkle with parmesan cheese. This can
be made ahead and reheated in the oven for
20 minutes at 350°.

Calories: 168.2
Fat (gm): 9.5
Protein (gm): 6.8
Cholesterol (mg): 8.0
Sodium (mg): 487.1

VARIATION: substitute 1 medium eggplant
(sliced) for the zucchini.

Cabbage Amandine

Preparation time: 25-30 minutes (includes
    cooking)
Yields: 4 servings

2 T butter
1/3 C slivered, blanched almonds
4 C shredded cabbage
1 to 2 T lemon juice

Heat butter in a large skillet until lightly
browned. Add almonds and saute, stirring
until golden. Remove with slotted spoon and
set aside. Add cabbage, cover and braise
until cabbage is crispy tender (about 5
minutes). Add lemon juice and if desired salt
to taste. Fold in almonds and serve.

Calories: 145.0
Fat (gm): 11.9
Protein (gm): 2.7
Cholesterol (mg): 16.5
Sodium (mg): 74.8

Summer Vegetables

Preparation time: 30-40 minutes (includes
shelling peas and cooking)
Yields: 4 servings

1 to 2 T oil
**1^1/$_2$ C summer squash (patty pan,
    crookneck, or zucchini), sliced**
1/2 C peas, shelled
**1 C cherry tomatoes or large tomatoes
    cut into 1 inch cubes**
1 C mung bean sprouts

Heat oil until sizzling in a wok or cast iron
pan. Saute squash, stirring constantly, for 1
minute. Add peas, tomatoes and sprouts.
Toss well, cover and turn down the heat.
Allow to steam until peas are just tender, but
still crisp. Don't overcook or tomatoes will be
mushy.

Calories: 92.2
Fat (gm): 4.9
Protein (gm): 2.2
Cholesterol (mg): 0
Sodium (mg): 6.8

Green Winter Vegetables

Preparation time: 20 minutes (includes
    cooking)
Yields: 6 servings

1 T oil
**2 C broccoli, cut into florets and thinly
    sliced stems (peel stem if tough)**
1 C chinese cabbage, shredded
1 C celery, thinly sliced on the diagonal
3 to 4 T vegetable stock (or water)

Heat the oil in a wok or cast iron pan. Add
the broccoli and stir well. Saute for 1 minute.
Add celery, stir well and saute for 1 more
minute. Add cabbage and vegetable stock.
Cover and steam 3 to 5 minutes over a
medium heat. Be careful not to burn the
vegetables.

Calories: 32.7
Fat (gm): 2.2
Protein (gm): .7
Cholesterol (mg): 0
Sodium (mg): 33.6

BAKED VEGETABLE DISHES

Broccoli Au Gratin

Preparation time: 20 minutes (includes
    cooking)
Yields: 4 servings

1 bunch broccoli
**1 C thick CHEESE SAUCE (p. 175) made
    with cheddar cheese**
2 T finely crushed dry bread crumbs

Peel stems of broccoli if they are tough. Cut
stems crosswise into thin slices and separate
florets. Steam until just tender. Place in
baking dish, cover with cheese sauce, and
sprinkle with bread crumbs. Bake at 450° for
10 to 15 minutes or until top is well browned
and casserole is heated through.

Calories: 136.3
Fat (gm): 8.3
Protein (gm): 7.0
Cholesterol (mg): 20.3

Sodium (mg): 251.1

VARIATION: Substitute other vegetables for
the broccoli, such as cauliflower or potatoes
or a combination.

Turnip Casserole

Preparation time: 15-20 minutes
Cooking time: 20-30 minutes
Yields: 6 servings

12 turnips
1/2 C sour cream or yogurt
1 t basil
1/4 t salt
paprika

Steam the turnips whole for 10 to 12 minutes.
Mix with sour cream, salt and basil. Sprinkle
with paprika and bake in a lightly oiled
casserole at 350° for 20 to 30 minutes until
tender.

Calories: 51.7
Fat (gm): 3.4
Protein (gm): .7
Cholesterol (mg): 6.7
Sodium (mg): 157.0

Baked Eggplant Slices

Preparation time: 40-70 minutes
Cooking time: 15-25 minutes
Yields: 4-6 servings

2 medium eggplants
6 T olive oil
2 T lemon juice
1/2 t oregano
1/2 t salt
**2 C grated parmesan or romano or dry
    jack cheese**

Cut eggplant crosswise into 3/4 inch slices.
Place slices one layer deep in a shallow
baking pan. Combine all other ingredients
except cheese. Spoon 1/2 of this marinade
over the eggplant (about 1/2 t per slice). Let
stand 15 to 30 minutes. Turn slices over and
spoon on remaining marinade. Let stand
another 15 to 30 minutes. Sprinkle

generously with cheese. Bake at 400° for 15 to 25 minutes until eggplant is soft.

Calories: 291.6
Fat (gm): 20.1
Protein (gm): 13.0
Cholesterol (mg): 21.3
Sodium (mg): 681.1

Winter Squash Supreme

Preparation time: 10 minutes
Cooking time: 60 minutes
Yields: 4 servings

2 medium acorn squash (or butternut, golden nugget or any medium squash)
2 t butter, melted
1/2 C cream
1/2 C maple syrup or honey

Cut squash in half lengthwise. Remove seeds and put halves cut side up in an oiled baking dish, positioned so they won't tip over. Bake uncovered at 350° for 30 minutes. Then brush the inside of each half with butter. Mix the cream and syrup and fill each squash cavity about half full. Bake another 20 minutes until tender.

Calories: 298.3
Fat (gm): 12.4
Protein (gm): 1.4
Cholesterol (mg): 47.5
Sodium (mg): 42.1

Candied Almond Squash

Preparation time: 45 minutes
Cooking time: 20 minutes
Yields: 6 servings

2 medium sized butternut squash (or 2$^1/_2$ pounds of any winter squash)
5 to 6 t butter or oil
1/2 to 3/4 C pure maple syrup or honey
1/2 C toasted, slivered almonds

Peel and seed squash. Cut into large pieces and steam until tender. Add butter and mash squash until very smooth. Stir in maple syrup and pour into an oiled 1 to 1$^1/_2$ quart

casserole. Sprinkle with almonds. Bake at 350° for 20 minutes until well heated.

Calories: 289.9
Fat (gm): 9.0
Protein (gm): 3.4
Cholesterol (mg): 10.1
Sodium (mg): 50.7

Note: this is an excellent way to use leftover cooked squash.

Nutty Candied Yams

Preparation time: 15 minutes
Cooking time: 60 and 30 minutes (yams are twice-baked)
Yields: 8 servings

6 medium yams
1/2 C honey
1/2 C water
1/2 t salt
2 T oil
1/2 t cinnamon
1/2 C walnuts

Bake yams in jackets at 350°-400° for 1 hour until almost tender. Cool slightly, peel and cut into thick slices. Boil all other ingredients together for 5 minutes. Pour syrup over yam slices in a shallow pan and bake uncovered at 375° for 30 minutes, occasionally basting slices with sauce in pan.

Calories: 300.8
Fat (gm): 7.1
Protein (gm): 3.2
Cholesterol (mg): 0
Sodium (mg): 146.9

VARIATION: Substitute pumpkin, winter squash, or sweet potatoes for the yams.

Orange Yam Casserole

Preparation time: 15-20 minutes
Cooking time: 30 minutes (add 1 hour if
  yams need to be baked first)
Yields: 8 servings

6 baked, peeled and sliced yams
1/4 C butter or oil
2 small oranges, sliced finely but not
  peeled
1/2 C honey
1/2 C orange juice
1/2 C bread crumbs, tossed with 1 T oil

Place 1 layer of yam slices in an oiled
casserole. Dot with butter and top with a
layer of orange slices. Repeat layers of yams
and orange slices until all are in the pan. Mix
honey with orange juice and pour over all.
Cover with slightly oiled bread crumbs.
Cover and bake 20 minutes at 375°. Then
uncover and cook an additional 10 minutes.

Calories: 311.6
Fat (gm): 6.0
Protein (gm): 2.3
Cholesterol (mg): 16.7
Sodium (mg): 97.7

Dilled Mashed Potatoes

Preparation time: 10 minutes
Cooking time: 20 minutes (add 30 minutes if
  potatoes are not already cooked and
  mashed)
Yields: 4 servings

4 C riced or mashed hot potatoes
1 C yogurt
2 t dried parsley
2 t lemon juice
2 t dill weed
1/2 t salt
1/4 C butter

Mix all ingredients except butter. Put into a
shallow 1 quart oiled baking dish and dot
with the butter. Bake at 350° for 20 minutes.

Calories: 286.5
Fat (gm): 12.9

Protein (gm): 4.6
Cholesterol (mg): 37.1
Sodium (mg): 441.5

STUFFED VEGETABLES

Most of the following stuffed vegetable
recipes have a unique stuffing mix which can
be used interchangeably with other stuffings
or dressings. Any vegetable or fruit with a
cavity except melons can be stuffed and
baked. Have fun experimenting!

Stuffed Baked Potatoes

Preparation time: 20 minutes
Cooking time: 60 and 20 minutes (twice
  baked)
Yields: 3 servings

3 russet baking potatoes (3 to 5 inches
  long)
1/3 C milk
3 T oil or butter
1/2 t salt
3 T sharp cheddar cheese, grated
  paprika

Thoroughly scrub potatoes and bake at 400°
until soft (about 1 hour). Slit potatoes
lengthwise and carefully scoop out the pulp.
Add the milk, oil and salt. Whip until fluffy.
Stuff potato shells with the mixture and
sprinkle with the cheese and paprika. Return
to the oven at 350° and bake until tops are
toasty.

Calories: 381.8
Fat (gm): 15.4
Protein (gm): 6.1
Cholesterol (mg): 9.5
Sodium (mg): 428.5

VARIATION: Potatoes can be cut into 2
halves and then stuffed. Omit 1 to 2 of the
shells and pile the stuffing on the other
shells. For a festive look, stuffing can be
piped on with the rosette tip of a pastry bag.
Paprika can be sprinkled on top for a
colorful accent.

Herbed Potato Boats

Preparation time: 20 minutes
Baking time: 60 and 20 minutes (twice baked)
Yields: 4 servings

Bake 4 potatoes and substitute 1/2 C cultured sour cream or thick yogurt for the milk, oil and cheese in STUFFED BAKED POTATOES (p.90). Add 1/2 t marjoram and 1/4 t thyme. Follow procedure in STUFFED BAKED POTATOES. Serve immediately or reheat at 350°.

Calories: 136.4
Fat (gm): 2.6
Protein (gm): 1.9
Cholesterol (mg): 5.0
Sodium (mg): 158.3

Stuffed Cabbage

Preparation time: 60 minutes (includes cabbage steaming time; brown rice must be cooked ahead)
Cooking time: 40 minutes
Yields: 6-8 servings

1 large firm cabbage about 6 to 7 inches in diameter
1/4 C oil
1 C minced celery
1/2 C minced bell pepper
2 to 3 C cooked brown rice (a larger cabbage takes more)
1 t to 1 T ITALIAN SEASONING (p. 221) or VEGETABLE HERBS (p. 222)
1 to 2 t salt
1/2 C finely chopped walnuts or almonds
2 C TOMATO SAUCE (p. 176) (or canned) seasoned to taste with basil

Steam the cabbage whole, on a rack in a large kettle, until tender but still firm. This may take as long as an hour for a big one. Meanwhile, heat oil and saute celery and bell pepper until celery is translucent. Add rice, herbs and nuts. If the mixture is too dry, add a little warm water. When the cabbage is done, remove the core and pull out the inner leaves until the shell is about one inch thick.

Be careful doing this so you do not make a hole in the top. Finely shred 1 C of the cooked cabbage and add to the stuffing mixture. (Add the rest of your cabbage to a soup or vegetable stock or serve at another meal.) Stuff cabbage firmly. Turn cabbage over, core side down, in a casserole dish. Coat with 1 T oil and bake at 350° for 40 minutes or until done. Cut in wedges and serve with tomato sauce.

Calories: 262.9
Fat (gm): 10.7
Protein (gm): 5.7
Cholesterol (mg): 0
Sodium (mg): 462.0

VARIATIONS: Stuff a squash or pumpkin or bell peppers (red ones are colorful) with this stuffing.

Stuffed Holiday Squash

Preparation time: 1 hour and 20 minutes (includes initial cooking of the squash and preparing the stuffing)
Cooking time: 45 minutes
Yields: 4 servings

Try a colorful Turk's Turban squash or a stuffed sweet pumpkin to replace the holiday turkey. Following are two stuffing recipes. Any of the stuffing recipes preceding this will also work.

one 6 to 8 inch winter squash

Pierce the top of your squash and steam it or bake it at 350° for 45 to 60 minutes until the sides can be pierced with a fork. Let cool until it is "handleable", and then cut out the top as for a jack-o-lantern. (If using a Turk's Turban, cut out the bottom of the top part of the turban). Remove all seeds and pithy insides. To get an idea of how much stuffing you will need, measure water into the squash. Pour out the water and drain squash upside down. The amount of water that filled it is the amount of stuffing you will need. Stuff with your choice of stuffings. After stuffing the squash, return it to the oven and bake for 45 minutes until the squash is very tender. Serve.

Stuffed Rainbow Cabbage

Preparation time: 50-80 minutes (includes
  cabbage steaming time)
Cooking time: 10-40 minutes
Yields: 8 servings

1 large cabbage (about 6 pounds)
2 medium summer squash, diced
2 medium turnips, grated
3 medium carrots, scrubbed or peeled
  and grated
1 potato or yam, grated
1 bell pepper, minced
 1 C fresh parsley
2 tomatoes, diced
1 t thyme
1/2 t salt
1 C TOMATO SAUCE (p.176) (or canned)

Steam cabbage whole until just barely tender.
(This will take 30 to 60 minutes.) Steam all
other vegetables except parsley and
tomatoes. When the cabbage is cooked, cool
it a bit until "handleable," then cut out the
core and carefully pull out the cabbage
leaves from inside, leaving 1/2 to 1 inch
walls. Chop about 1/4 of the inside leaves
and combine with the parsley, tomatoes,
other steamed vegetables and seasonings.
Carefully stuff cabbage, covering opening
with a leaf. Cover can be tied on with cotton
string. Coat cabbage with oil and reheat in a
350° oven 10 to 40 minutes (depends on
how hot stuffing is). The remaining inside
leaves can be reheated and served with
another meal or used in soup. Serve cabbage
core side down with tomato sauce lightly
dribbled on top. Cut into wedges to serve.

Calories: 148.2
Fat (gm): .2
Protein (gm): 3.9
Cholesterol (mg): 0
Sodium (mg): 532.5

Stuffed Zucchini

Preparation time: 20-30 minutes
Cooking time: 10 minutes
Yields: 4-8 servings

1 oversize zucchini, 1 to 2 feet long
1 medium potato, cubed
2 small carrots, scrubbed or peeled and
  finely sliced
1 C green beans, cut
1 C tomatoes, cubed
2 T oil
1/2 to 1 C cheese
1 t ITALIAN SEASONING (p. 221) (or 1/4 t
  each: thyme, marjoram, oregano and
  basil)
1/4 t salt
1/4 t paprika

Steam the potatoes, carrots and green beans
until almost tender. Steam the zucchini
whole. Cut the zucchini in half lengthwise.
Carefully hollow out the zucchini. Mix
steamed vegetables, tomatoes, oil, herbs, salt,
and 1 C of the zucchini insides together.
Omit the zucchini if the seeds are very large
and coarse. Fill zucchini halves with filling,
top with grated cheese and sprinkle with
paprika. Bake at 350° for 5 to 10 minutes
until the cheese is bubbly.

Calories: 175.0
Fat (gm): 8.6
Protein (gm): 6.0
Cholesterol (mg): 15.0
Sodium (mg): 193.7

VARIATION: Stuff other vegetables such as
winter squash with this stuffing.

Corn Stuffed Zucchini

Preparation time: 30-40 minutes
Cooking time: 30 minutes
Yields: 6-8 servings

6 medium zucchini
1¹/₂ C fresh corn
1 bell pepper, minced
1 stalk celery, minced
1/2 t salt
2 T oil
1/4 C minced fresh parsley
1/2 C grated cheese

Wash and cut off ends of zucchini but do not peel. Steam whole zucchini about 5 minutes (or if too large to steam, bake at 350° until just tender). Cut in half lengthwise and carefully remove pulp, leaving the shell about 1/4 inch thick. Place shells in a shallow baking dish. Finely chop pulp and combine with other vegetables and salt. Heat oil and saute vegetables until thick about 10 minutes. Fill shells with vegetable mixture and sprinkle with cheese. Bake uncovered at 350° for 30 minutes.

Calories: 130.3
Fat (gm): 7.1
Protein (gm): 3.7
Cholesterol (mg): 10.0
Sodium (mg): 247.2

Stuffed Bell Peppers

Preparation time: 30 minutes (rice and tofu
  must be cooked ahead)
Cooking time: 40 minutes
Yields: 6 servings

6 bell peppers
1 recipe SPANISH RICE (p. 168)
1 C browned tofu or commercial
  vegetarian sausage or cheese
1 C TOMATO SAUCE (p.176) (or canned)
6 three inch square thin slices of cheddar

Pick bell peppers that are reasonably round and have a flat bottom. Wash well. Cut out the top and remove seeds and inner partitions from peppers. Steam peppers for 5 minutes. While they are steaming mix the tofu and rice. When peppers are cool enough to handle, stuff them until full. Place in a lightly oiled baking dish and pour tomato sauce over the top. Top with slices of cheddar. Bake at 350° about 40 minutes until cheese is melted and peppers hot.

VARIATIONS: Remember when experimenting with your own stuffings or the following ones that each pepper will need about 1 to 1¹/₂ C stuffing. Also be aware of color and texture: a bright green pepper stuffed with yellow corn, red tomatoes and orange carrots is a delight to the eyes. Or start with a red pepper or the newer purple or golden yellow peppers (the purple ones turn green when cooked).

Calories: 385.9
Fat (gm): 20.0
Protein (gm): 16.8
Cholesterol (mg): 33.0
Sodium (mg): 396.5

STUFFING SUGGESTIONS:
- sauteed celery
  brown rice
  top with cheese and tomato sauce
- 1 part each:
  steamed minced celery
  tomatoes
  cooked brown rice
- 2 parts steamed vegetables
  1 part cooked grain
- equal parts:
  steamed corn
  steamed carrots
  chopped tomatoes

NOTE: Any vegetables can be stuffed with these mixtures.

Chestnut Stuffing

Preparation time: 20-30 minutes
Cooking time: 45 minutes
Yields: 3$\frac{1}{2}$ - 4 C

2 C dry chestnuts, hulled and peeled, roasted or boiled, and chopped (refer to NUTS AND SEEDS section, p. 215, for directions)
3 large carrots, scrubbed or peeled, thinly sliced and steamed
2 stalks celery, minced
3 to 4 C cooked brown rice or bulgur
2 T dry parsley
1/2 t marjoram
1/2 t thyme
1/2 t sage

Combine ingredients and stuff a steamed squash or whatever else you want to stuff.

Per cup:
Calories: 244.0
Fat (gm): .8
Protein (gm): 4.6
Cholesterol (mg): 0
Sodium (mg): 43.6

Bread Stuffing

Preparation time: 30-40 minutes
Cooking time: 45 minutes
Yields: 14 C

8 C dry bread cubes
1/2 C butter
2 C celery, minced
1 bell pepper, minced (red is colorful)
1 bunch spinach, finely cut (optional)
1 C walnuts, coarsely chopped
2 C commercially made seasoned baked tofu, or vegetarian sausage or browned tofu
1$\frac{1}{2}$ t sage
1/2 t pepper
1$\frac{1}{2}$ t thyme
1/4 t tarragon (optional)
1/2 C parsley
1 to 2 C vegetable stock or 2 bouillon cubes and 1 to 2 C water

Cut the commercial tofu squares into strips. Saute the tofu, celery, bell pepper and nuts in the butter. Add to the dry bread crumbs. Add seasonings and stir well. Heat the vegetable water to boiling and pour over bread mix. Add less water for a dryer stuffing and more for a more moist stuffing. Stir gently only until moistened. Stuff squash, allowing room for expansion. Bake at 350° for 45 minutes until squash is tender.

Per cup:
Calories: 201.5
Fat (gm): 12.6
Protein (gm): 7.0
Cholesterol (mg): 18.9
Sodium (mg): 380.8

NOTE: Any vegetables can be stuffed with this stuffing. Summer patty pan squash are excellent. This stuffing can also be cooked in a pan and not stuffed into anything at all.

EAST INDIAN VEGETABLE DISHES

The following recipes have all been derived from East Indian cuisine. However, none of them are at all hot. If you want to add cayenne or chilis, begin with 1/4 t or 1 small chili and season to taste from there. All of the following recipes are excellent served with puris or chapatis, and rice. They are also exceptional as stuffing in BO-PE (p. 159) or PARATHAS (p. 120).

Spicy Braised Vegetables

Preparation time: 35-55 minutes (includes cooking time)
Yields: 6 servings

2 C cauliflower florets (1 small head)
1 C cabbage, shredded
1 C bell pepper, diced
1 C carrots, scrubbed or peeled and thinly sliced on the diagonal
1/2 C lentil or other bean sprouts
2 T oil
1/2 t salt
1 t turmeric
1/2 t cinnamon
1 t ground coriander
3 to 4 cloves (or 1/4 t ground)
1/2 t black mustard seed
1/2 t cumin seed
1 t fenugreek (optional)
2 T water

Prepare and measure the vegetables, as noted above. Heat the oil and spices in a heavy saucepan (at least a 2 quart size, with a tight fitting lid). When the mustard seeds begin to "dance" (be careful, they may pop and burn you), reduce the heat and add the vegetables, all at once, stirring rapidly as you pour them in. Saute briefly, then add the water, cover, and let the vegetables steam until they are tender. This dish may be garnished with nuts or raisins and served with CHAPATIS (p.120) or a cooked grain. These vegetables are also excellent as the filling for PARATHAS (p. 120) or BO-PE (p. 159).

Calories: 79.0
Fat (gm): 4.4
Protein (gm): 1.3
Cholesterol (mg): 0
Sodium (mg): 204.4

Curried Vegetables

Preparation time: 35-55 minutes (includes cooking time)
Yields: 4 servings

This dish is excellent served as a main dish.

3 T oil
1 t black mustard seeds
1/2 t whole cumin seeds
2 t turmeric
1 t salt
6 C vegetables, diced

Heat the oil in a heavy pan. Add the seeds. When the mustard seeds begin to "dance" (be careful, they may pop and burn you), add the other ingredients, stirring quickly to avoid burning them. Turn the heat down, cover and simmer until vegetables are tender. (If you are using some vegetables with a high water content, such as zucchini or tomatoes, no water will be needed, but if your vegetables are all dry, such as cauliflower, add a little water before covering them so that the vegetables will not stick and burn.)

Calories: 158.2
Fat (gm): 9.7
Protein (gm): 2.7
Cholesterol (mg): 0
Sodium (mg): 600.0

VARIATIONS: Add other spices such as ginger, cinnamon, coriander, ground cloves, cardamom or green chilis.

Golden Squash

Preparation time: 40-50 minutes (includes
cooking time)
Yields: 6 servings

4 C winter squash, peeled and diced
(about 2 pounds)
1 bell pepper, minced
1/4 C oil
1/2 t black mustard seed
1/2 t whole cumin seed
1/2 t ginger
1 t paprika
1/2 t turmeric
1 t salt
2 T honey
juice of 1 lemon

Prepare vegetables as directed. Heat oil in a
heavy pan with a lid. Add seeds. When
mustard seeds "dance" (be careful, they may
pop and burn you), add all the other
ingredients except honey and lemon juice.
Cover the pot, lower heat and simmer squash
until very tender (about 15 minutes).
Uncover, add honey and lemon juice and
serve.

Calories: 162.4
Fat (gm): 9.0
Protein (gm): 1.2
Cholesterol (mg): 0
Sodium (mg): 358.0

Zucchini Vegetable

Preparation time: 30-40 minutes (includes
cooking time)
Yields: 6 servings

3 T oil
1 t salt
2 t turmeric
2 large (4 small) potatoes, cubed (not
peeled)
1 red bell pepper, minced
8 small zucchini, sliced
4 tomatoes, cubed

Heat oil in a heavy pan. Add turmeric and
salt. When oil is sizzling, add cubed potatoes.

Coat well in oil. Turn heat down, cover and
simmer 4-5 minutes. Add the bell pepper and
zucchini. Mix in thoroughly, cover and
simmer until vegetables are just tender. Add
tomatoes. Stir in well. Steam for another
minute or two.

Calories: 203.7
Fat (gm): 6.5
Protein (gm): 2.9
Cholesterol (mg): 0
Sodium (mg): 373.3

Alu Sabji

Preparation time: 40 minutes (includes
cooking time)
Yields: 6 servings

This is a hearty potato dish.

1/4 C oil
1/2 t whole cumin seeds
1 t black mustard seeds
1 t fennel
2 t turmeric
1 t salt
4 medium potatoes, cut into 1/2 inch
cubes
2 bell peppers, diced
1/4 C water

Heat the oil in a heavy pan. Add seeds.
When mustard seeds "dance" (be careful,
they may pop and burn you), add all the
other ingredients except water. Toss potatoes
well to coat with the hot oil and spices. Add
the water, cover and turn down heat.
Simmer, checking and stirring frequently until
potatoes are soft.

Calories: 172.0
Fat (gm): 8.7
Protein (gm): 1.5
Cholesterol (mg): 0
Sodium (mg): 361.3

Curried Peas and Cauliflower

Preparation time: 20-25 minutes (includes
    cooking time)
Yields: 4 servings (as a main dish) 6 servings
    (as a side dish)

3 T oil
2 t whole cumin seed
1 t black mustard seed
1/2 t salt
2 C fresh hulled green peas
3 C cauliflower, cut into little florets

Heat the oil in a heavy pan and add the
seeds. When the mustard seeds "dance" (be
careful, they may pop and burn you), add
the cauliflower and salt. Stir thoroughly,
cover and turn heat down very low. Simmer,
stirring occasionally for 10 minutes. Add peas
and simmer another 5 minutes until
vegetables are tender.

Calories: 120.5
Fat (gm): 6.5
Protein (gm): 3.2
Cholesterol (mg): 0
Sodium (mg): 720.3

Vegetables Pakora

Preparation time: 30-45 minutes (includes
    cooking time)
Yields: 4 servings

1 C garbanzo (chickpea) flour
1 t salt
1 t turmeric
3/4 C water
1/2 t chili powder (optional)
2$^1/_2$ C vegetables and/or fruits such as:
    eggplant cut in 1/4 inch slices
    carrot sticks
    broccoli florets
    potatoes, sliced very thin
    cauliflower florets
    bananas, cut in half both crosswise and
        lengthwise
    apples, thinly sliced
oil (preferably sesame or peanut)

Make a batter of all the ingredients except
the vegetables or fruits and oil. More water
can be added if it seems too thick. Heat the
oil in a deep pan until it is 375°. While it is
heating, dip the vegetables or fruits in the
pakora batter. When the oil is hot, very
carefully ease the coated vegetables or fruits
into the oil. Fry on one side until they are
golden brown. Carefully turn over and fry
until the other side is also golden brown.
Remove and drain on paper towels or on a
paper bag or on a rack over a paper bag. Be
very careful cooking these; the oil gets very
hot and can easily burn you. This is not a
recipe to cook with the help of young
children.

Calories: 339.0
Fat (gm): 26.6
Protein (gm): 10.5
Cholesterol (mg): 0
Sodium (mg): 534.6

Curried Brussel Sprouts and Cauliflower Casserole

Preparation time: 30 minutes (includes
   steaming vegetables)
Cooking time: 15 minutes
Yields: 6 servings

1$\frac{1}{2}$ C steamed cauliflower
1$\frac{1}{2}$ C steamed brussels sprouts
1 C vegetable stock or water
2 T oil
2 T CURRY POWDER (p. 223)
2 T whole wheat pastry flour
1 C thick YOGURT (p.213)
1/2 t salt
1/4 C slivered almonds or cashews

In a saucepan blend oil, curry powder and
flour. Simmer while stirring. Gradually add
vegetable stock, stirring until smooth and
thickened. Fold in yogurt and heat slowly
(too fast will cause curdling). Season to taste
with salt. Place vegetables in an oiled
1$\frac{1}{2}$ quart casserole. Pour sauce on top and
sprinkle with nuts. Bake at 400° for 15
minutes until well heated and the nuts are
browned.

Calories: 133.6
Fat (gm): 7.7
Protein (gm): 4.1
Cholesterol (mg): 2.7
Sodium (mg): 221.3

VARIATION: Substitute other vegetables for
the brussels sprouts and cauliflower.

ORIENTAL VEGETABLE DISHES

Sweet 'n Sour Vegetables

Preparation time: 30 minutes (includes
   cooking time)
Yields: 4 servings

Sauce: (make first)
  1/2 C pureed tomatoes
  1/2 C pineapple juice
  2 T honey
  1 t tamari (soy sauce)
  1 T arrowroot (mix with 2 T water to
    make a thick paste)
  1/4 C lemon juice

Mix above ingredients and simmer for 5
minutes.

2-3 T oil
1 C celery, sliced on the diagonal
1/2 bell pepper, cut into long strips
1 C snow peas (edible pod)
a few water chestnuts, sliced
2-3 stalks bok choy, chopped
1/2 C bean sprouts

Heat oil in a cast iron pan or wok until
sizzling hot. Add vegetables and keep stirring
them constantly for 2 to 3 minutes. Pour
sauce over vegetables, cover, and simmer
until vegetables are just tender.

Calories: 190.5
Fat (gm): 8.0
Protein (gm): 2.6
Cholesterol (mg): 0
Sodium (mg): 692.3

VARIATIONS: Use 4 to 6 C of any vegetable
or combination in this recipe. For a main
dish add 1 pound of tofu cut into 1 inch
pieces. This can be used fresh from the
package or stir fried.

Green Beans Oriental Style

Preparation time: 25 minutes (includes
  cooking time)
Yields: 4-6 servings

1/3 C water
1/4 t grated fresh ginger root
1 pound green beans (choose thin pods
  with undeveloped beans)
1 T oil

Combine water and ginger. Wash beans,
remove tips and string. Cut in half
lengthwise. Heat oil in a wok or cast iron
pan and add beans. Cook 3 to 4 minutes,
stirring constantly. Pour ginger and water
over beans. Cover and cook 5 to 6 more
minutes until cooked but still crispy tender.

Calories: 65.2
Fat (gm): 3.2
Protein (gm): 1.6
Cholesterol (mg): 0
Sodium (mg): 6.8

Tempura

Preparation time: 30-45 minutes (includes
  cooking time)
Yields: 4 servings

1 C whole wheat flour
2 t arrowroot
1/2 t salt
1¼ C water
5 C vegetables such as:
  broccoli florets
  cauliflower florets
  winter or summer squash slices
  fresh green beans
  carrots, scrubbed or peeled and sliced
    diagonally or slivered
  eggplant strips
  green pepper rings
oil (preferably sesame or peanut)

Combine all of the above ingredients except
the vegetables and oil and mix well. Heat at
least 2 inches of cooking oil in a deep pan to
374°. While the oil is heating, stir some of the
vegetables into the batter until they are

covered with it. When oil is hot, carefully
ease vegetables piece by piece into the oil.
Don't fill the pan so full that they stick
together. Fry on one side until golden brown
and then turn over and fry until the other
side is also golden brown. Remove and drain
on absorbent material (paper towel, paper
bag, etc.) or on a rack over a paper bag. Be
very careful while cooking these as the oil
gets very hot and can easily cause burns.
This is not a recipe to cook with the help of
young children. Eat while still warm. These
can be kept warm in the oven, but they will
lose some of their crispness.

Calories: 292.5
Fat (gm): 17.2
Protein (gm): 5.2
Cholesterol (mg): 0
Sodium (mg): 283.4

May be served with the following sauce:

  1 t hot prepared mustard
  1 t lemon juice
  1 t tamari (soy sauce)

Per teaspoon:
Calories: 6.7
Fat (gm): .2
Protein (gm): .6
Cholesterol (mg): 0
Sodium (mg): 350.3

Grains & Cereals

GRAINS & CEREALS

If possible, when purchasing grains and flours, smell them to see if they are rancid. Buy them from a store which refrigerates their flours or has a high enough turnover that the flours and grains are fresh. Of course, the best baked goods are made from freshly milled flour, which a few stores produce daily. Store your grains and flours in airtight containers in a dark, cool, dry spot. If possible, refrigerate or freeze them.

The following are brief descriptions of grains, cereals and flours to help you in identifying, selecting, and using these foods.

AMARANTH is a newly re-discovered grain of the Aztec. It has good amounts of protein, calcium, iron, phosphorus and fiber. It can be eaten as a hot breakfast cereal, sprouted like alfalfa seeds or used ground in baked goods. Amaranth is usually combined with other grains because it has a rather bitter taste alone.

BARLEY (whole) is used cooked in soups and stews. It can be used as a flour by people who are allergic to wheat. It imparts a sweet, moist, cake-like texture to quick breads, cakes and cookies. It does not have the gluten that wheat does, so yeast breads made with barley are dense and do not rise well. Barley grits can be quickly cooked as a cereal.

BRAN is the outer coating of a grain kernel. It usually refers to wheat bran, but in the last few years we have been hearing a lot about oat bran. Essentially any grain that is milled loses its bran in the milling. Bran is an excellent source of fiber and also a good source of vitamins and minerals.

BUCKWHEAT groats can be used cooked in stuffing, for breakfast cereal, or substituted for rice. It has a strong taste in the whole form, to which some people object. As flour it is used primarily in pancakes. It has a low gluten content and will not rise well with yeast. People allergic to wheat are not necessarily allergic to buckwheat.

BULGUR is cracked whole wheat that has been steamed and dried. It can be soaked in hot water for 30 minutes or so and used in salads or cooked as a cereal. It is similar to rice, and also good as a hot cereal.

CORN is used both as a vegetable and as a cereal grain. Cornmeal is coarser than corn flour and various grinds of each are available. The color of the flour varies according to the type of corn used. (Joy has a friend who grows, dries and grinds black corn which makes the most beautiful purple blue muffins.) Dried corn can be cooked and added to soups, but generally in the U.S. dried corn is used as cornmeal.

COUSCOUS is a finer ground version of bulgur.

CRACKED WHEAT is similar to bulgur except that it has not been steamed and dried. Unlike bulgur, it needs to be cooked before it is used. Its primary use is as a hot breakfast cereal.

GLUTEN FLOUR is wheat flour with the starch removed. It is used most often in making breads. The gluten forms cohesive elastic mass (developed by kneading) which traps the bubbles produced by the yeast. This results in a lighter bread. A high protein patty can be made by mixing gluten flour or whole wheat flour with water until a stiff dough is formed. Soak and knead in cold running water to remove the starch. When no more cloudy starch runs off with the water, you have pure gluten. This process takes much longer and yields a smaller amount when using whole wheat flour than white flour. The remaining ball of dough can be sliced, steamed or parboiled, then sauteed or ground and shaped into patties or loaves. It is basically tasteless but can be seasoned with miso and/or tamari (soy sauce) and spices. People allergic to wheat typically are allergic to gluten as well.

GRAHAM flour is a type of whole wheat flour, similar to pastry flour but with more bran. When a recipe calls for graham flour, pastry flour can be substituted unless the recipe calls for yeast, in which case whole wheat bread flour should be used.

GRITS are very coarsely ground grains that can be cooked into a cereal or used in cooking.

GROATS (whole kernels of grain) contain all the nutrients found in the grain, since nothing but the husk has been removed. Groats keep better than cracked or ground grains because the oil and other nutrients are protected from oxidation by the bran or outer coating.

KAMUT is a recently introduced grain that is reportedly of ancient origin. It has a high protein content of 17.3 grams of high quality protein in each 100 grams. It is cooked the same way as brown rice and can be used in place of rice or wheatberries.

MEALS are generally ground more coarsely than flours and provide more texture in baking. They may also be cooked as breakfast cereal.

MILLET (milo) is a tiny, pearl shaped grain which is usually white or yellow. It can be cooked as a whole grain or ground into a coarse meal. Millet is sweet and contains a reasonable amount of good quality protein. It is the most easily digestible grain.

OATS are usually used rolled or flaked in baking or breakfast cereal. The groats take an exceptionally long time to cook. Like other whole grains, they are a good source of fiber.

QUINOA (pronounced "keen-wa") is another ancient grain (from the Incas) which has recently been introduced into the U.S. It contains more high quality protein than any other grain, with all of the essential amino acids in a balanced state. It is considered by the National Academy of Sciences as "one of the best sources of protein in the vegetable kingdom." Quinoa can be used in all recipes calling for rice, and makes an interesting change from rice and other more ordinary grains. It is not sweet but does have a slightly nutty taste.

RICE is available in many forms and varieties. Brown rice is husked but not polished. Sweet rice is a glutinous rice used for oriental dessert dishes and breakfast cereal. Converted or quick-cooking rice is now available in brown rice. It has been parboiled or steamed and dried, much like bulgur.

Short grain rice tends to stick together a little more than long grain. Long grain tends to stay in individual grains. It is really a matter of individual preference which kind one uses. Try using a long grain Basmati-type rice, a fragrant and hearty rice which comes in white or brown varieties. If you have not eaten much brown rice, buy small amounts and try different varieties to see what you like best.

RICE POLISH is the inner layer of bran that is removed during the refining of white rice. It can be used in place of wheat germ or bran.

ROLLED and **FLAKED** cereals have been steamed and put through rollers. Quick cooking rolled grains are cut before being steamed and rolled.

RYE is most often used as a flour, and is frequently combined with wheat. It has a reasonable amount of gluten but lacks the elasticity of wheat, so used alone it makes a moist, dense loaf. If stored improperly, rye can develop a very toxic mold called ergot, so be certain your rye is fresh and stored in a dry, cool place.

SEMOLINA is a high gluten flour used to make pasta. It is available in some natural food stores and can be used in the NOODLE recipe (p. 113).

SPELT is an antique grain from Roman times with a great nutty taste. It is similar to wheat and can be cooked in the same way. It is also found in flour and pasta form, and in cereal flake combinations. People allergic to wheat are not necessarily allergic to spelt.

STONE-GRINDING (of flour) takes place at slower speeds than steel-grinding, and the resulting lower temperature saves many nutrients in the grains that are destroyed by heat.

TEFF, which has recently become available in the U.S., is reportedly the smallest grain in the world and has been the "staff of life" for the Ethiopian people for thousands of years. It has a slightly sweet taste and thus makes a good breakfast cereal. It is gelatinous and therefore works well as a thickener or to add body to stews or puddings.

TRITICALE is a cross between rye and wheat which is high in protein. Its flour can be substituted for part of the wheat flour in most recipes for a more nutritious food. It must be stored in a dry cool place so that it does not develop molds.

WHEAT is available in many different varieties. In this cookbook, references are made to whole wheat pastry flour and to whole wheat bread flour or whole wheat flour with no designation as to which kind of wheat is being referred to. Whole wheat bread flour is made from "hard" winter wheat and has a much higher gluten content, which helps yeast breads rise. Bread flour also has a more grainy texture and is not as appealing in cookies and quick breads as whole wheat pastry flour. Whole wheat pastry flour is made from "soft" spring wheat. It does not contain as much gluten, and the grain covering is softer, so it does not have a gritty texture in cakes and other pastries. Whole wheat pastry flour does not give satisfactory results in yeast breads. Whole wheat bread flour can be substituted for whole wheat pastry flour but more liquid will be needed and the texture will be coarser. If the recipe does not specify which type of flour to use, then either will do.

WHEAT GERM is the embryo of the wheat grain. It and the bran are removed from white flour during processing. Due to its high oil content, wheat germ becomes rancid very quickly and should be vacuum packed or refrigerated in the store where purchased.

WHITE WHOLE WHEAT has recently been introduced in the U.S. from Asia, where it is grown for noodles. According to the Center for Science in the Public Interest, white whole wheat is as nutritious as regular whole wheat but, when milled, is as mild-tasting as processed white flour. It is currently being grown in Kansas and will be available within the next year in supermarkets and natural foods stores.

WHOLE WHEAT BREAD FLOUR is covered under WHEAT.

WHOLE WHEAT PASTRY FLOUR is covered under WHEAT.

COOKING METHODS

There are numerous cooking methods for grains. We have listed a few which take into account the appliances found in most of our kitchens.

Some people prefer to wash their grains first, in which case you need to slightly cut down the amount of water used. Be sure to wash whole grains such as wheatberries and pick through them as you would beans to make certain that you are only cooking grain.

The amount of water used will determine how moist the grain will be when it is done. If you are cooking vegetables, nuts or dried fruits with the grain, add a little more water than you normally use. Grains are done when they are soft all the way through and no longer taste like raw starch. Usually they will also "puff" and the water will have all been absorbed.

Before cooking, grains can be toasted in a cast iron pan or sauteed in a little bit of oil, perhaps with some spices. This lends a distinctive flavor to the grain. Herbs and spices may be added to the cooking water.

Stove Top Method 1

Grains cooked this way will be light and fluffy. Bring water to a boil in a heavy pan with a tight fitting lid. Add grain so slowly that the water never stops boiling. Stir once, lower heat as much as possible and cover. Simmer without uncovering and without stirring until the water has been absorbed and the grain is tender. The reason for not stirring is that as the grain expands, it forms a network of steam tunnels. If these are disturbed, the grain will cook unevenly.

Stove Top Method 2

Place water and grain into a pan and bring to a boil. Stir once, turn heat down as much as possible, and cover. Cook as in Method 1. This method is faster but the grain will not have as nice a texture as in Method 1.

Microwave Method

Combine grain and minimum amount of water (shown in the following chart) in a glass or ceramic bowl with high sides. Cover with a glass top, plate or plastic wrap. Microwave on high for the time specified. Meals are best when stirred half way through the cooking time. Rice and whole grains are better not disturbed. This method is quicker but does not work for all grains (see chart on p. 107).

Crockpot Method

Place washed grain and minimum amount of water (shown in the chart) in a crockpot. Cover and cook on high until water is absorbed from the grain. It you are cooking the grain all day or all night, then cook on low. This method works best for whole groats. Rice does not turn out well using this method.

Pressure Cooker Method

Combine the grain and minimum amount of water as shown on the chart. Bring to full pressure, turn down to simmer and cook for time specified in the chart. Remove from heat and let pressure go down. Grain should be done when opened.

Thermos Method

This method doesn't work for whole grains except white rice and millet. However, it works well for cracked grains and meals. It is a marvelous method for backpackers and for an early riser's hot breakfast cereal. Soak 1 C grain for 5 to 6 hours. Then add additional water until you have 3 C grain and water mixture. Bring it to a boil. Pour into a preheated thermos. (To preheat, let hot water sit in it, then empty water out just before filling thermos with grain.) Cap thermos and lay it on its side. In 8 to 10 hours, the grain will be done. If camping, the thermos can double as a sleeping bag warmer!

QUICK REFERENCE GUIDE FOR COOKING GRAINS

1 C GRAIN	Water (Cups)*	Cooking time (in minutes)**	Pressure Cooker (in minutes)***	Microwave (in minutes)	Crockpot (in hours)
Amaranth	3	25	not rec.	n/a	n/a
Barley, hulled	2-2$\frac{1}{2}$	30-60	30-40	not rec.	2-3
Brown rice	1$\frac{1}{2}$-2	40-60	30-40	not rec.	not rec.
Buckwheat groats	2-2$\frac{1}{2}$	20-40	not rec.	not rec.	2-3
Bulgur	1-1$\frac{1}{2}$	15-20	not rec.	8	not rec.
Cornmeal & cream of grain cereals	4	20-30	not rec.	4-5	3
Cracked grains	1$\frac{1}{2}$-2	15-20	not rec.	8	1$\frac{1}{2}$
Kamut	2	45-60	not rec.	not rec.	n/a
Millet	2-3	20-30	25	not rec.	not rec.
Oats, rolled (oatmeal & other flaked or rolled grains)	2	5-15	not rec.	4-7	1$\frac{1}{2}$
Oats, whole	1$\frac{1}{2}$-2	40-60	30-40	not rec.	3-8
Quinoa	2	10-20	not rec.	n/a	n/a
Teff	3-4	15-20	not rec.	n/a	n/a
Wheat berries or Rye or Triticale	2-2$\frac{1}{2}$	60-90	45	not rec.	3-8[1]

* Amount of water varied according to method used for cooking.
** Amount of time required varies according to method used.
*** Certain grains, due to their size and consistency, tend to plug the safety valves of pressure cookers, which may cause them to explode. For this reason, we recommend that these grains NOT be pressure cooked. Be sure to read the manufacturer's instructions carefully before using a pressure cooker.
not rec.= not recommended.
n/a= information not available.
[1] Reduce water to 1$\frac{1}{4}$ C
NOTE: When cooking in the microwave, cook on high power and stir every 2 minutes.

GRAIN AND CEREAL RECIPES
(See also SPANISH RICE, p.168.)

Rice Cream

Preparation time: 45-50 minutes (includes
   cooking time)
Yields: 8 servings

2 C brown rice
water (see chart, p. 107)

Wash brown rice and dry roast it in a heavy
well-seasoned skillet until it is golden
colored and begins to pop. Grind it in an
electric blender at high speed or grind in a
grain mill until it is the consistency of
cornmeal (or finer for a baby). This powder
can be cooked like cornmeal in the chart on
p. 107.

Calories: 172.5
Fat (gm): .8
Protein (gm): 3.8
Cholesterol (mg): 0
Sodium (mg): 0

VARIATION: Use other whole grains in place
of the rice or in combination with the rice.

Cornmeal Mush

Preparation time: 25-35 minutes (includes
   cooking time)
Yields: 4 servings

1 C cornmeal
4 C cold water

Mix the cornmeal with 1 C water and make a
smooth paste. Boil the other 3 C water and
when boiling, gradually add the paste while
stirring constantly. Simmer approximately 20
to 30 minutes until the water is absorbed,
stirring frequently to avoid lumping.

Calories: 108.8
Fat (gm): 1.0
Protein (gm): 2.8
Cholesterol (mg): 0
Sodium (mg): 7.2

VARIATION: Add 1/2 C raisins.

Fried Cornmeal Mush

Preparation time: 20-30 minutes
Yields: 4 servings

Pour CORNMEAL MUSH prepared as above,
into a loaf pan and refrigerate. When solid,
turn out of pan, slice, dredge in flour and fry
on a lightly oiled, well seasoned griddle until
brown. Serve with syrup.

Calories: 253.8
Fat (gm): 13.8
Protein (gm): 3.7
Cholesterol (mg): 0
Sodium (mg): 7.9

VARIATIONS: Substitute leftover oatmeal,
rice cream or other cereal for the cornmeal.

Familia

Preparation time: 15 minutes
Yields: 7 servings

1 C oatmeal
1 C rolled wheat
1 C toasted wheat germ
2/3 C almonds, thinly sliced
1/2 C raisins
2/3 C date sugar
3/4 C dried apples, ground or finely
   minced

Mix the above ingredients and store in a
tightly closed container. Add milk just before
serving. For camping, add 1 C instant milk to
the above mixture and then add water when
serving. Use approximately 3/4 C per serving.

Calories: 329.5
Fat (gm): 6.5
Protein (gm): 9.0
Cholesterol (mg): 0
Sodium (mg): 26.5

Toasted Wheat Germ

METHOD 1: Place wheat germ in a loaf pan and bake in the oven at 300° for 10 to 20 minutes. Stirring frequently will allow a more even toasting. Watch carefully so that it does not burn.

METHOD 2: Place wheat germ in a well seasoned frying pan over medium heat. Stir until toasted. The wheat germ will continue browning after it is removed from heat if left in the pan.

Per 1/4 Cup:
Calories: 108.0
Fat (gm): 2.6
Protein (gm): 7.5
Cholesterol (mg): 0
Sodium (mg): 1.0

For sweet wheat germ, mix in 1/2 C warm honey to every 4 C wheat germ before toasting in the oven or after toasting in a frying pan. Warning: this variation can be habit-forming!

Per 1/4 C:
Calories: 140.5
Fat (gm): 2.6
Protein (gm): 7.5
Cholesterol (mg): 0
Sodium (mg): 1.5

Muesli

Preparation time: 5 minutes
Yields: 1 serving

1 T cream
1 t honey
1 T lemon juice
1 T rolled oats
1 large apple, grated
1 T finely chopped nuts

Mix cream, honey and lemon juice with the oats. Stir in the grated apple. Sprinkle nuts over the top.

Calories: 213.2
Fat (gm): 8.1

Protein (gm): 2.4
Cholesterol (mg): 13.0
Sodium (mg): 8.3

Granola

Preparation time: 15 minutes
Cooking time: 25-30 minutes
Yields: 4 servings

This is a basic recipe. Possible additional ingredients are listed in the ETHEREAL CEREAL recipe following this one.

1 T oil
1/2 C honey (or less)
3 C rolled oats
1/2 t vanilla
1/2 t cinnamon

Combine oil, honey and vanilla in one bowl. Combine the rolled oats and cinnamon in another. Combine the two mixtures. Roast in a shallow pan at 250° for 25 to 30 minutes in the oven or in an electric frypan for one hour. After roasting, dried fruit or nuts may be added.

Calories: 394.9
Fat (gm): 6.8
Protein (gm): 8.6
Cholesterol (mg): 0
Sodium (mg): 4.4

VARIATION: For crunchy granola, substitute 1 C unsweetened coconut and 1 C sesame seeds for 1$\frac{1}{2}$ C rolled oats.

Ethereal Cereal

Preparation time: 25-35 minutes
Yields: (varies)

If you like to experiment or have your own favorite ingredients for granola, you will probably enjoy working with this recipe. Refer to the GRANOLA recipe preceding this one for directions.

Use 4 to 6 C dry ingredients for each 1 C wet ingredients and (optional) 1 C dried fruit. Include the basic ingredients of the GRANOLA recipe, adding your choice of the ingredients listed below.

DRY INGREDIENTS: Oat, wheat, rye or triticale flakes; wheat germ, bran, meals, grits, sesame, pumpkin, sunflower, chia or flaxseed; chopped or sliced nuts, shredded coconut, powdered milk, date sugar, salt, etc.

WET INGREDIENTS: Melted butter, oil, molasses, honey, warm water, vanilla, coconut, dairy, soy or nut milk, etc.

FRUIT: Shredded apples, fresh shredded coconut, raisins, chopped dates, minced apricots, or other dried fruit.

Tomato Wheat

Preparation time: 15 minutes
Cooking time: 3-4 hours
Yields: 4 servings

Joy's daughter likes this with plenty of broth for a soup.

1 C whole wheatberries
3 C tomato juice
1/2 t powdered cumin
1 bell pepper, minced
1/2 t oregano

Wash wheatberries and add to boiling tomato juice. Cover, reduce heat, and simmer for 3 to 4 hours. Add other ingredients and continue simmering until bell peppers are tender.

Calories: 89.6
Fat (gm): trace
Protein (gm): 2.4
Cholesterol (mg): 0
Sodium (mg): 696.2

CROCKPOT COOKING: In the morning place all ingredients in a crockpot and cook all day on low. It will be ready for dinner.

Burt's Buckwheat

Preparation time: 15 minutes
Cooking time: 40 minutes
Yields: 4 servings

1 bell pepper, minced
2 T oil
1 C buckwheat groats
1 tomato, cubed (optional)
1/2 t salt
2$^1/_2$ C water

Heat oil in a heavy pan. Add buckwheat groats and minced bell pepper. Saute over high heat until buckwheat smells toasted. Be careful not to burn bell pepper. Add salt, water and tomato. Cover and simmer until done.

Calories: 238.2
Fat (gm): 7.2
Protein (gm): 3.8
Cholesterol (mg): 0
Sodium (mg): 784.9

Fried Rice

Preparation time: 25 minutes (includes
   cooking time; rice must be cooked ahead)
Yields: 4 servings

3 T oil or butter
3 slices fresh ginger or 1/4 t dried ginger
3 C cooked rice (or other grain)
1 stalk celery, thinly sliced on the
   diagonal
1/2 bell pepper, cut in thin slices
1 C fresh peas or other vegetables
1 t tamari (soy sauce)

Heat the oil and ginger in a wok or heavy
frying pan. Add vegetables. Saute until barely
crispy tender. Add rice and cook, stirring
frequently until rice is hot. Add tamari (soy
sauce) before serving.

Calories: 301.0
Fat (gm): 10.4
Protein (gm): 5.9
Cholesterol (mg): 0
Sodium (mg): 93.8

VARIATIONS: Melt jack or cheddar cheese
over the rice and vegetables at the end, or
add grated cheese when serving.

Rice Pilaf

Preparation time: 20 minutes
Cooking time: 60 minutes
Yields: 6 servings

2 T olive oil or butter
1 1/4 C brown rice
3/4 C uncooked whole grain spaghetti
   (broken into 1 inch pieces)
3 C boiling water or vegetable stock
1/2 C celery, minced
1 bell pepper, minced (or 1 C other
   vegetables)
1/2 t salt
1/2 C yogurt (optional)
2 T parsley (for garnish)

Heat oil in a medium sized saucepan. Add
rice and toast over medium heat until it is
lightly browned (about 10 minutes). Add

spaghetti, boiling water, vegetables and salt.
Bake in a covered casserole for 50 minutes at
350°. Fold in yogurt, top with parsley and
bake another 10 minutes or until tender.

(With yogurt):
Calories: 211.2
Fat (gm): 8.8
Protein (gm): 4.2
Cholesterol (mg): 23.4
Sodium (mg): 287.6

Yogi Rice

Preparation time: 10-15 minutes
Cooking time: 45 minutes
Yields: 4 servings

This is a sweet rice dish.

2 1/2 C water
1/2 C raisins
1/4 t ginger
1 cinnamon stick
5 whole cloves
3 pods cardamom, seeded
2 T honey
1 C brown rice (or other grain)

Bring water, raisins, spices and honey to a
boil. Add rice, stir once, cover tightly and
turn heat as low as possible. Cook until
liquid is absorbed and rice is tender (about
45 minutes).

Calories: 218.8
Fat (gm): .7
Protein (gm): 3.2
Cholesterol (mg): 0
Sodium (mg): 4.7

VARIATIONS:

CURRIED YOGI RICE: Cook as above
adding 1 apple (finely sliced), 1/2 t curry
powder, 1/4 t turmeric, and 1 T butter.

SWEET MILLET: Follow basic YOGI RICE
recipe substituting 1 C millet for the brown
rice. This will cook in 15 to 20 minutes.

Lemon Rice

Preparation time: 30-35 minutes (includes
    cooking time; rice must be cooked ahead)
Yields: 6 servings

*This is a delightfully flavored and colorful
grain dish.*

**1/4 C butter, oil, ghee, or BUTTER OIL
    SPREAD (p. 153)**
1 t salt
1 t black mustard seeds
2 t turmeric
1/2 C red bell pepper, minced
1 C eggplant, diced
1/2 C green peas
3 C cooked brown rice
3 T lemon juice (juice of 1 lemon)

Melt butter in a heavy frying pan. Add salt,
mustard seeds, and turmeric to butter. Heat
and stir until the mustard seeds "dance" (be
careful, they may pop and burn you).
Immediately add vegetables and cook until
almost tender. Add rice. Stir until all is
heated, then add lemon juice and serve.

Calories: 211.7
Fat (gm): 8.5
Protein (gm): 3.4
Cholesterol (mg): 22.0
Sodium (mg): 439.0

NOTE: This dish can be made ahead and
heated in the oven or microwave in a
covered casserole. It also freezes well. Add
the lemon juice before serving.

Chinch Bhat
(Rice And Yogurt)

Preparation time: 25-30 minutes (includes
    cooking time; rice must be cooked ahead)
Yields: 4 servings

2 T oil
1/2 t black mustard seeds
1/2 t fennel seeds
1/2 t cumin seeds
1 t turmeric
1/2 t salt
1/4 to 1/2 t cayenne
3 C cooked rice
1 C YOGURT (p.213)

Pour oil in the bottom of a heavy 10 inch
frying pan, add seeds and heat. When the
mustard seeds "dance" (be careful, they may
pop and burn you), add the other spices.
Add the cooked rice. When heated
thoroughly, add yogurt. Stir and serve.

Calories: 276.2
Fat (gm): 8.4
Protein (gm): 6.6
Cholesterol (mg): 4.1
Sodium (mg): 310.8

NOTE: This dish can be made ahead and
instead of being heated in the frying pan, the
contents can be transferred to a baking
casserole (yogurt included) and heated in the
oven.

Herbed Rice

Preparation time: 15 minutes
Cooking time: 45 minutes
Yields: 4 servings

2 C water
1/2 t salt
1/2 t rosemary
1/2 t marjoram
1/2 t thyme
1 T butter
1 C brown rice (or other grain)

Bring water to a boil. Add butter and herbs. Add rice very slowly. Stir once, cover and turn down heat as far as possible. Cook for approximately 45 minutes until all the water has been absorbed and the rice is tender.

Calories: 178.2
Fat (gm): 3.7
Protein (gm): 3.0
Cholesterol (mg): 8.2
Sodium (mg): 299.0

NOTE: If using other grains, the cooking time may have to be adjusted (see chart on p.107).

Noodles

Preparation time: 60-90 minutes
Cooking time: 20 minutes (includes time to boil water)
Yields: 6-12 servings

These take time but are so much fun to make. And making them is excellent exercise for upper arm muscles. Do give them a try. The dough can be used to make little raviolis (refer to LASAGNA recipe, p. 162, for a stuffing), manicotti cylinders, lasagna sheets or just plain noodles. The dough can be changed by adding spices and herbs. Have fun!

3 C whole wheat bread flour
1½ C cold water
1 t salt

Mix ingredients well. Add additional water if necessary to make a workable dough. Knead dough 10 to 15 minutes. (This is important to develop the gluten.) Roll out on a well floured board as thin as possible for noodles. Roll thicker for ravioli, etc. Cut into strips. Cook immediately or let dry completely and store until needed. To cook while fresh, boil 1 to 2 gallons of water. Add noodles and cook until they rise to the surface of the boiling water. Drain and serve. To dry, place a single layer over a clean wooden clothes-drying rack. Let dry until brittle. Cook as for regular noodles.

Calories: 200.0
Fat (gm): .9
Protein (gm): 8.0
Cholesterol (mg): 0
Sodium (mg): 359.1

VARIATIONS: You may substitute up to 1 C of the whole wheat bread flour with any other flour. The noodles won't hold together as well.

SPINACH NOODLES: Add to dough before kneading 1 package defrosted spinach (squeezed dry) or 1 bunch of spinach, chopped, steamed, cooled and squeezed dry. Proceed with regular instructions above.

CURRY NOODLES: Add 2 T CURRY POWDER (p. 223) to the dough.

HERB NOODLES: Add 2 T ITALIAN SEASONING (p. 221) or basil to the dough. If using fresh basil, add 1 C minced fresh basil.

Poppy Seed Noodles

Preparation time: 20 minutes (includes
   cooking time)
Yields: 6 servings

6 C noodles (8 ounces)
1 T butter
2 T poppy seeds

Cook noodles in boiling water until tender.
Drain and return to pan. Add butter and
poppy seeds, tossing lightly to mix.

Calories: 233.0
Fat (gm): 4.1
Protein (gm): 7.5
Cholesterol (mg): 5.5
Sodium (mg): 31.5

VARIATION: Substitute 2 T sesame seeds for
the poppy seeds.

Crisp Fried Pasta

Preparation time: 20-25 minutes (includes
   cooking time)
Yields: 6 servings

This is a great way to serve leftover pasta.

1 T butter
6 C cooked pasta

Melt butter in a heavy skillet over low heat.
Add pasta and cook on one side until
browned. Using a dinner plate, invert pasta
so that the browned side is on the top. Slip
pasta back into the pan, cooking until the
other side is brown (about 5 to 10 minutes).

Calories: 224.0
Fat (gm): 3.7
Protein (gm): 7.0
Cholesterol (mg): 7.3
Sodium (mg): 37.3

VARIATION: Add poppy seeds, or ITALIAN
SEASONING (p. 221) to butter.

GRAIN NUTRITION COMPARISON

GRAIN (1C)	WEIGHT (gm)	FOOD ENERGY (calories)	PROTEIN (gm)	CHOLESTEROL (gm)	CALCIUM (mg)	IRON (mg)	VITAMIN A (I.U.)	THIAMIN (mg)	RIBOFLAVIN (mg)	NIACIN (mg)	FAT (gm)
All-purpose flour (enriched)	125	455	13.1	95.1	20	3.6	0	.55	.33	4.4	1.3
Barley	200	698	16.4	157.6	32	4.0	0	.24	.10	6.2	2.0
Bran flakes (enriched)	35	106	3.6	28.2	19	12.4	1,650	.41	.49	4.1	.6
Cornmeal, yellow	122	433	11.2	89.9	24	2.9	620	.46	.13	2.4	4.8
Farina, enriched	180	668	20.5	138.6	45	76.3	0	.79	.47	6.3	1.6
Oats, rolled	80	312	11.4	54.6	42	3.6	0	.48	.11	.8	5.9
Rice, brown	200	720	15.0	154.8	64	3.2	0	.68	.10	9.4	3.8
Rice, par-boiled (enriched)	185	683	13.7	150.4	111	5.4	0	.81	.07	6.5	.6
Rice, white, (enriched)	195	708	13.1	156.8	47	5.7	0	.86	.06	6.8	.8
Rice polish	105	278	12.7	60.6	72	16.9	0	1.93	.19	29.6	13.4
Soy flour (full fat)	85	358	31.2	25.8	169	7.1	90	.72	.26	1.8	17.3
Wheat germ	96	368	28.8	48	48	8	160	1.76	.8	4.8	11.2
Whole wheat flour	120	400	16	85.2	49	4	0	.66	.14	5.2	2.4
Wh Wht Pastry Flr	?	540	18	123	6	30	tr	45	12	30	3

Breads & Crackers

BREADS & CRACKERS

ABOUT CRACKERS

The thinner the crackers are rolled, the crisper they will be. Holes can be pricked in them to improve crispness.

Rolling is easiest between 2 pieces of waxed paper or plastic wrap. The dough can also be rolled out on a greased cookie sheet and cut into squares.

Rice Crackers

Preparation time: 40-50 minutes
Cooking time: 12-15 minutes per pan
Yields: about 3 dozen 2 inch round crackers

2 C cooked rice, cooled
$3^1/_2$ T oil
1 C whole wheat bread flour
1 T water
1 t salt

Crumble the cooked rice until the grains are separated. Mix it thoroughly with the other ingredients. Knead the mixture well until it sticks together. Roll out on a very well floured board as thin as possible so that the grains of rice stick up from the dough. Cut into circles or squares. Bake on a lightly oiled baking sheet at 400° about 12 to 15 minutes, until golden brown.

Each:
Calories: 32.4
Fat (gm): 1.3
Protein (gm): .7
Cholesterol (mg): 0
Sodium (mg): 59.5

Cheese Crackers

Preparation time: 60 minutes (includes 30 minutes in freezer)
Cooking time: 10 minutes
Yields: about 3 dozen crackers

1/2 C butter
2 C grated cheddar cheese
1 C whole wheat bread flour
1 t dill weed (optional)

Mix ingredients and knead until the mixture holds together. Work into 2 oblong rolls. Wrap in waxed paper and chill in the freezer for 30 minutes. Slice wafer thin. Bake on a slightly oiled baking sheet for 10 minutes at 400°.

Each:
Calories: 60.5
Fat (gm): 4.9
Protein (gm): 2.1
Cholesterol (mg): 14
Sodium (mg): 66.4

NOTE: The cracker dough may be frozen for longer periods of time than 30 minutes. It should be wrapped securely so that it doesn't get freezer burn. When ready to cook, proceed as directed in recipe. If very hard, the rolls may have to be slightly defrosted before slicing.

VARIATIONS: Substitute another type of cheese for the cheddar. Swiss is good. If parmesan is used, it should be freshly grated and combined with cheddar. 1/2 C of rye flour can be substituted for 1/2 C whole wheat flour and caraway seeds can be substituted for the dill.

Sweet Millet Crackers

Preparation time: 40-50 minutes
Cooking time: 8-10 minutes per pan
Yields: approximately 3 dozen 2 inch round
   crackers

3¹/₂ T oil
2 C cooked millet, cooled
1 C whole wheat bread flour
1/4 C honey

Crumble the cooked millet until the grains
are separated. Mix it thoroughly with the
other ingredients. Knead the mixture well
until it forms a ball. Roll out as thin as
possible until the millet grains stick out from
the dough. Cut into squares or circles. Place
on a lightly oiled baking sheet and bake at
400° 8 to 10 minutes, until golden brown.

Each:
Calories: 52.4
Fat (gm): 1.5
Protein (gm): 1.1
Cholesterol (mg): 0
Sodium (mg): .4

Graham Crackers

Preparation time: 40-50 minutes (includes
   baking time)
Yields: about 40 crackers

2 C graham flour
1¹/₂ C whole wheat flour
1/4 t salt
1/2 t cinnamon
1/4 C oil
3/4 C milk
1/4 C molasses
1/4 C honey

Combine flours, salt and cinnamon. Work in
the oil. Mix the milk, molasses and honey
together. Add to dry ingredients and mix
well. Knead on a lightly floured board and
roll out 1/8 inch thick. Cut into 2 inch
squares, place on a cookie sheet and prick
with a fork. Place on a lightly oiled baking
sheet. Bake at 400° for 12 to 14 minutes until
golden brown.

Each:
Calories: 60.4
Fat (gm): .1
Protein (gm): 1.6
Cholesterol (mg): .3
Sodium (mg): 16.8

FLAT BREADS

Flour Tortillas (Chapatis)

Preparation time: 45-60 minutes (includes
   cooking time)
Yields: 10

These take time to make but are worth it.

2 C whole wheat bread flour
1/2 t salt
1 C water
oil

Combine the flour and the salt. Dribble in the
water, mixing with your fingers until an
elastic dough is formed. Knead it roughly for
a few minutes. Then divide into 10 pieces.
Roll out into circles as thin as you can. (With
practice, they become more circular.) Lightly
coat the griddle or frying pan with oil. Fry
about 30 seconds, until brown, on the first
side. Flip and brown the second side.

Each:
Calories: 128
Fat (gm): 5.5
Protein (gm): 3.0
Cholesterol (mg): 0
Sodium (mg): 109.3

VARIATIONS: Up to 1 C of whole wheat
flour can be replaced with another flour or
cornmeal.

PARATHAS: Brush rolled out chapati with
ghee (clarified butter) and fold in half; brush
again and fold in half again. You will now
have a triangular shape. Roll this into a circle
and fry as before.

NOTE: Chapatis can be made a little thicker
(increase the cooking time slightly) and right
after cooking rolled into a cone. A napkin or

paper is rolled around the cone and the cone is filled with thick beans. No plate is needed!

East Indians use chapatis (flour tortillas) and puris (deep-fried flour tortillas) to scoop up food. They can be served with CURRIED VEGETABLES (p. 95), LEMON RICE (p. 112), EAST INDIAN DAL (p.145), SPLIT PEA AND POTATO STEW (p. 148) or any soups or stews.

Puris
(East Indian Deep Fried Bread)

Preparation time: 60-70 minutes (includes cooking time)
Yields: 12 puris

2 C whole wheat bread flour
1/2 t salt
1/2 to 2/3 C water
2 T oil

Mix the flour and the salt in a bowl. Mix in oil until the mixture is the size of peas. Gradually drip in the water, mixing it in with your fingers until you form a ball. Knead until smooth, about the consistency of an earlobe (really!). Cover and let sit for approximately 30 minutes.

Place about $1^1/_2$ inches of oil in a heavy pan large enough to hold the puris. Divide the dough into 12 balls. Roll a ball between your palms until smooth. Flatten a little into a rounded patty, coat each side sparingly with flour and place on a board. Gently roll from the center out into a circle, turning over frequently and re-flouring as needed. Stop rolling when it is slightly less than 1/8 inch thick. If you are making them ahead of time, oil lightly and do not stack more than 3 high, or place waxed paper in between them.

Heat the oil to between 375° and 400°. Slip a puri into the oil from the side so that it doesn't spatter on your hand. With a spatula, hold the puri under the oil to encourage the bubbles to expand. Small bubbles should start and then spread so that the puri becomes one big puff. About this time it should be turning golden brown. Carefully

turn it over so you don't spatter the oil, and fry the other side. When bubbles stop in the oil around the edges of the puri, it is time to take it out.

Drain the cooked puris on edge in a bread pan with a layer of paper towels on the bottom.

Each:
Calories: 86.7
Fat (gm): 2.4
Protein (gm): 2.7
Cholesterol (mg): 0
Sodium (mg): 89.3

NOTE: Don't be discouraged if you can't get them to puff the first time you try. Try varying the way that you roll them, the temperature of the oil, the amount of water used, or the mixing and kneading of the dough. Even if they don't puff, they are still good.

Native American Fry Bread

Preparation time: 30-40 minutes
Yields: 10

This recipe was shared with Joy by her good friend Patty Parker. The original Native American version uses white flour and lard because that is what was available to them. These are the favorite "flat bread" in Joy's family, especially when made into Native American Tacos!

2 C whole wheat flour
2^1/$_2$ t baking powder
1/2 t salt
2 T oil
1 C warm water

Mix flour and baking powder. Add oil and mix until the mixture is in pieces the size of peas. Add water until a workable dough is formed. Knead well. Divide into 10 equal pieces. Roll out into circles about 1/8 inch thick. Fry in 1/8 inch of oil until brown. Turn and brown the other side. Serve with pinto beans. Refer to NATIVE AMERICAN TACOS (p. 168) recipe for serving suggestions.

Each:
Calories: 153.0
Fat (gm): 8.0
Protein (gm): 3.0
Cholesterol (mg): 0
Sodium (mg): 215.8

MUFFINS, BISCUITS, AND OTHER QUICK BREADS

Quick breads are leavened with baking soda or baking powder. They are called "quick" because they do not need to rise as yeast breads do.

Honey Muffins

Preparation time: 15 minutes
Baking time: 20-30 minutes
Yields: 12 medium muffins

2 C whole wheat pastry flour
1/2 t salt
1 T baking powder
1 C milk
1/4 C honey
2 T oil

Mix together dry ingredients. In a separate bowl mix together wet ingredients. Make a depression in the center of the dry ingredients. Add the wet ingredients, stirring only until just moistened. Fill oiled muffin tins almost full. Bake at 400° for 20 to 30 minutes until delicately browned.

Each:
Calories: 119.7
Fat (gm): 2.8
Protein (gm): 1.5
Cholesterol (mg): 1.5
Sodium (mg): 178.0

VARIATIONS:

EVE'S HONEY NUGGETS: Add 1 C grated apple, 1/2 C blueberries, 1/2 C walnuts and cut down milk to 3/4 C.

BLUEBERRY MUFFINS: Add 1 C fresh blueberries to the dry ingredients and proceed with the recipe instructions.

FRUIT MUFFINS: Add 3/4 C chopped citron to the batter. Brush muffins lightly with honey before baking.

HONEY FILLED MUFFINS: Put a small spoonful of crystallized honey in the center of the batter of each muffin.

PEANUT BUTTER MUFFINS: Blend 1/4 C peanut butter with the honey and add to the milk mixture.

SOYBEAN MUFFINS: Replace 1/2 C flour with 1/2 C soy flour.

ORANGE MUFFINS: Replace the milk with orange juice and add 1 t dried orange rind.

Carrot Molasses Muffins

Preparation time: 20-25 minutes
Baking time: 40-45 minutes
Yields: 12

1¹/₂ C whole wheat pastry flour
1 T baking powder
1 t cinnamon
1 C packed, finely grated raw carrot
  (scrub or peel first)
1 C chopped nuts
1 C chopped dates
1/2 C soy flour
1/2 C molasses
2 T oil
1/4 C water

Combine the dry ingredients, stirring well to separate the carrots and the dried fruit. In a separate bowl, mix wet ingredients. Make a depression in the center of the dry ingredients and add the wet ingredients. Mix just until the dry ingredients are moistened. Fill oiled muffin tins almost full. Bake at 350° for 40 to 45 minutes.

Each:
Calories: 232.4
Fat (gm): 8.6
Protein (gm): 4.1
Cholesterol (mg): 0
Sodium (mg): 121.6

VARIATIONS: These can be made into excellent unleavened muffins by eliminating the baking powder.

ZUCCHINI MUFFINS: Substitute shredded zucchini for the carrots. The zucchini work best if they have been shredded and frozen, then defrosted and drained. That way they do not have too much liquid. This is a great way to use zucchini from your garden in the winter.

Apple Nut Muffins

Preparation time: 20-25 minutes
Baking time: 40-45 minutes
Yields: 12

1¹/₂ C whole wheat pastry flour
1/2 C soy flour
1/2 t cinnamon
1 T baking powder
1 C nuts, finely chopped
1 C raisins, chopped figs or dates
1¹/₂ C packed grated raw apple
  (1 large apple)
1/2 C molasses
2 T oil
1/4 C water or apple juice

Combine dry ingredients. Add fruit, stirring well to separate the dried fruit and apples and coat them with flour. Make a depression in the center of the dry ingredients. Mix wet ingredients together and add to the dry, mixing just until dry ingredients are moistened. Fill oiled muffin tins almost full. Bake 40 to 45 minutes at 350°.

Each:
Calories: 235.7
Fat (gm): 8.8
Protein (gm): 5.2
Cholesterol (mg): 0
Sodium (mg): 115.3

Fig Rye Muffins

Preparation time: 20-30 minutes
Baking time: 30 minutes
Yields: 12

2$^1/_2$ C rye flour
1/2 t salt
1 t baking soda
1 C ground dried figs
1/4 C molasses
2 T oil
1 C water

Mix dry ingredients thoroughly. Add figs and stir enough to coat the fruit with flour. Make a depression in the center of the dry ingredients and add wet ingredients. Stir just until dry ingredients are moistened. Spoon into oiled muffin pans. Smooth dough down. Top may be oiled slightly. Bake 30 minutes at 350°. Remove immediately from pan and cool on a rack.

Each:
Calories: 178.3
Fat (gm): 2.8
Protein (gm): 3.1
Cholesterol (mg): 0
Sodium (mg): 162.9

VARIATIONS: Substitute other dried fruit for the figs, such as raisins or prunes. Substitute milk or fruit juice for the water. Substitute whole wheat flour or other for rye. Add 1 t cinnamon or allspice or lemon peel.

Bran Raisin Muffins

Preparation time: 25 minutes
Baking time: 25 minutes
Yields: 12

1$^1/_2$ C bran
1$^1/_2$ C milk
1/2 C molasses
1/4 C oil
2 C whole wheat pastry flour
1 T baking soda
1 C raisins

Soak the bran in the milk for 10 minutes. Add the oil and molasses. Combine flour, soda, and raisins and add to the wet ingredients. Bake at 400° for 25 minutes.

Each:
Calories: 213.6
Fat (gm): 5.4
Protein (gm): 4.1
Cholesterol (mg): 2.2
Sodium (mg): 228.9

VARIATIONS: Substitute prunes or apricots for the raisins.

Biscuits

Preparation time: 20-25 minutes
Baking time: 10-12 minutes
Yields: 12

2 C whole wheat pastry flour
1 T baking powder
1/2 t salt
1/4 C butter
2/3 C milk

Mix the dry ingredients together. Melt the butter and pour it on top of the dry ingredients. Using a strong fork, mix the butter in thoroughly until the whole mixture has a texture like cornmeal. Add the milk and stir. The dough should be just wet enough to hold together but not sticky. Roll out to a half inch thickness on a well floured board. Cut out biscuits. Place on an oiled baking sheet and bake 10 to 12 minutes at 400°.

Each:
Calories: 75.4
Fat (gm): .6
Protein (gm): 3.2
Cholesterol (mg): 1.2
Sodium (mg): 175.2

VARIATIONS:

BUTTERMILK BISCUITS: Substitute 1$^1/_2$ t baking soda for the baking powder and substitute buttermilk for the milk. If the buttermilk is very thick, you may need to add more.

YOGURT BISCUITS: Reduce the milk to 1/4 C and add 1/2 C plain or flavored yogurt. Substitute 1$^1/_2$ t baking soda for the baking powder.

CHEESE BISCUITS: Add 1/2 C grated cheese (cheddar or swiss) to flour mixture.

CARROT ZUCCHINI FLECKED BISCUITS: Add 1/4 C grated carrot, 1/4 C shredded zucchini, and 1/2 t dill.

DROP BISCUITS: Increase the milk to 1 C. Drop the dough by tablespoons onto a lightly oiled baking sheet.

Quick and Easy Sweet Rolls

Preparation time: 30-35 minutes
Baking time: 20-30 minutes
Yields: 12

1 recipe BISCUIT dough (p. 124)
2 T soft butter
1/4 C honey
1 C raisins
1/2 C chopped walnuts
1 t cinnamon

Roll the biscuit dough out to 1/4 inch thick. Spread with the soft butter and sprinkle with the cinnamon. Evenly spread with honey and sprinkle with cinnamon again. Evenly cover with raisins and chopped walnuts. Roll up tightly and cut into 1 inch slices. Stand cut edge up in a lightly oiled 8 inch square pan or pie pan. Bake at 400° for 20 to 30 minutes.

Each:
Calories: 183.4
Fat (gm): 5.2
Protein (gm): 4.6
Cholesterol (mg): 6.7
Sodium (mg): 197.6

Cornbread or Corn Muffins

Preparation time: 15-20 minutes
Baking time: 15-20 minutes
Yields: 12 muffins or one 8 inch square pan

3/4 C whole wheat pastry flour
1$^1/_4$ C cornmeal
1/2 salt
1 t baking powder
1 C milk
2 T oil
2 T honey

Mix dry ingredients together thoroughly. In a separate bowl, mix wet ingredients together. Make a depression in the middle of the dry ingredients and add wet ingredients. Stir just until moistened. (If you are using cast iron muffin pans or corn stick pans, heat them in the oven before adding batter to make the outside of the muffins crispy.) Bake at 425° for 15 to 20 minutes.

Each:
Calories: 111.2
Fat (gm): 3.0
Protein (gm): 2.9
Cholesterol (mg): 1.5
Sodium (mg): 167.9

Apple Fritters

Preparation time: 20-25 minutes
Frying time: about 20 minutes
Yields: 18 small fritters

1 C whole wheat pastry flour
1/2 t salt
1/2 t baking soda
1 t cinnamon
1/4 C honey
6 T yogurt
2 C grated apples
oil

Combine dry ingredients well. In a separate bowl, mix wet ingredients well; then add to dry ingredients. Stir until well moistened. Add grated apples and stir until well coated. Drop by tablespoons into one or more inches of oil heated to 375° to 400°. Cook until medium to dark brown. Pull one apart to make certain that the inside is getting done. Remove from oil with a slotted spoon and drain on a paper towel, paper bag or rack.

Each:
Calories: 100.6
Fat (gm): .1
Protein (gm): 1.2
Cholesterol (mg): .3
Sodium (mg): 86.1

VARIATIONS:

CORN FRITTERS: Substitute 1 t thyme or 1/2 t chili powder for the cinnamon. Reduce the honey to 2 T. Substitute 2 C corn for the apples or $1^1/_2$ C corn and 1/2 C minced bell peppers.

VEGETABLE FRITTERS: Substitute 1/2 t dill for the cinnamon and omit the honey. Substitute for the apples: 1 C grated zucchini, 1/2 C grated carrots and 1/2 C corn or minced bell pepper.

Jyoti's Banana Bread

Preparation time: 20-25 minutes
Baking time: 45-60 minutes
Yields: one loaf (12 large slices)

1 C mashed bananas
1/4 C oil
1/2 C honey
1 t vanilla
1/2 C date sugar (or honey)
1/2 t salt
1 t soda
1 t mace or nutmeg
1/2 t dried lemon peel
1$^3/_4$ C whole wheat pastry flour
1 C chopped walnuts

Add the ingredients to the bananas in order listed, mixing well after each addition. Pour into an oiled loaf pan. This makes 1 large loaf or 2 small ones. Bake at 350° for 45 to 60 minutes for large loaves, 35 to 40 minutes for small loaves.

Slice:
Calories: 267.8
Fat (gm): 10.1
Protein (gm): 3.6
Cholesterol (mg): 0
Sodium (mg): 161.3

VARIATIONS:

PUMPKIN BREAD: Substitute 1 C pureed cooked pumpkin or winter squash for the bananas. Follow mixing and baking directions.

PERSIMMON BREAD: Substitute 1 C persimmon puree for the bananas. Follow mixing and baking directions.

Boston Brown Bread

Preparation time: 20-25 minutes
Cooking time: 3 hours
Yields: two 1 pound coffee cans (24 slices)

2 C cornmeal
3 C sour milk (or 3 C fresh milk and 1 T
    lemon juice)
1/2 C butter
1 t salt
2 C graham flour or whole wheat pastry
    flour
1 C molasses
2 t soda
1 C raisins

Combine the dry ingredients in a bowl. In a separate bowl, combine the wet ingredients. Make a depression in the dry ingredients and add the wet ingredients. Mix until just moistened. Fill lightly oiled coffee cans 1/2 full. Cover with aluminum foil and tie on with string or rubber bands. Set on rack above water in large kettle. Cover. Steam for 3 hours.

Slice:
Calories: 169.6
Fat (gm): 5.0
Protein (gm): 3.4
Cholesterol (mg): 13.2
Sodium (mg): 219.9

YEAST BREADS

About Yeast Bread Ingredients

Hearty, nutritious bread is an important part of a vegetarian diet. To make a good bread, it helps to know a little about the ingredients that will be used.

FLOUR is the basis for a yeast bread. There are two types of wheat: soft wheat and hard wheat. Flour made from soft wheat feels silky when rubbed between the fingers; hard wheat feels slightly gritty. Soft wheat flour is called pastry flour and is not the best choice for yeast bread because there is not as much gluten as in hard wheat flour. Whole wheat flour contains the germ or live part of the wheatberry and the bran or outer coating. Unbleached white flour has had the bran and the wheat germ removed and does not contain as many nutrients as whole wheat flour. Bleached enriched flour has also had the wheat germ and bran removed and then has had some of the natural vitamins replaced by synthetic ones.

Flours from large commercial firms are ground quickly by heavy steel rollers which generate a great deal of heat. This tends to "burn" off the heat sensitive vitamins and the oil in the grain. Stone ground flours are better in this respect because the stones stay much cooler, but these flours can contain minute particles which over a lifetime can wear down teeth. Freshly ground flour tastes better and is more nutritious than stale flour. For information on storing flours and grains to preserve their nutrition and flavor, refer to the section on GRAINS AND CEREALS (p. 101).

Each grain adds its distinctive taste and texture to bread. Following are descriptions of some flours readily available. Refer also to the description of grains and their products in GRAINS AND CEREALS (p. 101).

GLUTEN flour is made from wheat flour. Gluten is a stringy, elastic substance that gives body to dough. During kneading the gluten forms a structure that catches and holds in the bubbles of carbon dioxide made by the growing yeast, enabling the bread dough to rise. Wheat flour has the highest proportion of gluten of all the flours; therefore breads made with wheat flour are usually lighter than those made with other flours. When using flours with a low gluten content, gluten flour can be added to help make the bread lighter and hold together better.

RYE flour is next to wheat in gluten content. Rye flour is silky and helps work in other granular grains such as cornmeal and rolled oats. Pure rye flour tends to make a sticky dough.

SOY flour adds protein. Breads containing it will brown faster and remain fresher.

CORN flour adds sweetness and a more crumbly texture.

MILLET flour makes bread crunchier as well as sweeter.

ROLLED OATS (oatmeal) make the bread stay moist longer. They add to the texture and make the bread slightly chewy and sweeter.

BARLEY flour added to breads makes them more cake-like. For non-yeast breads, cakes and pastries, barley flour is an excellent substitute for wheat flour. The finished product will be slightly heavier than if it were made from wheat, and it will be more cake-like than bread-like. The flavor is not very different from that of wheat.

BUCKWHEAT (not related to wheat) makes breads very heavy. It is best used in small amounts. It adds a good flavor and an interesting texture.

BRAN adds flavor, texture and fiber. It is best soaked an hour or so before it is added to the bread.

YEAST causes the bread to rise. There are basically two types of yeast which are used in making bread: cake yeast and dry powdered yeast. (Sourdough starter is different and will be discussed later.) Nutritional yeast, torumel and brewer's yeast are not "active yeasts" and will not cause bread to rise. Cake yeast must be fresh. If the cake is beige in color, smells yeasty and crumbles easily, it is probably fresh. Dry yeast lasts longer and, purchased in bulk form, is most economical. Both types of yeast should be stored in the refrigerator.

Yeast produces carbon dioxide as a byproduct of its growth. The carbon dioxide causes the bread to rise. The yeast feeds on the sweetener in the bread (the amount of sugar present in grain is usually not enough). White sugar feeds the yeast, but we recommend a natural sweetener such as honey, sorghum, molasses or barley malt. These add nice flavors and minerals in addition to helping keep the bread moist. When converting recipes to honey, cut down the liquid in the recipe by 1/4 C for each cup of honey substituted for a cup of sugar.

SALT controls the yeast's activity in the bread. If not enough salt is used, the bread will rise too quickly and perhaps run out of its pan, producing large-holed, coarsely textured bread. If too much salt is used, the bread will not rise enough, and it will be heavy.

LIQUID is the last necessary ingredient. A little water (at least 1/4 C) must be used to activate the yeast. The rest of the liquid can be water, milk, fruit or vegetable juice, vegetable or bean stock, or whatever else you choose. Breads made with milk are more nutritious (powdered milk works well) and have a velvety texture. Raw milk needs to be scalded to kill off any bacteria or undesirable types of wild yeast that might sour the bread. (Scalding means to heat to just below the boiling point; the milk steams and tiny bubbles rise at the edges of the pan.)

Breads made with all water as the liquid have a thicker, crisper crust and resemble French bread in texture. Within reason, the less liquid used, the better the texture of the bread. If you are converting recipes using white flour, more liquid is required when using whole grain flours as the bran of the grain absorbs more liquid than the rest of the grain. Also the amount of water that the flour can absorb depends on the temperature, the humidity and the amount of gluten present in the flour.

FAT is added to the bread (3/4 to 1 T per cup of flour) to give a richer flavor and to keep the bread from drying out too fast. The fat can be eliminated from the bread. If used, use unrefined, cold-pressed oil. Butter may not be the healthiest choice, but it does add a nice flavor and a rich brown crust.

OTHER ADDITIONS include chopped or ground nuts; sunflower, sesame, chia, caraway or other seeds; dill or other herbs; grated apples; minced dried fruit; grated coconut; and steamed vegetables, whole or pureed. Dry additions require increasing the amount of liquid. Wet additions require more flour or less liquid.

You may also want to add whole or cracked grains to your bread. These must be soaked, or better yet, cooked before adding. Whole grains can also be sprouted and added (whole or ground) to the bread dough.

1 T lecithin per 4 C flour can be added to the bread as a preservative and nutrient.

To enrich bread nutritionally: for each cup of flour add 1 T soy flour, 1 T powdered milk and 1 T wheat germ.

Basic Yeast Bread Procedures

STEP 1: YEAST

The first step in making bread is to add the yeast to lukewarm water. To test the water, drop some on the back of your wrist. If you can't feel the temperature or if it feels lukewarm, it is the right temperature. Too hot, and the yeast will die. Too cold, and the yeast will not grow as easily. Add the sweetener to this water and let it sit for 10 to 15 minutes while you get everything else ready. This will give the yeast a chance to begin growing. Add the salt and the liquid to the yeast mixture and then add as much flour as you can mix in. Add nuts, etc. (see BREAD INGREDIENTS, p. 127) with the flour. Mix it vigorously to develop the gluten.

STEP 2: KNEAD

Now you are ready to knead the bread. Your working surface should be at a height at which your hands rest comfortably. If you are using a board on top of another surface, a wet towel underneath will keep it from slipping. Spread some flour on a clean smooth surface. (A cutting board is not suitable because the bread dough will work into the cuts and perhaps mold.) Dump the bread dough out onto the flour; push it down, fold it over, turn; push it down, fold it over, turn; and repeat. This process is called kneading. Add more flour to the kneading surface occasionally to replace the flour picked up by the dough. Do not add flour to the top of the bread as it will get folded in and make a pocket of dry flour. The bread will tell you when it has had enough flour added by not picking up any more from the table. The purpose of kneading is to develop the gluten in the flour. Breads with little or no wheat flour in them require longer kneading. The kneading is done when the dough is smooth, satiny and not sticky. It should be the consistency of an earlobe or a plump baby's bottom: warm, rounded, soft yet springy. Touch lightly with a finger —the mark should not disappear. Usually ten minutes of kneading the dough is enough. Over-kneading is possible but doesn't happen often; it results in a poorly textured bread. Under-kneading prevents the bread from rising properly.

STEP 3: RISE

Oil the kneaded bread and place it in a clean large bowl (large enough so when the dough doubles, it won't go over the top). Cover with a paper or cloth towel. Leave the dough in a warm place, free of drafts, to rise (near a pilot light is good). Depending on the bread and the weather, it will take from 30 minutes to several hours for the bread to rise. If you do not have a warm nook for the bread, put the bowl in your sink and fill around the bowl with warm water. Place the dough in the bowl, adding hot water as the water in the sink cools. Be careful not to get the bread dough wet. The bread should be evenly warmed while rising, especially while in the pans. If bread rises unevenly, it will crumble when sliced. Protect it from too much heat in the summer.

The bread is ready to shape into loaves when you can insert two fingers half an inch into the dough and have the indentations remain. If the dough has risen too long, punch it down (which lets the gas out so the yeast doesn't suffocate), cover as before and let rise again. Remember that each time the bread rises, it does so in a shorter period of time.

STEP 4: SHAPE

To shape loaves, pull off a piece of dough that half fills the bread pan. There are several methods to shape the loaf. The bread dough may be stretched out and two edges folded under, then you may put it in the pan. Or, first roll the folded bread up the long way and then put it in the pan. Or, without folding, round the dough in your hands, tuck any rough edges under and put it in the pan. The important thing to remember is to put all rough edges and seams on the bottom and oil the pans well. Butter or ghee will keep the bread from sticking better than oil. When the dough is stretched out, before folding or rolling, you can butter it and add surprises such as nuts, fruit, honey, raisins, etc. Oil the tops of the loaves. You can also sprinkle seeds or finely chopped nuts on the top of the loaves, but don't put honey on the top as it may burn.

A note on bread pans: If you don't have bread pans, any oven proof dish or can will work. Round or freeform loaves can be baked on cookie sheets. For easy baking, all the loaves should be about the same size. Larger bread pans take $2^1/_2$ pounds of bread; medium ones take $1^1/_4$ pounds; a 2 pound coffee can holds $2^1/_2$ pounds of bread dough.

STEP 5: RISE AGAIN

Let the bread rise again in the pans until barely double. If you allow the bread to more than double, it will have a coarse texture. Breads with a low gluten content should not be allowed to rise even double or they will fall during baking.

While the bread rises the second time, preheat the oven to 375° to 400°. If a large part of your bread is soy flour or if your baking pans are glass or ceramic, lower all baking temperatures by 25 degrees from that stated in the recipe.

When your bread has risen, put it in the preheated oven and bake your bread at 375° to 400° for the first 10 to 15 minutes and then lower the temperature by 50 degrees. This will make a good crust. Bake the loaves until they are brown and sound hollow when thumped. For a crisper crust, remove the bread from pans when it is almost done and finish baking without pans. For a soft crust, brush crust with milk when done, or put a small pan of water in the oven while baking. For a butter crust, instead of buttering the bread when it is hot from the oven, slash the uncooked loaf from one end to the other and put thin slices of butter in the slash.

If you do not have an oven, yeast breads can be steamed in coffee cans with aluminum foil tops tied on with string or rubber bands. The foil needs to be ballooned up over the tops to allow room for the bread to expand. Fill them 1/2 full and let rise until double. Steam for 3 hours on a rack over water in a large covered kettle. Be very careful when checking the water level as the steam can cause very bad burns. Steamed yeast breads are exceptionally light but do not have a crust.

Cool the loaves on racks. If no racks are available, take the bread out of the pans and cool it balanced on the edges of the pans.

STEP 6: STORE

Store your bread in plastic bags, but make certain that it is cool before putting it in bags.

If you make several loaves at once, it's best to freeze them. They will dry out in the refrigerator.

Raw bread dough can be frozen but shouldn't be kept frozen for more than 2 to 3 weeks. The yeast won't be as active. Freeze in loaf shapes but before letting it rise the second time. When a standard-sized raw loaf of bread is taken from the freezer, it will take at least 6 hours to thaw and rise.

Baking With Children

Yeast bread dough is the best play dough that has ever been invented. Children love to punch and form it into shapes. They like to watch it grow and love to eat it baked. After the dough has risen once and is ready to form into loaves, give each child an adult-sized handful. Establish the most minimal ground rules: It must stay on the table, they can't eat it until it is baked, and their hands must be clean. Then let them make whatever they want. After they are through playing, place their creations on a lightly oiled cookie sheet and let rise. The only trick in baking them is to make certain that the pieces baked in the same pan are approximately the same size so that they will be done at the same time. Let them have fun and then let them eat their creations when they are done.

Children also like to help with the regular baking, especially making sweet rolls.

YEAST BREAD RECIPES

For most yeast bread, count on spending about four hours from start to finish.

Mom's Bread

Preparation time: 60 minutes (plus 1-2 hours rising)
Baking time: 60 minutes
Yields: 4 loaves

Joy says: I grew up with my mother making this bread (or a white bread version of it) at least once a week. When my mom was sick, my dad made it. Now my brother makes it

every week. We always made at least one little loaf that would bake faster than the big ones. When it was done, we would tear it into pieces and devour it right out of the oven. Needless to say, it was great!

2 C milk
4 t salt
1/4 C butter
1/2 C molasses
2 C cold water
2 T active dry yeast
10 to 12 C whole wheat bread flour

In a saucepan, add the salt, butter and molasses to milk. Heat, stirring until butter melts. Remove from heat. Add cold water and cool to lukewarm. Beat in yeast. Add 6 C flour. Beat smooth (about 2 minutes). Add remaining flour. Knead 7 to 10 minutes. Let rise one hour or until double. Punch down and let rise again until double. (If you are in a hurry, the second rising can be omitted.) Form loaves. Let rise one hour or until double. Bake at 400° for 1 hour. Cool on racks.

Slice:
Calories: 76.3
Fat (gm): 1.0
Protein (gm): 2.8
Cholesterol (mg): 2.3
Sodium (mg): 130.5

VARIATIONS: See also SWEET ROLL recipe (p. 136).

BRAIDED BREAD: Roll one quarter of MOM'S BREAD into a long rope. Divide the rope into 3 or 4 pieces and braid. Place on a lightly oiled baking sheet tucking the ends under to secure them. Oil and let rise until almost double. Bake as for regular bread.

Dinner Rolls

Use one quarter of the dough from the preceding recipe for MOM'S BREAD. Instead of making it into a loaf, make it into dinner rolls. There are several shapes with which you can experiment. After forming, unless otherwise noted, place on a lightly oiled baking sheet about 2 inches apart. Let rise until almost double. Brush the tops with melted butter and bake at 425° for 10 to 12 minutes until browned.

CLOVER LEAF rolls are made by placing 3 one inch balls in each lightly oiled muffin tin.

PARKER HOUSE rolls are made from rolling out the dough 1/4 inch thick and cutting it into 2 inch by 1 inch rectangles or 2 inch circles. Brush with melted butter and fold one edge almost over to the other side.

MINI BRAIDS can be made with 1/4 to 1/2 inch coils. Make the braids about 3 inches long. Tuck ends under.

SOFT BREAD STICKS can be made by rolling out 1/2 inch thick coils and cutting them about 8 inches long.

KNOTS can be made with 1/2 inch coils tied in an overhand knot.

PULL-APART rolls are made by rolling out the dough to 1/4 inch thick and buttering it, then cutting in $1^1/_2$ inch strips. Stack these strips and cut the other way in $1^1/_2$ inch segments. Place in lightly oiled muffin tins with a cut edge up.

CRESCENT rolls are made from dough rolled out to 1/4 inch thick. Lightly butter the dough. Cut triangles about 3 to 4 inches on a side. Roll them up from the wide end toward the point. Place on a lightly oiled baking sheet on the point so that they don't unroll.

Digger Bread

Preparation time: 45 minutes (plus 1-2 hours rising)
Baking time: about 60 minutes
Yields: 2 loaves

According to the man who taught Joy how to make it, this is the bread that fed thousands in San Francisco's Haight Ashbury district in the "Summer of Love" in the '60's.

2 clean two pound coffee cans (for measurements and baking)
1/2 C lukewarm water
large spoonful whole wheat bread flour
1 t to 1 T salt
1/8 can powdered milk
1 T dry yeast
large spoonful honey
1 level can whole wheat bread flour
2 handfuls raisins

Mix the water, yeast, salt, honey and spoonful of flour in one coffee can. Let stand while you combine the other ingredients in a large pan. Add the wet mixture and blend until it reaches a uniform consistency. Cover. Let rise in a warm place until it increases to $1^1/_2$ times the original size. This may take an hour or two. Wash, dry, and oil the cans (be careful to oil the edges and bottom). Knead the dough (you may need more flour). Divide the dough and knead the halves into balls. Put all rough edges under and pop into cans. Oil the tops of the loaves. Let rise until even with the tops of the cans. Put the cans upright in an oven preheated to 400° and bake for 1 hour or so. After baking, let the cans cool 5 to 10 minutes. Then, with potholders, give the bread a twirl in the can to dump it out on the counter. Cool on racks.

Slice:
Calories: 180.0
Fat (gm): .6
Protein (gm): 8.3
Cholesterol (mg): 1.5
Sodium (mg): 176.1

NOTE: A small amount of salt is needed to regulate the growth of the yeast so that the bread is a uniform texture (the 1 t). The larger amount of salt (1 T) is needed to make the bread taste like we are accustomed to having bread taste.

Light Rye Bread

Preparation time: 60 minutes (plus 1-1$\frac{1}{2}$ hours rising)
Baking time: 60 minutes
Yields: 2 loaves (20 slices)

1 quart hot water
1 C dark molasses
1 T salt
1 T oil
2 T dry active yeast
3 C rye flour
6 to 9 C whole wheat bread flour
1 to 1$\frac{1}{2}$ t caraway seeds (optional)

Dissolve the molasses, salt and oil in the water. Let it sit until it is lukewarm. Stir in the yeast. Let sit 5 to 10 minutes until the yeast is foamy. Mix in all the rye flour and enough of the wheat flour to make a stiff batter. Let sit for 15 minutes. Mix in more wheat flour to make a stiff dough. Knead very well to develop the gluten. Finally, knead in the caraway seed. Form into 2 small round loaves. Place on a lightly oiled baking sheet. Cover with a damp cloth and let rise until double in bulk. Bake at 350° about an hour.

Slice:
Calories: 251.7
Fat (gm): 1.5
Protein (gm): 7.6
Cholesterol (mg): 0
Sodium (mg): 335.2

All Rye Yeast Bread

Preparation time: 40 minutes (plus 1 to 1$\frac{1}{2}$ hours rising)
Baking time: 60 minutes
Yields: 1 large loaf (18 slices)

2 T dry active yeast
2 C lukewarm water
2 T honey
2 t salt
2 T oil
5 C rye flour

Dissolve the yeast in the lukewarm water. Add the honey, salt and oil. Add the flour slowly, beating well. Knead thoroughly. Shape into a loaf and place it in a well-oiled baking pan. Oil the top lightly and cover. Let rise in a warm place until 1$\frac{1}{2}$ times the original size. If you let it rise too high, you will produce a crumbly bread which may fall during baking. Bake at 375° for 50 to 60 minutes. Remove from pan and let cool on a rack.

Slice:
Calories:124.4
Fat (gm): 1.7
Protein (gm): 3.0
Cholesterol (mg): 0
Sodium (mg): 238.5

VARIATION:

TRITICALE BREAD: substitute 5 C triticale flour for rye flour in the ALL RYE YEAST BREAD recipe.

Barley Bread

Preparation time: 40 minutes (plus 1 hour rising)
Baking time: 60 minutes
Yields: 1 loaf (12 slices)

This has a good taste but is crumbly.

1 T dry active yeast
2 t honey
1 C lukewarm water
3 C barley flour
1 t salt
2 t oil
1/4 C soy flour
more barley flour

Dissolve the yeast in the lukewarm water with the honey. Add half of the flour and beat vigorously until air is mixed into the batter and the gluten is developed. It has been beaten enough when the batter follows the spoon around without falling off. Stir in the salt, oil and soy flour. Add more of the barley flour until you have a stiff enough dough to turn out on a floured board and knead until smooth and elastic. Shape into a loaf and place on a lightly oiled baking sheet. Oil the loaf, cut a slash or X across the top and let it rise until it is double in size. Bake at 350° for 1 hour.

Slice:
Calories: 122.8
Fat (gm): 1.6
Protein (gm): 4.1
Cholesterol (mg): 0
Sodium (mg): 180.1

Batter Bread

Preparation time: 20-25 minutes (plus 45 minutes rising)
Baking time: 60 minutes
Yields: one loaf (16 slices)

Yeast bread in a jiffy!

$1^1/_2$ C lukewarm water
3 T barley malt, molasses or honey
$1^1/_2$ BUTTER OIL SPREAD (p. 153) or melted butter
$1^1/_2$ t salt
$1^1/_2$ T dry active yeast
3 C whole wheat bread flour

Mix the first five ingredients well and then mix in the flour. Let rise until tripled, about 45 minutes. Pour into a lightly oiled loaf pan. Bake at 350° for 1 hour. Do not let rise after putting it into the pan.

Slice:
Calories: 96.1
Fat (gm): 1.4
Protein (gm): 3.3
Cholesterol (mg): 3.1
Sodium (mg): 215.1

VARIATIONS:

HERBED BATTER BREAD: Add 1/2 C minced fresh parsley and 1 t dill or 1 t rubbed thyme.

SWEET BATTER BREAD: Add 1/2 C to 3/4 C raisins and 1 t cinnamon. Sweetener may be doubled.

Sprout Bread

Sprout 1 C triticale, rye or wheatberries until 1/4 inch long (refer to directions under SPROUTS, p. 78). Grind coarsely. Mix with the "remaining flour" in MOM'S BREAD (p. 131) and proceed with the recipe directions.

Bagels

Preparation time: 60-70 minutes (plus 20 minutes rising)
Cooking time: 30-35 minutes
Yields: 16

1 C warm milk or water
2 t salt
2 T butter or oil
1/4 C molasses or honey
1 C cold water
2 T dry active yeast
5 to 6 C whole wheat bread flour

Mix the liquid ingredients together. Add yeast and let sit 2 minutes until softened. Mix well and then add flour gradually while stirring, until a ball forms in the bowl. Turn out onto a floured board and knead, adding more flour if necessary, until it is a smooth, heavy dough that will keep its shape. Place in an oiled bowl, cover and let rise once. Cut dough into 16 pieces and form each piece into a smooth ball. Make a hole in the ball with your fingers and shape it into a doughnut shape. Cover and let rise for 20 minutes. In a large pan, combine a gallon of water and 1 T honey or 1 T salt, and bring to a boil. Cook bagels in the water a few at a time for seven minutes. Flip them half way through. Remove from the water and top with sesame seeds or poppy seeds if desired. Place on baking sheets and bake at 375° for 30 to 35 minutes until done. Can be served with cream cheese.

Calories: 175.7
Fat (gm): 2.3
Protein (gm): 6.4
Cholesterol (mg): 5.2
Sodium (mg): 295.1

Pocket Bread (Pitas)

Preparation time: 60 minutes (plus 1-2 hours rising)
Cooking time: 10 minutes
Yields: 8

1 T dry active yeast
1$^1/_4$ C lukewarm water
1/2 t honey
3$^1/_2$ C whole wheat bread flour
1/2 t salt

Dissolve the yeast in water. Add honey and leave in a warm place until bubbly. Mix salt and flour thoroughly and add to the yeast mixture. A bit of additional water may be necessary, but the dough should be very firm. Knead thoroughly for 15 minutes. This length of time is necessary to develop the gluten. Oil the dough, place in an oiled bowl and cover with a cloth. Let rise in a warm place about 1 to 2 hours until double in bulk.

Punch down and knead briefly. Roll into a log shape and cut into 8 equal pieces. Roll each piece out on a lightly floured board into rounds slightly less than 1/4 inch thick. Place on well floured baking sheets and cover well with a floured towel. Let rise about 45 minutes until slightly puffy. They should look like they are going to "pocket" and be higher in the middle. Sprinkle with water on both sides and place on the racks in a 500° preheated oven. Cook as near the source of heat as possible without over-browning. Bake about 10 minutes. The strong yeasty smell will change to the smell of baked bread when they are done. Remove from the oven and immediately enclose completely in foil to keep them soft.

Calories: 179.5
Fat (gm): .8
Protein (gm): 7.4
Cholesterol (mg): 0
Sodium (mg): 137.4

SWEET YEAST BREADS

Sweet Rolls

Preparation time: 20 minutes (BASIC YEAST BREAD or other bread dough must be made ahead)
Yields: 12 sweet rolls

1/2 loaf of raw bread dough that is ready to be raised in the pan
2 T soft butter
1/4 C honey
1 C raisins
1/2 C chopped walnuts
1 t cinnamon

Roll the bread dough out to 1/4 inch thick. Spread with the soft butter. Spread with honey and sprinkle with cinnamon. Evenly cover with raisins and chopped walnuts. Roll up tightly and cut into 1 inch slices. Stand cut edge up in an 8 inch square pan or pie pan. Let rise until almost double. Bake at 350° for 30 minutes.

Calories: 165.3
Fat (gm): 5.5
Protein (gm): 3.1
Cholesterol (mg): 7.2
Sodium (mg): 120.7

NOTE: This dough can also be baked uncut in a loaf pan. When done, it can be frosted with CREAM CHEESE FROSTING (p. 204).

Doughnuts

Preparation time: 50-60 minutes (plus 30-45 minutes rising)
Frying time: 30 minutes
Yields: 2 dozen doughnuts plus holes

1 1/2 C warm water
1 T dry active yeast
1/4 C honey
4 1/2 to 5 C whole wheat bread flour
1 t salt
2 T oil
2 t dried orange peel
1 t dried lemon peel
1 quart frying oil

Dissolve the yeast in the warm water. Add the honey, salt, and oil. Stir in as much of the whole wheat flour as can easily be stirred in. Turn out onto a floured board and knead until smooth (about 5 minutes). Let rise until double in bulk in an oiled bowl. Split in half and roll out to 1/2 inch thick. Cut with a doughnut cutter or cut into circles with the top of a glass and form the hole with your fingers. Place on an oiled baking sheet and let rise in a warm place for 30 to 45 minutes until almost double in size. Deep fry at 375°. Drain on paper towels, paper bags or a rack. If the oil is the right temperature, the doughnuts should not be oily after they are drained. Frost with CAROB FROSTING (p. 205) or any other glaze or frosting or sprinkle with date sugar. These are excellent fresh but as with almost all homemade donuts, they do not keep well.

One doughnut with hole:
Calories: 121.0
Fat (gm): 3.5
Protein (gm): 6.2
Cholesterol (mg): 0
Sodium (mg): 90.6

VARIATION: Add 1 t cinnamon and 1 C raisins.

SOURDOUGH

Sourdough is a yeast culture which is used to make bread rise. It usually has a sour taste, hence its name. Originally it was "caught" from wild yeast in the air. Starters can be bought, obtained from a friend, or made from ordinary yeast. Some of the purchased strains are almost a hundred years old.

Starter Notes

Always store your starter in a glass or ceramic container. If the container has a metal lid, cover the container first with plastic and then put on the lid. Always use a wooden or stainless steel spoon or rubber spatula to stir it. Never use aluminum. Some people say the starter should be stirred or beaten each day, but if used at least once a week, this is unnecessary. If you do not use it once a week, it should be fed in the same way you would if you were going to use it (see below). Starters will separate when they are finished fermenting. This is a sign that they need to be fed again. In hot weather, don't leave your starter out of the refrigerator too long. If the starter smells like wine, it is happy and healthy.

Bread must be baked and tasted to determine the sourness of the starter. Letting the starter ferment longer outside the refrigerator will make it more sour.

NOTE: Nutritional Analyses are not available for the recipes in this section, as sourdough starters vary.

Sourdough Starter
(making your own)

Preparation time: 15 minutes (5 days rising time)
Cooking time: 30 minutes

1 T active dry yeast
1 T honey
2 C warm water
2$^1/_2$ C whole wheat bread flour

Combine the yeast and warm water. Add honey. Beat in the flour and water. Place in a large pottery or stainless bowl. Cover with a damp cloth tied over the top of the bowl. Keep the cloth damp so that the starter doesn't dry. (It needs to be tied down to keep wild yeasts or bacteria from reaching it as easily.) Allow to ferment for 5 days. Each day stir it down. On the fifth day, add 1/4 C flour and 1/4 C warm water. Beat. Cover as before and leave one more day. Then it may be used or refrigerated. It should not have mold growing on it and it should smell like wine. If it smells bad or is moldy, discard, and after thoroughly cleaning your utensils, try again.

BASIC SOURDOUGH BATTER: The "Basic Sourdough Batter" in the following recipes refers to this starter after it has fermented for 5 days and had the 1/4 C flour and 1/4 C water added OR any basic sourdough batter made according to the directions included with the purchased starter. The starter must be fed and left overnight before using (see below).

NOTE: Nutritional analysis of sourdough is not available.

Basic Care And Feeding

Put the starter in a pottery or stainless bowl (never aluminum). For every cup of starter, beat in 2 C lukewarm water and 2 to 2$^1/_2$ C flour. Leave it out overnight in a warm place. In the morning put at least 1 C back in the refrigerator to save as your starter for next time. Don't forget!

Simple Sourdough Bread

Preparation time: 40 minutes (plus several
hours rising)
Baking time: 60-90 minutes.
Yields: 1 large loaf

3 C BASIC SOURDOUGH BATTER (p. 137)
1$^1/_2$ T barley malt or honey
1 t salt
1$^1/_2$ T oil
3 T water
**4$^3/_4$ C flour (this can be part whole wheat
bread flour, and part rye, triticale, rice,
barley, or whatever)**

Mix ingredients in order given, adding flour
until the bread pulls away from the edges of
the bowl. Knead until it is no longer sticky
and feels elastic. Oil and let rise until
doubled. Shape into a loaf, oil and let rise
until it doubles again. Depending on the
strength of the starter, this may take all day.
Bake at 350° for 1 to 1$^1/_2$ hours.

PANCAKES AND WAFFLES ETC.

Pancake Hints

Preheat the griddle until it is hot enough that
a drop of water will sizzle and dance. Cook
only one pancake at first; if it turns out oily,
wipe the excess oil out with a paper towel or
increase heat as necessary.

If the batter contains enough added oil,
pancakes can be cooked on a dry griddle.
When there is little or no added fat, the
griddle must be lightly oiled between each
couple of batches. This can be done most
easily by spreading the oil with a paper
towel or pastry brush.

Use a scant 1/4 C batter for each pancake
leaving 2 to 3 inches between cakes to allow
for spreading.

Turn the cakes only once. They are usually
ready to turn when the bubbles have popped
and the top is no longer shiny. Turning
before the bubbles pop will make the inside

doughy. Cooking them too quickly will leave
doughy insides. Cooking them too slowly
causes them to be tough.

Toppings

The most common toppings for waffles and
pancakes are maple syrup or honey. Jams
and jellies, BANANA HONEY DRESSING
(p. 46) , FRUITY FRUIT DRESSING (p. 46),
SPICED CREAM AND HONEY SAUCE
(p. 206) or the toppings in the section on
DESSERTS (p. 179) also make good toppings.
For a low calorie, less sweet topping, blend a
banana with a little juice in the blender and
pour on like syrup. Any kind of berry and
many kinds of fruit can be minced and
heated to boiling with honey to make a
flavored syrup. For a dinner pancake, try
serving with CHEESE SAUCE (p. 175) or
WHITE SAUCE (p. 175) and vegetables.

Sourdough Pancakes

Preparation time: 20 minutes
Cooking time: 3-4 minutes each
Yields: about 40

3 C BASIC SOURDOUGH BATTER (p. 137)
3 T powdered milk
3/4 t soda
1$^1/_2$ t oil
3/4 t salt
1$^1/_2$ T honey

Mix ingredients together in order listed. Let
rise 5 minutes. Bake on a hot griddle in
dollar-sized cakes.

Sourdough Waffles

Make this recipe the night before for an easy
breakfast.

Use above recipe adding an extra tablespoon
of oil. Cook in a waffle iron.

Buckwheat Pancakes

Preparation time: 20-25 minutes (plus
  overnight rising)
Cooking time: 3-4 minutes each
Yields: 4 servings (15 pancakes)

*This recipe needs to be made the night before
and keeps well in the refrigerator for several
days.*

1/2 T dry active yeast
1 C warm milk
1 C buttermilk or thin yogurt
2 T oil
1½ C buckwheat flour
1 t soda
1 t salt

Soak the yeast in warm water. Add
buttermilk and oil. Add flour and beat until
smooth. Let stand in a warm place overnight.
In the morning, add the salt and soda and
bake on a hot, oiled griddle.

Each:
Calories: 69.5
Fat (gm): 2.3
Protein (gm): 2.4
Cholesterol (mg): 1.8
Sodium (mg): 222.5

Buckwheat Corn Cakes

Preparation time: 20-25 minutes (plus
  overnight rising)
Cooking time: 3-4 minutes each
Yields: 3 servings (6 large cakes)

*This recipe needs to be made the night before
and keeps well in the refrigerator for several
days.*

1/3 C cornmeal
2 C milk
2/3 t salt
1¼ C buckwheat flour
1 t yeast
1/3 C lukewarm water
2 T honey
2 T oil
1/4 t soda

Soak the cornmeal in the milk. Add the salt
and the flour. Soften yeast and honey in
lukewarm water. Add oil and mix into other
ingredients. Put in a pitcher or covered bowl
and let rise all night. In the morning add the
soda and bake on a hot griddle.

Each:
Calories: 222.3
Fat (gm): 6.4
Protein (gm): 6.6
Cholesterol (mg): 6.0
Sodium (mg): 310.7

Sesame Grain Pancakes

Preparation time: 20-25 minutes
Cooking time: 2-3 minutes each
Yields: about 2 dozen

1/2 C sesame seed
4 to 4½ C water
3/4 C rolled grain (oats, rye, wheat,etc.)
3/4 C cornmeal
1/2 t salt
1 t oil

Blend all ingredients until smooth in a
blender. Bake on a hot, well oiled griddle.
They will be thin.

Each:
Calories: 42.3
Fat (gm): 1.8
Protein (gm): 1.2
Cholesterol (mg): 0
Sodium (mg): 46.2

Waffles

Preparation time: 20 minutes
Cooking time: 5 minutes each
Yields: 20 individual waffles

2 C whole wheat pastry flour
4 t baking powder
1/2 t salt
2 C milk
1/4 C oil
2 T honey

Mix the flour, baking powder and salt
together in a bowl. Mix milk, oil and honey
together in another bowl. Add wet
ingredients to the dry mix and stir only until
blended but still slightly lumpy. Pour 3/4 to
1 C batter onto a well seasoned and oiled
waffle iron. Bake until brown.

Each:
Calories: 97.9
Fat (gm): 3.3
Protein (gm): 2.7
Cholesterol (mg): 1.8
Sodium (mg): 150.8

VARIATIONS:

PANCAKES: Reduce oil to 2 T. Mix as
directed above. Use 1/4 C batter for each
pancake. Makes 20.

YOGURT PANCAKES: Follow the above
waffle recipe substituting 1 C yogurt for 1 C
of the milk. Reduce the baking powder to 2 t
and add 1 t baking soda.

French Toast

Preparation time: 10 minutes
Cooking time:10-15 minutes
Yields: 2 servings

4 slices bread
1/2 C milk or cream
3 T cashew or almond butter (or finely
   ground nut meal; see below)
1/4 t cinnamon

Blend milk, cashew butter and cinnamon
together until smooth in a blender. Dip slices
of bread in the mixture. Do not soak. Brown
in butter until golden. Serve with maple
syrup or honey.

Slice:
Calories: 155.8
Fat (gm): 7.3
Protein (gm): 6.0
Cholesterol (mg): 2.2
Sodium (mg): 196.8

NOTE: If you do not have a nut butter,
substitute 3 T finely ground cashews and
1/2 T oil.

Soups, Sandwiches
& Spreads

SOUPS, SANDWICHES, AND SPREADS

SOUPS AND STEWS

Vegetable Stock

Preparation time: 20-40 minutes
Cooking time: 2-3 hours (depending on
   quantity)

**vegetable scraps (ends, outer leaves, limp
   but not moldy vegetables, pulp from
   juicing)**
water to cover

Mince vegetables. Cover with water and
bring to a boil. Turn down and simmer until
the vegetables are soft and the broth dark.
Strain and discard vegetables.

NOTE: This can be made in a crockpot. If
you do not have enough vegetables at once,
you can keep them in a container in the
freezer until you have enough vegetables and
the time.

Tomato Soup

Preparation time: 45 minutes
Cooking time: 40-50 minutes
Yields: $3^1/_2$ quarts

**5 quarts tomatoes, cubed (about 10
   pounds)**
2 large stalks celery and tops, minced
2 medium bell peppers, minced
1/4 C fresh parsley, minced
1 T dried basil
3 bay leaves
2 t salt
1/4 t cloves
2 to 3 T honey
7 T flour
**7 T BUTTER OIL SPREAD (p. 153) or
   butter or oil**
1 T lemon juice

Combine all ingredients except flour,
BUTTER OIL SPREAD and lemon juice.
Simmer until soft. Cool slightly and puree.
Return puree to pan and bring to a boil.
Blend together the butter and flour and
gradually stir into tomato puree. Reheat on
low until hot. Stir in lemon juice just before
serving. This may be thinned with cream or
milk right before serving.

Calories: 146.1
Fat (gm): 6.3
Protein (gm): 2.5
Cholesterol (mg): 16.5
Sodium (mg): 401.2

NOTE: This soup is excellent canned or
frozen. Do not add cream or milk if
preserving. To can, process pints for 15
minutes in a boiling water bath. Refer to
CANNING AND PRESERVING (p. 225) for
detailed instructions.

Borscht

Preparation time: 30 minutes
Cooking time: 40 minutes
Yields: about 1$\frac{1}{2}$ quarts (4 servings)

2 C finely shredded beets
1 C finely shredded carrots
1 C minced celery
1 C minced bell pepper
1 C finely shredded cabbage
4 C vegetable stock or water
1 C minced fresh parsley
1 t cumin
1/2 C yogurt or sour cream

Place carrots and beets in a pan with just
enough water to cover them. Cover tightly
and bring to a boil, stirring occasionally. Add
other vegetables, cover and simmer until
thick. Season with parsley, basil, and salt.
Serve topped with a spoonful of thick yogurt
or sour cream.

Calories: 77.4
Fat (gm): .6
Protein (gm): 2.7
Cholesterol (mg): 2.0
Sodium (mg): 117.6

VARIATIONS: Add tomato puree along with
the beets, or 1/2 C tomato puree may be
substituted for 1 C shredded beets.

Cream Of Broccoli Soup

Preparation time: 30 minutes (includes
   cooking)
Yields: 4 servings

1 recipe WHITE SAUCE (p. 175) made
   with whole milk or half light cream
   and half milk
1/2 t thyme or 1/4 t nutmeg
3 C steamed broccoli (stems are fine)
1$\frac{1}{2}$ C vegetable stock or water and 2
   bouillon cubes
3 T parsley

Make the white sauce using thyme as the
seasoning. Set aside. Puree the steamed
broccoli and vegetable stock in a blender.

Mix with the white sauce and heat. Do not
boil. Serve and garnish with the parsley.

Calories: 147.6
Fat (gm): 7.5
Protein (gm): 5.6
Cholesterol (mg): 16.0
Sodium (mg): 293.9

VARIATION: 3 C of any steamed vegetables
can be substituted for the broccoli.

CORN CHOWDER: Follow the above recipe
using the nutmeg instead of the thyme,
substituting 3 C corn for the broccoli and
adding 1 to 2 t honey. Make as directed.

Parvati's Zucchini Cheese Soup

Preparation time: 30 minutes (includes
   cooking)
Yields: 4 servings

This soup is quick, easy and tasty.

4 C water
5 small zucchinis, sliced
3 to 4 C sharp cheddar cheese (about 1
   pound)

Boil squash in water until tender. While
boiling, grate the cheese. Let the zucchini
cool slightly. Add grated cheese to taste.

Calories: 476.5
Fat (gm): 34.9
Protein (gm): 31.3
Cholesterol (mg): 120.2
Sodium (mg): 719.7

NOTE: If the water is too hot when the
cheese is added, the cheese will be stringy.
This soup can be seasoned with dill or thyme
or SOUP HERBS (p. 222). It does not freeze
well.

Curry Soup

Preparation time: 20 minutes
Cooking time: 25 minutes
Yields: about 1½ quarts

1 C YOGURT (p.213)
3 C water
1 T garbanzo flour
4 T ghee (clarified butter) or oil
1/2 t mustard seeds
1/2 t cumin seeds
1/4 t ground fenugreek
3 to 4 whole cloves
1 inch cinnamon stick
1 t salt
1 t turmeric
1 t ground coriander
2 T honey
1 C peas, fresh or frozen
1 C corn, fresh or frozen
1 C tomatoes, cubed

Beat the yogurt, water and garbanzo flour together until smooth. Heat the ghee and add to it the mustard seeds, cumin seeds, fenugreek, cloves and cinnamon. When mustard seeds "dance" (be careful, they may pop and burn you), add the yogurt mixture and stir well. Lower heat and add the salt, turmeric, coriander and honey. Simmer for 20 minutes and then add the vegetables. When vegetables are heated through, serve.

Calories: 184.7
Fat (gm): 9.4
Protein (gm): 4.2
Cholesterol (mg): 2.7
Sodium (mg): 393.6

NOTE: This does not freeze well at all. It does make an excellent sauce over grain.

East Indian Dal

Preparation time: 15 minutes
Cooking time: 40-60 minutes
Yields: 6 servings

This is good as a soup or as a gravy over grains.

1 C Indian dal (mung or toor) or yellow
    split peas, sorted and washed
4 to 6 C water
2 T oil
1 T hot green peppers, minced (optional)
4 whole cloves
1 t salt
1 t turmeric
1 t cumin seeds
1/2 t black mustard seeds

Cook dal in water until mushy. In a separate pan, heat the oil and seasonings. When the mustard seeds "dance" (be careful, they may pop and burn you), add to dal and water. Bring to a boil again and serve.

Calories: 141.7
Fat (gm): 4.5
Protein (gm): 6.1
Cholesterol (mg): 0
Sodium (mg): 361.7

VARIATION: Add 2 to 3 C steamed vegetables.

NOTE: This is excellent served with a spoonful of rice in the center and topped with a spoonful of yogurt. Freezes well.

Black Bean Soup

Preparation time: 15 minutes (soak beans
    overnight)
Cooking time: 3 hours
Yields: 8 servings

2 C black beans
2 to 3 quarts water
2 T olive oil
2 bell peppers, minced
4 bouillon cubes
1¹/₂ T cumin
1¹/₂ T oregano
2 T vinegar

Sort and wash the black beans and soak
them overnight. The next day drain, rinse
and cook in 2 quarts of water. When tender
but not mushy, saute in the olive oil 2 bell
peppers. Add the sauteed bell peppers and
all other ingredients except the vinegar to the
beans. Simmer for 45 more minutes. Just
before serving add the vinegar. Serve with
rice and tortillas.

Calories: 163.3
Fat (gm): 4.1
Protein (gm): 7.4
Cholesterol (mg): 0
Sodium (mg): 46.2

NOTE: To cook in a crockpot, eliminate the
soaking time. Cook the beans on low
overnight and add other ingredients, except
the vinegar, in the morning. Cook until
dinner. Add the vinegar just before serving.
Or, this soup can be started in the morning,
adding the vegetables and seasonings to the
beans an hour before dinner.

Minestrone

Preparation time: 25 minutes (soak beans
    overnight)
Cooking time: 3 hours
Yields: 6 servings

1 C garbanzo beans
4 C water
2 stalks of celery, minced
1 carrot, scrubbed or peeled and thinly
    sliced
4 to 5 tomatoes, cubed or 2 C canned
2 medium zucchini, thinly sliced
1/2 bell pepper, minced
2 T SOUP HERBS (p. 222)
1 t salt
2 T lemon juice

Sort and wash the garbanzo beans and soak
overnight. The next day, rinse and cook in
fresh water. When beans are tender, add
other ingredients except lemon juice, and
simmer until vegetables are just tender. Add
the lemon juice and serve garnished (if
desired) with grated parmesan cheese.

Calories: 125.1
Fat (gm): 1.1
Protein (gm): 5.4
Cholesterol (mg): 0
Sodium (mg): 390.7

NOTE: If cooking this in a crockpot, cook
the beans overnight, eliminating the soaking.
Do not cook the vegetables all day or they
will lose their texture and flavor. The
vegetables will take about an hour
depending upon your crockpot. This soup
freezes well.

Cream Of Bean Soup

Preparation time: 25-30 minutes (soak beans
    overnight)
Cooking time: 3 hours
Yields: 6-8 servings

$1^1/_2$ C Great Northern beans
2 C tomatoes, cubed
3 stalks celery, minced
3 small zucchini, sliced
3 large carrots, scrubbed or peeled and
    thinly sliced
1 T SOUP HERBS (p. 222)
1/2 T salt
3 T lemon juice (of 1 lemon)

Soak beans overnight. Cover with almost
double the amount of water as beans and
cook until beans are mushy. Puree them.
Add all other ingredients except the lemon.
Cook 20-30 minutes more until vegetables
are tender. Add lemon juice just before
serving.

Calories: 153.4
Fat (gm): .4
Protein (gm): 7.7
Cholesterol (mg): 0
Sodium (mg): 579.0

NOTE: If using a crockpot, eliminate soaking
and cook beans for 8 hours or so. Puree and
add vegetables. Vegetables will take about 1
hour in the crockpot depending on how hot
the puree is. Do not overcook. This soup
freezes well.

Lentil Soup

Preparation time: 30 minutes
Cooking time: 90 minutes
Yields: 8 servings

$1^1/_2$ C lentils
2 quarts vegetable stock or water
3 tomatoes, cubed
2 carrots, scrubbed or peeled and grated
3/4 C fresh parsley, minced
3/4 C shredded cabbage
1 bunch spinach, chopped
6 stalks celery and tops, minced
1 T SOUP HERBS (p. 222)
1 or 2 bay leaves
1 t salt
3 T lemon juice

Sort and wash the lentils, then cook them in
vegetable stock until tender. Add other
ingredients except lemon juice and simmer
until vegetables are tender and flavors are
mingled. Add lemon juice just before serving.
Freezes well.

Calories: 115.4
Fat (gm): .3
Protein (gm): 6.7
Cholesterol (mg): 0
Sodium (mg): 320.1

Split Pea Soup

Preparation time: 10 minutes
Cooking time: 40-50 minutes
Yields: 4 servings

2 C split peas
4 C water
2 carrots, scrubbed or peeled and diced
2 stalks celery, diced
1 t vegetable or celery salt

Sort and wash the split peas. Add other ingredients except salt and cook until everything is tender and creamy. When done, add salt and cook a few more minutes. Blend for a cream soup or serve as is.

Calories: 251.0
Fat (gm): .6
Protein (gm): 6.5
Cholesterol (mg): 0
Sodium (mg): 416.0

NOTE: This can be made in a crockpot in the morning and served for dinner. Add all ingredients except salt at once. This can also be made in a pressure cooker. Cut water to 3 C and process 15 minutes. Freezes well.

Chili

Preparation time: 20 minutes (soak beans overnight)
Cooking time: 3 hours
Yields: 6 servings

This is a mild chili.

2 C red beans
3 C tomatoes, fresh and cubed or canned
3/4 C tomato paste (or a six ounce can)
8 bouillon cubes
2 T chili powder
1/2 T basil
1/2 T oregano

Sort and wash the beans. Soak overnight, rinse and cook in fresh water until done (double the amount of water as beans). When tender but not mushy, add other ingredients and simmer for 1 hour. Serve with CORNBREAD (p. 125) or TORTILLAS (p. 120) or NATIVE AMERICAN FRY BREAD (p. 122).

Calories: 237.8
Fat (gm): 2.0
Protein (gm): 12.1
Cholesterol (mg): 0
Sodium (mg): 339.8

NOTE: To make in a crockpot, eliminate the soaking and cook beans overnight. In the morning, add the other ingredients and cook all day. This freezes well.

Split Pea and Potato Stew

Preparation time: 25 minutes
Cooking time: 90 minutes
Yields: 4 servings

1 C yellow split peas, sorted and washed
4 C vegetable stock
4 t oil
2 large potatoes, cubed
1 t salt
1/4 t turmeric
2 t GARAM MASALA (p. 222)
1 t honey
2 large tomatoes, cubed

Sort and wash the split peas, then simmer them in vegetable stock until mushy. In a frying pan, heat the oil and add the potatoes, salt and turmeric. Stir until potatoes are well coated. Add to the split peas. Add garam masala and honey. Simmer until the potatoes are tender. Add tomatoes and simmer a few more minutes. May need to be thinned with a little water. Serve with CHAPATIS (p. 120) or PURIS (p. 121).

Calories: 283.9
Fat (gm): 4.6
Protein (gm): 9.1
Cholesterol (mg): 0
Sodium (mg): 555.1

NOTE: If making this in a crockpot, start the split peas the night before. In the morning, add all other ingredients (eliminating the frying pan step) and cook on low all day. This freezes excellently.

SANDWICHES AND BURGERS

Cold Sandwich Suggestions

NUT BUTTER AND JELLY: Try substituting cashew or almond butter for the peanut butter on a sandwich. Use honey or BANANA HONEY SPREAD (p.154) instead of jam or jelly.

NUT BUTTER AND MAYO: This sandwich is not sweet, a pleasant change from jam and peanut butter. Spread peanut butter on one slice of bread and mayonnaise on the other. Place a crisp leaf of lettuce or grated carrot in the middle and enjoy.

CREAM CHEESE AND DATE BUTTER served on a sweet bread.

SOY SPREAD on toast with lettuce and with or without grated carrots.

CHEESE with lettuce, tomatoes, sprouts, and avocado. Try different kinds of cheese and different kinds of bread. If you are not eating the sandwich right away, slice the tomato and put it in a bag to add just before eating. Add sunflower seeds for some crunch.

Hot Sandwiches And Burgers

Grilled Cheese

Lightly butter two pieces of whole wheat bread. Place a slice of cheddar cheese between the unbuttered sides of the bread. Brown on a skillet over medium heat until the cheese is partially melted and the bread is toasted. Flip over and continue cooking the other side. These can be pulled apart quickly and lettuce inserted if desired.

Calories: 222.0
Fat (gm): 13.1
Protein (gm): 8.5
Cholesterol (mg): 34.5
Sodium (mg): 367.5

Broiled Open-faced Cheese

Place a slice of cheddar cheese on a slice of whole wheat bread or toast. Place cheese-topped bread on a broiler pan. Broil until cheese is bubbly. These can be served with 2 pieces together to make a regular type sandwich or they can be topped open-face with sprouts, lettuce and tomato and eaten as is.

Calories: 118.0
Fat (gm): 6.2
Protein (gm): 6.5
Cholesterol (mg): 18.0
Sodium (mg): 206.0

Olive Cheese on Rye

On a slice of rye bread, layer black chopped olives, tomato slices and swiss. Broil until the cheese melts.

Calories: 168.9
Fat (gm): 7.6
Protein (gm): 7.3
Cholesterol (mg): 14.0
Sodium (mg): 325.3

PB and Cheese

Make an open-face toasted cheese sandwich, spread peanut butter on a piece of toast and place together.

Calories: 284.0
Fat (gm): 20.2
Protein (gm): 14.5
Cholesterol (mg): 18.0
Sodium (mg): 208.0

Grilled Tofu

Saute thin slices of hard or firm style tofu until well browned. Season with tamari (soy sauce). Serve on bread or toast or buns with lettuce, tomato, sprouts, avocado, mayo, etc. Refer to the section on CASSEROLES, BEANS, AND OTHER HEARTY ENTREES (p. 157) for more tofu recipes which can be used in sandwiches.

Calories: 201.9
Fat (gm): 9.4
Protein (gm): 8.65
Cholesterol (mg): 2.5
Sodium (mg): 296.4

Sloppy Joys

Preparation time: 10 minutes (basic soyburger must be made ahead)
Cooking time: 20-30 minutes
Yields: 6 servings

2 C BASIC SOYBURGER (p. 168)
6 ounces tomato paste
15 ounces tomato sauce
1 t basil
1/2 t oregano
1/2 t thyme
1/2 t cumin powder
1/4 t chili powder
1 C grated cheddar cheese
6 french rolls or burger buns

Mix together all ingredients (except cheese and buns) and simmer for 20 to 30 minutes. This may need to be thinned with a little water. Serve on toasted buns topped with cheese. This freezes well.

Calories: 374.7
Fat (gm): 17.3
Protein (gm): 18.6
Cholesterol (mg): 20.0
Sodium (mg): 506.7

Tofu Burgers

Preparation time: 20 minutes (plus 1-2 hours pressing)
Cooking time: 20 minutes
Yields: 4-6 servings

Joy's favorite burger.

2 C TOFU (1 pound) (p. 162)
1 T miso
1/2 t ITALIAN SEASONING (p. 221)
1$\frac{1}{2}$ t tamari (soy sauce)
1/4 t pepper
2 T sunflower seeds
1 T sesame seeds
1/4 C finely grated carrots
1/4 C finely minced bell peppers
3 T oil (for frying)

Cut the tofu into 1 inch thick slices. Place on a clean absorbent towel on a waterproof surface. Cover with another towel. Place a board on top and a heavy weight such as a cast iron pan or gallon jar of water. Press in this manner for one to two hours. While pressing the tofu, prepare vegetables and measure all other ingredients. After pressing, mash tofu. A potato masher works well for this. Add all other ingredients except oil and knead well until the mixture holds together. The greater the proportion of tofu to other ingredients, the better it will hold together. Form 6 patties and either deep fry or pan fry until brown and crusty.

Calories: 316.1
Fat (gm): 20.1
Protein (gm): 22.0
Cholesterol (mg): 0
Sodium (mg): 211.4

VARIATION: Try other seasonings; top with melted cheese.

SPAGHETTI BALLS: Make the above recipe substituting 1/2 C finely cut fresh bread crumbs for the seeds and carrots, and add 1/4 C parmesan cheese. Knead very thoroughly and roll into 3/4 inch balls. Deep fry.

NOTE: TOFU BURGERS and SPAGHETTI BALLS freeze wonderfully. Place a piece of waxed paper between them so that they don't stick together and can be removed individually. Joy makes 5 to 8 pounds of tofu in the above recipe at once. Then she freezes them inside one-pound coffee cans or other cans with lids about that size.

Macroburgers

Preparation time: 20-40 minutes (soybeans and millet must be cooked ahead)
Cooking time: 20 minutes per pan (4 patties)
Yields: 12 burgers

$2^1/_2$ C cooked soybeans, drained
$1^1/_2$ C cooked millet
1 carrot, scrubbed or peeled and finely grated
1 bunch spinach, finely chopped
1 stalk celery, minced
$1^1/_2$ C grated cheddar cheese
1/2 C raw wheat germ
4 t tamari (soy sauce)
1 t dry mustard
1/2 t chili powder
1 t dill
1 t thyme
1 T ground cumin
1 t celery seeds
1/2 t black pepper
3 T oil

Combine all ingredients except oil and mix well. This can be done in a food processor or by hand. Form into 12 patties and fry, over low medium heat, in as little oil as possible. Do not turn frequently. Brown one side and then flip and continue cooking until brown on both sides. Serve on toasted burger buns with avocado, tomato slices and alfalfa sprouts.

Calories: 229.1
Fat (gm): 11.3
Protein (gm): 12.4
Cholesterol (mg): 15.0
Sodium (mg): 206.2

NOTE: These freeze well and also make great lunches. To freeze, place waxed paper between the patties and then they can be removed individually for lunches. They warm well in a microwave.

Green Burgers

Preparation time: 30 minutes (brown rice and wheatberries must be cooked ahead)
Cooking time: 20-30 minutes each pan (4 patties)
Yields: 10 burgers

$2^1/_2$ C cooked brown rice
1 C cooked wheatberries
1 bunch or 4 C chard, washed and minced
$1^1/_2$ t ITALIAN SEASONING (p. 221) (or 1/2 t thyme, 1/2 t oregano, and 1/2 t basil)
1/2 t black pepper
1 t tamari (soy sauce)
1 C grated cheese

Steam the chopped chard and cool. Mix all ingredients well in a blender or food processor. Form into 10 balls and flatten. Fry in as little oil as possible until brown and not gooey inside.

Calories: 168.7
Fat (gm): 8.8
Protein (gm): 4.9
Cholesterol (mg): 12.0
Sodium (mg): 140.2

NOTE: These freeze well. For easy removal, place plastic wrap or waxed paper between the burgers when freezing.

Falafels

Preparation time: 30 minutes (beans must be
    cooked ahead)
Cooking time: 20 minutes
Yields: 4 servings

2 C well-cooked garbanzo beans, mashed
2 C fresh whole grain bread crumbs
1/2 C minced bell pepper
1 t cumin
1/2 t chili powder
4 PITAS (p. 135)

Mix all ingredients (except pitas) until
smooth. Mixture should be a consistency that
can be formed into balls. Set aside for about
1 hour so that the outside can dry. Deep fry
in oil heated to 375° until brown.

NOTE: FALAFELS can also be pan fried in
less oil. These are excellent served with
ALFALFA SPROUT DRESSING (p. 65). They
freeze well.

Calories: 409.0
Fat (gm): 10.2
Protein (gm): 14.5
Cholesterol (mg): 1.5
Sodium (mg): 446.2

Tostadas

Preparation time: 20 minutes (beans must be
    made ahead)
Cooking time: 20 minutes
Yields: 12 tostadas (6-8 servings)

12 tostada shells or tortillas
3 C REFRIED BEANS (p. 169)
3 C shredded lettuce
2 tomatoes, quartered and thinly sliced
1 avocado, thinly sliced
1¹/₂ C grated cheddar or jack cheese
Salsa or hot sauce (optional)

Cook tortillas in a heavy dry frying pan until
crisp or heat tostada shells in a 200° oven
while preparing the other ingredients. Heat
the refried beans. Cover a tostada shell with
a thin layer of refried beans and then cover

with cheese. Top with lettuce, tomatoes and
avocado. Season with salsa if desired.

Each:
Calories: 193.2
Fat (gm): 8.1
Protein (gm): 7.6
Cholesterol (mg): 18.8
Sodium (mg): 363.5

Tacos

Preparation time: 30 minutes (soyburger must
    be made ahead)
Cooking time: 20 minutes
Yields: 12 tacos

12 taco shells
2 C BASIC SOYBURGER (p. 168)
1 t cumin
1 t oregano
1/2 t chili powder
1 C thinly sliced or cubed tomatoes
1 avocado, peeled, pitted and thinly
    sliced
3 C shredded lettuce
1¹/₂ C grated cheddar or jack cheese
1/4 C green chilis, minced (optional)
1/2 C chopped ripe olives (optional)
Salsa or hot sauce

Crisp the taco shells in the oven at 200° for
20 minutes. Heat soyburger in a frying pan
and add the cumin, oregano and chili
powder. If your soyburger is very thick, it
may need to be thinned with a little water.
Simmer for 20 minutes while preparing the
rest of the ingredients. Serve by putting
soyburger in the bottom of the taco shell,
then topping with cheese. Add the
vegetables and, if desired, hot sauce. Serve
immediately. Try putting all the ingredients
on the dinner table and letting everyone
make their own just the way they like them.

Each:
Calories: 216.4
Fat (gm): 14.2
Protein (gm): 7.8
Cholesterol (mg): 15.0
Sodium (mg): 282.7

SPREADS AND DIPS

Tofu Mayonnaise

Preparation time: 15 minutes
Yields: 2^3/$_4$ C

1 pound hard or firm tofu
2 T lemon juice
1 C oil
1/2 t salt

Blend until smooth in a blender. Store in the refrigerator. This will keep about a week.

Per Tablespoon:
Calories: 58.8
Fat (gm): 9.5
Protein (gm): 1.4
Cholesterol (mg): 0
Sodium (mg): 25.8

Butter Oil Spread

Preparation time: 30 minutes
Yields: 6 C

1 pound butter, softened
1 quart Canola oil
1 to 2 t lecithin (optional, helps emulsify)
1 to 2 t salt (optional)

Add lecithin and salt to softened butter. Beat in oil, put into containers and refrigerate immediately. Stir well (occasionally) during cooling. This freezes well and is soft when cold, so it spreads easily. This spread can be used in place of butter. Store in the refrigerator.

Per teaspoon:
Calories: 38.8
Fat (gm): 4.2
Protein (gm): 0
Cholesterol (mg): 3.5
Sodium (mg): 13.2

Honey Butter

Preparation time: 15 minutes
Yields: 1^1/$_2$ C

1 C honey
1/2 C butter

Have both ingredients at room temperature. Add honey slowly to softened butter while beating. When well blended, pour into a jar and cover. Use as a topping for breads, waffles, pancakes and french toast.

Per Tablespoon:
Calories: 79.3
Fat (gm): 3.9
Protein (gm): trace
Cholesterol (mg): 11.0
Sodium (mg): 41.7

Orange Honey Butter

Preparation time: 15 minutes
Yields: about 3/4 C

1/2 C butter
2 T honey
2 T frozen concentrated orange juice

In a small bowl, cream butter until softened. Gradually add the honey and beat until light and fluffy. Continue beating while slowly adding orange juice concentrate. Serve on pancakes, etc.

Per Tablespoon:
Calories: 87.5
Fat (gm): 7.8
Protein (gm): .1
Cholesterol (mg): 22.0
Sodium (mg): 82.3

Banana Honey Spread

Preparation time: 10 minutes
Yields: 3 C

1 T honey
1 banana, pureed
1/4 t mace or dried lemon peel

Combine and serve on pancakes or yogurt.

Per Tablespoon:
Calories: 24.4
Fat (gm): .1
Protein (gm): .2
Cholesterol (mg): 0
Sodium (mg): .3

Guacamole

Preparation time: 15-20 minutes
Yields: 4 generous servings as a salad (may
  also be used as a dip or on sandwiches as
  a spread)

$1^1/_2$ C mashed avocado (about 3 medium)
1 medium to large tomato, diced or 2 T
  lemon juice (or both for a tangy taste)
1 large bell pepper, finely minced
1/2 t coriander
1/2 t cumin
1/2 t oregano
1/2 t salt

Combine ingredients thoroughly.

Calories: 150.6
Fat (gm): 11.6
Protein (gm): 1.8
Cholesterol (mg): 0
Sodium (mg): 279.1

VARIATION: May have other vegetables
added to it such as parsley, celery, sweet bell
peppers, and sprouts.

Avocado Dressing and Spread

Preparation time: 15-20 minutes
Yields: about 3/4 C

1/2 C mashed avocado (1 medium
  avocado)
2 T oil (optional)
1 T lemon juice
1/4 t salt
1 t oregano
1/4 t sage
1/4 t savory
1/4 t dill weed
1/8 t coriander
1/8 t thyme

Blend the above ingredients until smooth.
Use as a dip with chips and vegetables, or as
a spread on sandwiches or as a salad
dressing. It may need to be thinned for a
salad dressing.

Calories: 36.3
Fat (gm): 3.4
Protein (gm): .2
Cholesterol (mg): 0
Sodium (mg): 45.7

Saffron Spread

Preparation time: 20 minutes
Cooking time: 20 minutes
Yields: about 4 C

This is good as a sandwich spread or as a dip with raw vegetables or chips.

5$^1/_2$ to 6 C cooked carrots
1$^1/_2$ to 2 C cooked corn
1 t thyme
1/4 t salt

Puree corn, carrots, and seasonings in blender or food processor. Store in refrigerator.

Per 1/4 C:
Calories: 30.7
Fat (gm): 0
Protein (gm): 6.1
Cholesterol (mg): 0
Sodium (mg): 63.7

Soyspread

Preparation time: 25-30 minutes (soybeans must be cooked ahead)
Yields: 3$^1/_4$ C

2$^1/_2$ C cooked soybeans
3/8 C oil
1 T tamari (soy sauce)
1/4 C lemon
1/2 C dried parsley
1/2 t paprika
1/2 t ground cumin

Puree in a blender or food processor the soybeans with the oil, salt and lemon juice. Stir in herbs and spices. Use as a spread for sandwiches. Freezes well.

Per Tablespoon:
Calories: 29.1
Fat (gm): 2.1
Protein (gm): 1.2
Cholesterol (mg): 0
Sodium (mg): 19.9

Nut Butters

Preparation time: 15 minutes
Yields: about 1/2 C

For those of you who cannot find a particular nut butter or want to experiment with them at home, they can be made in a blender. Nutritional analysis is not given due to the variety of nuts or seeds which may be used.

1 C unsalted nuts or seeds
1$^1/_2$ T oil
1/4 t salt (optional)

Grind nuts in a blender on high. Add a little oil at a time until the nuts begin to thicken into a spread. Salt may be added if desired.

Curried Cheese Dip

Preparation time: 20 minutes
Yields: about 3/4 C

This makes a great gift around holiday time.

3 ounces cream cheese
3 T YOGURT (p.213)
1/4 t curry powder
1/2 t lemon juice
1 t parsley
1/4 C sunflower seeds, finely chopped almonds or pistachios (optional)

Cream yogurt and cream cheese and add remaining ingredients. Serve in a bowl surrounded with crisp celery and carrot sticks, raw cauliflower florets and cucumber strips for dipping.

Per Tablespoon:
Calories: 27.6
Fat (gm): 2.5
Protein (gm): .8
Cholesterol (mg): 8.3
Sodium (mg): 24.1

Sage Cheese Crock

Preparation time: 20-30 minutes (tofu
  mayonnaise must be made ahead)
Yields: about 1$^1/_2$ C

*This is similar to the spreads which come in
pottery crocks at Christmas, but is made
without any preservatives. Besides being tasty,
it makes a great holiday gift.*

2 C grated cheddar cheese
3 ounce package of cream cheese
2 T TOFU MAYONNAISE (p. 153) or heavy
  cream
1 t dried sage, crumbled
1/2 t dry mustard
1 T lemon juice

Blend cheese and mayonnaise until smooth.
Add sage, mustard, and lemon. Continue
mixing until well blended. Store in the
refrigerator, removing about 30 minutes
before serving. Serve as a spread for
sandwiches or crackers or stuff celery with it.

Per Tablespoon (made with heavy cream):
Calories: 54.1
Fat (gm): 4.4
Protein (gm): 2.9
Cholesterol (mg): 15.1
Sodium (mg): 69.6

NOTE: This can be shaped into logs or balls
and rolled in finely chopped nuts for a very
beautiful appetizer or gift.

Casseroles, Beans
& Other Hearty Entrees

CASSEROLES, BEANS & OTHER HEARTY ENTREES

CASSEROLES, BEANS & OTHER HEARTY ENTREES

These are hearty recipes for substantial meals. Most of them freeze well and can be made in advance for quick meals for after work or unexpected company. For other entrees, refer to the section on VEGETABLES (p. 67) and the section on SOUPS, SANDWICHES AND SPREADS (p. 141).

FILLED PASTRIES

Bo-pe

Preparation time: 60-75 minutes (plus 3 hours rising)
Cooking time: 20-30 minutes
Yields: 24, serving 12

These are filled pastries originating in the Orient.

Dough:
1 T dry active yeast
4 C whole wheat bread flour
2 T oil
1½ C warm water
1 t salt
2 T honey

Filling:
4 C ricotta cheese
1 bunch of spinach, chopped, steamed and drained
2 C grated mozzarella cheese

Mix the yeast, oil, honey and water together well. Mix the flour and salt. Make a depression in the center and pour the yeast mixture into it. Mix well and knead for 10 minutes. Cover and let rise about 3 hours.

While it is rising, make the filling by mixing the ricotta and mozzarella cheeses with the spinach. Divide dough into 24 small pieces. Roll out each piece until it is about 4 inches in diameter. Place 1/4 C filling on each piece. Draw up the edges, overlapping them as if wrapping a package. Place them seam side down about 4 inches apart on a lightly oiled baking sheet. Continue until all are stuffed. Let rise until double. These can now be baked, deep fried or steamed:

- Bake on cookie sheets at 400° for 20 minutes or
- Deep fry in 2 inches of hot oil heated to 375° (be careful deep frying, the hot oil can cause severe burns) or
- Steam on a steaming rack over boiling water 30 minutes. Do not overcook.

Baked:
Calories: 164.1
Fat (gm): 5.8
Protein (gm): 10.0
Cholesterol (mg): 18.0
Sodium (mg): 186.9

NOTE: We like them prepared all of the 3 different ways. The steamed ones are delicious fresh but don't keep as well. The fried ones are not as healthy. The baked ones store well and make great lunches. Because it makes so many, you might want to cook some each way, or at least steamed and baked.

VARIATIONS: These can be stuffed with basically anything. Try brown rice and steamed vegetables, or curried vegetables or one of the stuffings in the section on VEGETABLES (p. 67). They are also delicious sweet, stuffed with dried fruit, APPLE TURNOVER filling (p. 97), or the fillings for FILLED COOKIES in the DESSERTS section (p. 184). Make some sweet and some savory. Young children love making BO-PE. Experiment and do have fun!

Vegetable Pie

Preparation time: 60-90 minutes (includes making crust)
Cooking time: 60 minutes
Yields: 6 servings

1 PIE CRUST, top and bottom (p.195)
4 to 5 C assorted chopped vegetables (such as corn, zucchini, tomatoes, broccoli, cauliflower, peas, potatoes, etc.)
2 C grated cheese (all cheddar or cheddar & swiss or jarlsberg)
1/2 t oregano or herbs of your choice
1/2 t salt
1 to 2 C WHITE SAUCE (p.175)

Mix the vegetables with sauce and cheese. Place in crust and cover with top crust. Poke a hole in the top and bake at 350° for about one hour.

Calories: 677.0
Fat (gm): 38.1
Protein (gm): 21.6
Cholesterol (mg): 114.4
Sodium (mg): 1304.4

NOTE: If using tomatoes, drain the liquid from them so that they don't make the pie soggy. The amount of white sauce will depend upon the amount of vegetables used and how saucy you like your pies. It is best to start with 1 C and add to suit your taste.

Curried Vegetable Pies

Preparation time: 75 minutes
Cooking time: 20 minutes
Yields: 12 pies

1 recipe FLOUR TORTILLAS (p.120), uncooked
1 recipe CURRIED VEGETABLES (p.95), cooked

Divide the tortilla dough into 12 pieces and roll out. Place on top of each tortilla 1/3 to 1/2 C curried vegetables. Moisten the edges of the tortilla with water. Fold over and seal the edges by rolling them up and pressing

them down. Place on a lightly oiled baking pan and lightly coat tops with oil. Bake pies at 400° for 20 minutes until brown.

Calories: 164.4
Fat (gm): 8.3
Protein (gm): 3.4
Cholesterol (mg): 0
Sodium (mg): 291.1

NOTE: These are excellent cold in lunches. They can be deep fried instead of baked but are not nearly as healthy prepared that way.

PASTA DISHES

Stovetop Mac 'n Cheese

Preparation time: 30 minutes
Yields: 3-4 servings

Try using tricolored vegetable spirals. They are colorful and catch the cheese.

4 C cooked macaroni
3/4 to 1 C nonfat yogurt
1 to 2 T milk
3 C grated cheese (whatever is available)
1 T butter or margarine
1/4 t thyme
1/4 t freshly ground pepper

In a large kettle bring approximately 4 quarts of water to a boil. Add macaroni. Boil rapidly, uncovered, stirring occasionally, until tender (about 10 minutes depending on the size of the macaroni used). Drain and rinse. In the pan that was used for cooking the macaroni, melt the butter and add the milk, cheese and yogurt. When the cheese is melted and mixed with the milk and yogurt, add the macaroni. Season with the thyme and pepper. Gently stir to reheat the macaroni and serve.

Calories: 584.3
Fat (gm): 29.2
Protein (gm): 32.0
Cholesterol (mg): 99.5
Sodium (mg): 592.2

Fettucine

Preparation time: 30-35 minutes
Yields: 4-6 servings

8 ounces spinach noodles
1 recipe WHITE SAUCE (p.175)
2 C grated jack cheese
1 C grated dry jack or parmesan cheese

In a large kettle bring approximately 4 quarts of water to a boil. Add noodles. Boil rapidly, uncovered, stirring occasionally, until tender (about 10 minutes). Drain and rinse. While the noodles are cooking, make the white sauce. Add the cheeses and cook over a very low flame until the cheeses are melted. Pour over noodles. Toss gently and serve.

Calories: 506.9
Fat (gm): 21.1
Protein (gm): 29.6
Cholesterol (mg): 54.7
Sodium (mg): 642.0

Baked Pasta and Cheese

Preparation time: 30 minutes
Cooking time: 40 minutes
Yields: 4-6 servings

$2^1/_2$ C uncooked pasta (we prefer shapes
with nooks to catch the cheese)
2 T oil
1/4 C whole wheat pastry flour
1 t salt
1/2 t dry mustard
$1^1/_4$ C milk
2 C grated cheddar or other cheese
1 T oil
3/4 C dry bread crumbs

In a large kettle bring approximately 4 quarts of water to a boil. Add pasta. Boil rapidly, uncovered, stirring occasionally, until tender (about 10 minutes depending on the size of the pasta used). Drain and rinse. While the pasta is cooking, make the sauce. Mix the 2 T oil, flour, salt and mustard. When smooth, heat over a medium flame. Gradually stir in the milk. Cook, stirring constantly, until mixture just begins to boil.

Turn down the heat immediately and stir in the cheese. When the cheese is melted, mix the sauce with pasta in an oiled 2 quart casserole. Toss bread crumbs with the 1 T oil and sprinkle over the top of the casserole. Bake uncovered at 350° about 40 minutes until the cheese is golden and the bread crumbs brown.

Calories: 461.6
Fat (gm): 16.1
Protein (gm): 20.4
Cholesterol (mg): 44.4
Sodium (mg): 707.8

Good Karma Casserole

Preparation time: 45-55 minutes
Cooking time: 40 minutes
Yields: 4-6 servings

$1^1/_2$ C thick CHEESE SAUCE (p.175)
3/4 C tomato paste
3 C cooked noodles
1/4 C ripe olives, sliced or chopped
1 C cauliflower florets
1 C broccoli florets
1 C grated carrots
1/2 minced bell pepper
2/3 C grated cheddar cheese
2/3 C grated jack cheese
1/2 C finely chopped walnuts
2 tomatoes, sliced

Lightly steam vegetables (except tomatoes). Mix cheese sauce, tomato paste, noodles, vegetables (except tomatoes), and nuts. In a separate bowl, mix the cheeses. Pour half the noodle mixture into a 3 quart casserole. Sprinkle half the cheeses on top. Pour in the rest of the noodle mixture. Top with the sliced tomatoes and the rest of the cheese. Bake at 350° for 40 minutes or until the cheese in the center is bubbly.

Calories: 553.4
Fat (gm): 22.9
Protein (gm): 24.0
Cholesterol (mg): 43.1
Sodium (mg): 459.7

Lasagna

Preparation time: 45 minutes
Cooking time: 40-60 minutes
Yields: 8 servings

Every time our son Josh comes home from college on a visit, he asks if there are any individual casseroles of frozen lasagna that he can take back to school with him. It's a favorite with all of us.

12 cooked lasagna noodles (3/4 to 1 pound)
2 C ricotta or cottage cheese or mashed tofu
2 C grated mozzarella cheese
1 bunch spinach, cut, steamed and drained
1¹/₂ pint SPAGHETTI SAUCE (p. 177)

In a large kettle bring approximately 4 quarts of water to a boil. Carefully add lasagna noodles. Cook the noodles until barely done, so they remain sturdy and do not rip. While the noodles cook, mix the ricotta, spinach and 1 C of the mozzarella. Then, when the noodles are cooked and drained, layer the ingredients in a 9 x 12 inch rectangular pan, beginning with a thin layer of sauce, then noodles, then the cheese-spinach mixture. Repeat for 3 layers of each, ending with sauce on top. Sprinkle with reserved mozzarella. Bake at 350° for 40 to 60 minutes or until the cheese in the middle is bubbly.

Calories: 499.1
Fat (gm): 13
Protein (gm): 25.5
Cholesterol (mg): 41.3
Sodium (mg): 272.9

VARIATIONS: Substitute manicotti or large stuffing shells for the lasagna. Cook the pasta until almost done and then stuff with a mixture of cheeses and spinach. Place single layer in a lightly oiled 9x12 inch pan. Pour sauce over the top leaving much of the pasta exposed. Sprinkle with cheese. Allow 2 manicotti or 3 shells per person.

NOTE: This freezes excellently. Make several pans of it at once and freeze them uncooked for easy meals later. Remove from the freezer in the morning and bake as directed in the afternoon or early evening.

TOFU DISHES

Tofu

Preparation time: 2-3 hours
Yields: 1¹/₂ pounds

Tofu is a versatile high-protein food. To help you convert meat dishes to vegetarian, tofu can be used with success in any recipe calling for chicken or fish. Some people think that tofu alone is not very flavorful, but freshly made tofu is a treat by itself and worth the effort to make it. Try it for yourself!

6 quarts SOYMILK (p. 30) See below for additional instructions.
2 t epsom salts or 1/4 C lemon juice or 1/4 C vinegar

Make a double recipe of plain soymilk so that you have 6 quarts. Do not add any vanilla, honey, salt or lecithin. Remove soymilk from heat and let it sit until it cools down to 180°. While it cools, dissolve 2 t epsom salts in 1/2 C hot water (or use the lemon juice or vinegar). Use 1 t epsom salts for each cup of dry soybeans that you started with when you made the soymilk. Stir the epsom salts into the soymilk and let it sit without disturbing it for 15 to 20 minutes. The curd and the whey will separate and the whey will become straw colored. While it sits, wash the muslin (from making the soymilk) to remove all soy pulp, and then place it over a colander in the sink. Slowly pour the tofu into it. The curd is apt to come out in a big lump. Pull the edges of the muslin up as you did when making the soymilk. Put a plate or flat bowl on top and a weight such as a big container of water. Let it drain for an hour or so, then remove the weight. The firmness of the tofu depends on the amount of weight used. It may be eaten as is, browned in oil or butter, or used in recipes calling for tofu.

1 pound, using lemon juice:
Calories: 408.0
Fat (gm): 17.8
Protein (gm): 33
Cholesterol (mg): 0
Sodium (mg): 18.7

NOTE: Although the flavor will change, tofu will keep about a week to 10 days in the refrigerator. It must be kept covered with water. Change the water every day and it will keep longer. Tofu can be frozen in water; however, the texture will be significantly altered.

VARIATIONS: Try seasoning it: Add 2 T dried parsley and 1 t thyme or minced bell pepper and 1 t salt to the soymilk before adding the epsom salts.

Pan Fried Tofu

Preparation time: 5 minutes
Cooking time: 30-45 minutes
Yields: 3 servings

This is a great teenage snack food. Both my teenaged kids and a few of their friends like to eat this cold right out of the refrigerator container!

1 pound tofu (Joy always makes 2 or 3 times this much for snacks)
1 to 2 T oil
1 t tamari (soy sauce)

Cut tofu into little cubes or crumble it. Fry it in a heavy frying pan over a medium heat, stirring occasionally until the outside is dark and crispy. When done, sprinkle with tamari (soy sauce) and stir. Excellent with rice, in dishes calling for tofu or in hot or cold pita bread sandwiches.

Calories: 271.9
Fat (gm): 21.8
Protein (gm): 8.5
Cholesterol (mg): 0
Sodium (mg): 186.8

Nama Age
(Deep Fried Tofu)

Preparation time: 20 minutes
Cooking time: 20 minutes
Yields: 6 servings

$1^1/_2$ pounds tofu
oil (sesame oil is preferable)

Cut tofu into 3x1x1 inch slices. Drain tofu and dry between paper towels while oil heats so that the oil will not spatter. Heat 1 to 2 inches oil in a heavy pan to 375°. Fry the tofu, turning once. (Be very careful when deep frying and do not let young children help as the oil is very hot and causes severe burns.) Remove from the oil and put into cold water to dispel the oil. Remove from the water when cool and drain on paper towels. Use in recipes calling for tofu, serve in sandwiches, with vegetables, or alone as a snack.

Calories: 312.0
Fat (gm): 20.4
Protein (gm): 17.0
Cholesterol (mg): 0
Sodium (mg): 18.0

VARIATION:

STUFFED NAMA AGE: After cooking the Nama Age, slit each slice down one edge (as if you were opening a pocket). Fill the inside with any stuffing. (Refer to stuffings in the VEGETABLES section, p. 90). Heat and serve.

Floured Deep Fried Tofu

Preparation time: 20-25 minutes
Cooking time: 20 minutes
Yields: 4 servings

1 pound tofu
1/3 C whole wheat flour
2 T arrowroot
1/4 t salt
oil

Cut tofu into 1 inch squares. Dry on paper towels so the oil doesn't spatter when cooking it. While it is drying, heat 1 to 2 inches of oil in a heavy pan to 375°. In a paper bag mix the flour, arrowroot and salt. Toss the tofu in the bag to lightly dredge it in the flour. Fry the tofu, turning once. (Be very careful when deep frying and do not let young children help as the oil is very hot and can cause severe burns.) Drain well on paper towels. (Do not place in water as the coating will get soggy). Use in recipes calling for tofu or serve with rice or in pita bread sandwiches with lettuce.

Calories: 345.0
Fat (gm): 20.6
Protein (gm): 18.2
Cholesterol (mg): 0
Sodium (mg): 152.1

Tofu Curry

Preparation time: 30 minutes
Cooking time: 20-25 minutes
Yields: 3-4 servings

Prepare CURRIED VEGETABLES (p. 95), substituting 1 pound cubed tofu for 1½ C of the vegetables. Cook as directed. This is good served with rice and a green salad.

Asian Stir Fry

Preparation time: 20 minutes
Cooking time: 30 minutes
Yields: 4 servings

2 T oil
1 to 1½ pounds tofu cut into 1/2 inch squares
1/4 C slivered almonds or halved cashews
3 stalks celery, finely sliced on the diagonal
1 bell pepper, slivered
2 C shredded Chinese cabbage
3 C mung bean sprouts
3 T arrowroot diluted in 1 to 2 T water
1 to 2 t tamari (soy sauce)

Heat the oil in a wok or heavy frying pan. Brown tofu well on all sides. Add nuts and brown them also. Remove from wok. Stir fry celery in wok until almost done. Add other vegetables and a sprinkle of water. Cover. When all vegetables are crispy tender, add diluted arrowroot and tamari (soy sauce). Stir in tofu and nuts and serve immediately.

Calories: 310.4
Fat (gm): 15.8
Protein (gm): 16.1
Cholesterol (mg): 0
Sodium (mg): 187.6

VARIATIONS: Substitute other vegetables such as peas, sliced jicama or water chestnuts.

Tofu Teriyaki

Preparation time: 30-60 minutes (plus 6 to 8 hours marinating)
Cooking time: 30 minutes
Yields: 6 servings

2 pounds hard TOFU (p.162)
1/2 C oil
1 C tamari (soy sauce)
1/4 C molasses
3 inch piece of fresh ginger root, grated
1/2 C lemon juice
1/2 t dried chilis or 1 small hot chili, minced
2 bell peppers (one red and one green provide a nice color combination)
1 small can water chestnuts, rinsed and drained

Cut tofu into 1 inch cubes. Press the tofu by placing it on a clean absorbent towel. Place another towel on top. Cover with a cutting board and something heavy such as a gallon of water. Let sit for 30 to 60 minutes. This forces the water out of the tofu, allowing more marinade to penetrate it. While pressing the tofu, make the marinade. Combine the oil, tamari (soy sauce), molasses, ginger, and chili in a gallon container. Cut the bell peppers into 1 inch squares. Place the tofu, water chestnuts, and bell peppers in the marinade. Refrigerate at least 6 to 8 hours and preferably overnight. Gently turn the tofu and vegetables over in the marinade every few hours. After marinating, skewer the tofu and vegetables, alternating between the tofu, different colors of peppers and water chestnuts. Broil in the oven or over charcoal.

Calories: 155
Fat (gm): 8.2
Protein (gm): 8.6
Cholesterol (mg): 0
Sodium (mg): 677.4

VARIATIONS: Add cherry tomatoes or other vegetables.

Tofu Loaf

Preparation time: 30 minutes
Cooking time: 60 minutes
Yields: 6-8 serving.

$1^1/_2$ C TOFU (p.162)
1 C grated cheddar cheese
1/2 C almonds, finely chopped
1/2 C walnuts, finely chopped
1/4 C finely minced bell pepper
1/2 C grated carrot
1/4 C celery, minced
1 T tamari (soy sauce)
1 T prepared mustard
1/4 C wheat germ
1/2 t pepper
1/2 t thyme
1/2 t marjoram
1/2 t sage

Combine all ingredients, kneading thoroughly until they hold together. Press into a loaf pan. Bake at 350° for 1 hour.

Calories: 346.2
Fat (gm): 22.7
Protein (gm): 19.4
Cholesterol (mg): 20.0
Sodium (mg): 398.5

NOTE: This freezes well, so Joy frequently makes several batches and freezes it. Try it pan fried with ketchup or gravy or cold in sandwiches, for lunch.

VARIATIONS: Substitute cooked beans or brown rice for the tofu or substitute brown rice for the nuts, leaving the tofu in.

BEANS (LEGUMES)

Dried beans are an important and inexpensive source of dietary protein. The protein in beans is more readily utilized by the body if the beans are combined with grains, seeds or cheese. Sprouting also increases the nutritive value of beans.

For cooking purposes, beans can be divided into five groups. Those within any of the first four groups can be substituted for others in the same group. The fifth group is comprised of beans with distinctive characteristics which can not be substituted for one another.

- Group 1: pink, black, cranberry, pinto, Santa Maria, and Anasazi
- Group 2: white beans including Great Northern, small whites, navy and pea beans
- Group 3: kidney and red
- Group 4: lentils, dal, split yellow or green peas
- Group 5: soy, aduki and limas.

Cooked Beans: The Basic Process

AMOUNT TO COOK: Allow approximately 1/4 to 1/3 C of dry beans per serving. Soybeans increase $2^{1}/_{2}$ times in volume during cooking. Other beans approximately double their bulk. Cooked beans freeze very well, so if they are a type that you use for more than one recipe or meal, make enough for the freezer. Measure them before freezing and freeze them (in the quantities needed for the recipes in which you use them) with or without the cooking broth.

PREPARATION FOR COOKING: First, sort the beans carefully, removing any broken beans, rocks or other foreign particles. Then wash them until the washing water is clear. After washing, soak the beans using one of the following methods. Group 4 beans cook fairly rapidly and need not be soaked ahead of time.

OVERNIGHT SOAKING: Soak the beans in 3 to 4 times as much water as beans. In warm weather, beans may ferment (especially soybeans) and should be refrigerated while soaking.

QUICK SOAK: Boil the beans for 2 minutes using 4 C of water for every cup of beans and then let them sit for an hour.

FREEZER METHOD: Soak the beans for an hour or two. Drain them and freeze. The freezing helps soften the structure so that they cook faster.

NOTE: If using a crockpot to cook the beans, only soybeans need to be soaked.

After soaking the beans, drain and rinse. (Although the soaking water does have some nutritional value, using it may make the taste of the beans a little strong and increase the flatulence they tend to cause.) Add 4 times as much water as there are beans. Vegetable stock may be used for cooking the beans. However, do not add salt, tomatoes, or lemon juice until the beans are tender; the acids and salt toughen the skin of the beans and they may never become tender.

Beans should be simmered, as a full boil will break them up. Cooking with a lid on the pot reduces the amount of time necessary for cooking, keeps the liquid from evaporating and conserves energy. Stir the beans enough to keep them from sticking to the bottom and burning. Avoid over stirring as this tends to break up the beans.

Adding 1 t oil per cup of dry beans will help reduce the foaming with most varieties of beans. Vegetables may be added while the beans are still cooking. Salt, herbs, and acid foods should be added after the beans are tender and then simmered for 30 minutes or so. Beans are done when they can easily be squashed with a finger. The cooking time usually takes from 3 to 5 hours after soaking. The Group 4 beans cook much more quickly, usually within 45 to 60 minutes.

NOTE: Beans tend to cause flatulence (intestinal gas). There are several things that can be done to eliminate or at least reduce this problem. Adding fenugreek, fennel and dill alone or in combination seems to help. Longer cooking (12 to 14 hours) also helps. For that reason, beans cooked in a crockpot overnight (or even as long as 24 hours) cause the least flatulence of all. Serving potatoes and tomatoes with beans tends to increase the gas, therefore not serving them together will decrease the gas.

Boston Baked Beans

Preparation time: 30 minutes (beans must be soaked overnight)
Cooking time: 7-9$^1/_2$ hours
Yields: 6-8 servings

2 C small white beans
water
1/2 C oil
1/2 C molasses
1 t salt
1 t ginger
1 t dry mustard

Sort, wash and soak the beans overnight in enough water to cover them generously. The next day, drain and rinse them. Cover beans with water and simmer about 1 to 1$^1/_2$ hours (adding water as needed) until the beans are tender and the skins burst. When done, drain the beans, saving the cooking liquid. Mix all other ingredients and pour over beans. Place in an oiled ovenproof casserole. Cover and bake at 300° for 6 to 8 hours, adding reserved bean liquid as necessary to keep beans moist. Remove the cover the last hour to brown and crisp the top of the beans, taking care to not let them dry out.

Calories: 295.6
Fat (gm): 13.2
Protein (gm): 7.1
Cholesterol (mg): 0
Sodium (mg): 275.6

NOTE: This is very simple to make in a crockpot. Eliminate the soaking step, cooking the beans on low overnight. In the morning, drain the excess liquid, add other ingredients and continue cooking all day. If you want the top brown, the beans can be put in

another pan and broiled for a few minutes in a regular oven.

Soybean Curry

Preparation time: 25 minutes (brown rice must be cooked ahead)
Cooking time: 30 minutes
Yields: 4 servings

Curry concentrate:
2$^1/_2$ C cooked soybeans
1 T CURRY POWDER (p. 223)

Puree the soybeans and add curry powder. Simmer for 30 minutes. This curry concentrate then can be frozen in 1 C quantities. Makes 2 C.

To serve:
1 C curry concentrate
1/2 to 1 C yogurt
1 C chopped tomatoes
3 C cooked brown rice

To serve, add the yogurt and tomatoes to the curry concentrate and heat. Serve over the brown rice.

Calories: 304.5
Fat (gm): 5.9
Protein (gm): 13.9
Cholesterol (mg): 3.0
Sodium (mg): 37.3

VARIATIONS: Add 1/4 C raisins or 1/4 C cashews or almonds, coconut or vegetables.

Basic Soyburger

Preparation time: 45-55 minutes (beans must be soaked overnight)
Cooking time: 28 hours in a crockpot
Yields: about 5 C

2 C soybeans
8 C water
8 bouillon cubes or VEGIE HERB BOUILLON (p. 223)
1/4 C oil

Sort and wash the soybeans. Soak overnight in the refrigerator. Drain and rinse, discarding the soaking water. Drain again and grind in a food grinder using a medium blade. Cook in the 8 C water in a crockpot on high for 24 hours. Add the bouillon cubes and oil and continue cooking for approximately 4 hours more, stirring frequently until the beans get very brown. Cool and freeze for use in other dishes such as SLOPPY JOYS (p. 150), SPAGHETTI (p. 171) or TACOS (p. 168).

Per 1/2 C:
Calories: 183.2
Fat (gm): 11.2
Protein (gm): 10.7
Cholesterol (mg): 0
Sodium (mg): 63.2

MEXICAN FLAVOR DISHES

Spanish Lentils

Preparation time: 20 minutes
Cooking time: 40 minutes
Yields: 6-8 servings

3 C cooked lentils
2 C chopped tomatoes
1 bell pepper, minced
3/4 C grated cheddar or jack cheese
2 T oil
2 T soy flour
1/2 t salt
1 t basil
1 t Italian seasoning
2 crushed bay leaves

Combine the above ingredients and bake in a lightly oiled 12x8 inch casserole for 40 minutes at 325°.

Calories: 240.3
Fat (gm): 9.4
Protein (gm): 12.9
Cholesterol (mg): 15.0
Sodium (mg): 273.4

VARIATION:

SPANISH RICE: Use 3 C cooked (but not mushy) brown rice instead of the lentils.

Native American Tacos

Preparation time: 45 minutes (beans must be cooked ahead)
Cooking time: 30 minutes
Yields: 6-10 servings

1 recipe NATIVE AMERICAN FRY BREAD (p. 122)
6 C cooked pinto beans
1$^{1}/_{2}$ t ground cumin
1 t oregano
1/2 t chili powder
1/2 t salt
2 C grated cheddar cheese
6 to 8 C shredded lettuce
3 tomatoes, cubed
salsa or hot sauce (optional)
1 avocado, sliced (optional)

Simmer pinto beans with the cumin, oregano, chili powder and salt for 30 minutes while you roll and cook the fry breads. When fry breads are cooked and pintos have simmered, spread 1/2 C or so pinto beans on each fry bread. Top with cheese, lettuce, tomato and (if desired) salsa and avocado. Serve immediately.

Calories: 400.3
Fat (gm): 15.3
Protein (gm): 16.9
Cholesterol (mg): 24.0
Sodium (mg): 472.7

NOTE: In our family we all like to make our own tacos, so we put all the ingredients on the table and we assemble them there.

Mexican Beans

Preparation time: 25-30 minutes
Cooking time: 3 hours
Yields: 8-10 servings

3 C pinto beans, washed and sorted
8 to 10 C water
2 C tomatoes, chopped
3 stalks celery, minced
1 bell pepper, minced
1/2 T salt
2 t cumin
2 t oregano
1 t ginger
$1^1/_2$ C fresh or 1/3 C dried parsley

Heat the water to boiling. Slowly add the washed pintos. Cook at a low boil in a covered pan for 2 to 3 hours until the beans are very soft. At this point, add the vegetables and salt. Cover and continue cooking. When vegetables are tender, add the last 4 ingredients. Cook 1/2 hour more. Serve with tortillas and a green salad.

Calories: 195.8
Fat (gm): .6
Protein (gm): 9.8
Cholesterol (mg): 0
Sodium (mg): 432.1

VARIATION: Add 2 thinly sliced carrots or other vegetables.

NOTE: These can be easily cooked in one day in a crockpot. All ingredients except salt can be added in the morning. Add the salt about 45 minutes before serving and have for dinner.

Refried Beans

Preparation time: 20 minutes
Cooking time: 3 hours
Yields: 6-8 servings

2 C dry pinto beans, washed and sorted
6 C water
1/2 C oil or butter
1/2 C grated cheese
1/2 t salt

Simmer pinto beans in the water in a covered pan for 2 to 3 hours until the beans are very soft and thick. Mash beans thoroughly. Stir in oil and salt. Place mashed beans in a large frying pan and fry, stirring constantly, until beans pull up from the edges of the pan. Sprinkle cheese on top and serve.

Calories: 354.0
Fat (gm): 20.2
Protein (gm): 10.6
Cholesterol (mg): 10.0
Sodium (mg): 237.3

VARIATION: Do not mash beans. Omit salt and add 2 t cumin,1 t oregano, 1/2 t chili powder and 4 vegetable bouillon cubes or 1 T VEGIE HERB BOUILLON (p. 223). Serve in bowls with grated cheese and avocado slices on top.

NOTE: To make refried beans in a crockpot, follow the same procedure, cooking them in a crockpot instead of on the stove. They can be started in the morning for that night.

Enchiladas

Preparation time: 45-60 minutes
Cooking time: 20-40 minutes
Yields: 6 servings

Sauce:
2 T oil
1/2 C celery
1/2 C minced bell pepper
2 C chopped tomatoes
2 small green chili peppers, minced
  (optional)
1 t cumin
1/2 t oregano
1/2 t salt
1 T flour

Filling:
2 C grated jack cheese
2 C ricotta
1 bunch spinach, cut, steamed and
  drained
1/2 to 1 C chopped black olives
12 corn tortillas
1 C grated cheddar cheese

Saute celery and peppers in the oil. Stir in the other sauce ingredients and simmer until thick. While the sauce is cooking, make the filling by mixing together the jack, ricotta, spinach and black olives. Then dip tortillas in the warm sauce. Place a large spoonful of filling on each tortilla and roll up. Continue with all the tortillas. Arrange side by side in a rectangular 9x12 inch pan. Cover with sauce and top with cheddar. Bake at 350° for 20 to 40 minutes until the cheese in the middle is melted and bubbly.

Each:
Calories: 557.1
Fat (gm): 32.2
Protein (gm): 29.8
Cholesterol (mg): 78.7
Sodium (mg): 775.7

NOTE: Enchiladas do freeze but the consistency changes. The tortillas do not stay intact and it turns into a casserole. The flavor is still very good. When Joy makes enchiladas, she triples this recipe, and there is one pan for dinner while 2 go in the freezer for later.

Flautas

Preparation time: 25-35 minutes
Cooking time: 30 minutes
Yields: 6-12 servings (depends on size of
  tortillas)

12 large tortillas
1 recipe REFRIED BEANS (p. 169)
3 C grated cheddar cheese

Place 1/3 to 1/2 C beans in the middle of a tortilla. Sprinkle with 1/4 C cheese. Fold ends of tortilla in and then fold in the sides. Secure the tortilla with a toothpick and deep fry at 350° until the tortilla is brown. Remove from oil and remove toothpick. These can be made without deep frying by brushing the outsides lightly with oil, placing in a pan and baking 30 minutes at 350°. They can be garnished with GUACAMOLE (p. 154), yogurt or sour cream, lettuce and tomato.

Each:
Calories: 384.3
Fat (gm): 22.9
Protein (gm): 13.8
Cholesterol (mg): 35.1
Sodium (mg): 520.1

ITALIAN FLAVOR DISHES

Pizza

Preparation time: 40-50 minutes (plus 2 hours rising)
Cooking time: 25-35 minutes
Yields: 6-8 servings (2 12-inch pizzas)

Dough:
4 C whole wheat bread flour
1 T yeast dissolved in 1^{1}/$_{3}$ C lukewarm water
1 t honey, dissolved in the water
2 T oil
1 t salt

Combine the above ingredients and knead 10 minutes. Cover and let rise about 2 hours until double. Divide the dough into 2 parts and roll it out until it is about 14 inches in diameter. Place on pizza pans or cookie sheets. Make a "collar" to hold in the filling by rolling up 1 inch of the edge. Prick the dough with a fork in a few places.

Topping:
3 pints SPAGHETTI SAUCE (p. 177)
4 C grated cheese, all mozzarella or a combination of cheddar, mozzarella and jack

Optional ingredients:
1 to 2 C BASIC SOYBURGER (p. 168) or SPAGHETTI BALLS (p. 150) or commercial vegetarian sausage
sliced tomatoes
sliced ripe olives
minced bell pepper
broccoli, slightly steamed
artichoke hearts

Spread the dough with spaghetti sauce. Sprinkle cheese on top. Then top with your choice or all of the optional ingredients. Bake at 400° for 25 to 35 minutes until the cheese is bubbly and the crust is brown.

With cheese, no soyburger; each slice:
Calories: 448.0
Fat (gm): 17.9
Protein (gm): 21.3
Cholesterol (mg): 44.0
Sodium (mg): 650.2

Spaghetti Dinner

Preparation time: 20 minutes (spaghetti sauce must be made ahead)
Cooking time: 20-30 minutes
Yields: 6 servings

1 quart SPAGHETTI SAUCE (p. 177)
1 pound spaghetti noodles (a 2 inch circle of spaghetti)
2 C SPAGHETTI BALLS (p. 150) (optional)
2 C steamed broccoli and/or cauliflower, (optional)
1/2 C parmesan cheese

Heat at least 4 quarts of water. When the water begins to boil, add the spaghetti noodles and boil for 8 to 10 minutes until tender but not overcooked. (When a noodle is bitten in two, there should not be any white or light core visible). While spaghetti cooks, warm sauce and spaghetti balls. Serve sauce on noodles with spaghetti balls and steamed vegetables on top, and sprinkle with cheese. Serve with bread and a green salad.

With soyburger:
Calories: 375.7
Fat (gm): 8.4
Protein (gm): 18.3
Cholesterol (mg): 2.7
Sodium (mg): 431.1

NOTE: If you use spaghetti balls, do not use soyburger in the spaghetti sauce.

Eggplant Parmesan

Preparation time: 50-60 minutes (spaghetti
    sauce must be made ahead)
Cooking time: 40 minutes
Yields: 4-6 servings

**1 eggplant (dark in color and light in
    weight)**
2 C grated mozzarella cheese (1/2 pound)
1^1/$_2$ pints SPAGHETTI SAUCE (p. 177)
2 C ricotta cheese or 2 C mashed tofu
1 C wheat germ
1/4 C parmesan cheese

Cut eggplant as thin as possible. (If it is
green right inside the peel, peel it, slice,
lightly salt and place on paper towels to
leach out the bitter juices). Moisten eggplant
slices in water or milk and dip in the wheat
germ. Brown in as little oil as possible over a
medium-low flame until wheat germ is
brown and eggplant is limp. Continue until
all the eggplant is done. When the eggplant
is all cooked, cover the bottom of a 2 quart
casserole with a thin layer of the spaghetti
sauce, cover with a layer of eggplant, another
layer of sauce, next a layer of ricotta or tofu
and then a layer of mozzarella. Alternate the
layers until the eggplant is all used, ending
with a layer of mozzarella. Sprinkle on the
parmesan and bake at 350° for about 40
minutes, until the casserole is bubbly in the
middle and slightly brown.

Calories: 356.0
Fat (gm): 18.2
Protein (gm): 25.8
Cholesterol (mg): 57.7
Sodium (mg): 421.4

NOTE: This freezes excellently, either baked
or unbaked.

Sauces & Gravies

SAUCES & GRAVIES

Gravy

Preparation time: 20 minutes (includes
    cooking)
Yields: 2 C

3 T oil
3 T whole wheat pastry flour
**1 t Marmite® or other yeast extract or 1
    crushed vegetable bouillon cube or 1 T
    VEGIE HERB BOUILLON (p.225)**
2 C milk

Mix the oil and the flour together. Heat over
low while stirring with a wire whisk for
about 5 minutes until the flour has browned.
Remove from heat and stir in the yeast
extract and about 1/4 C milk. Stir until
smooth. Return to heat and continue adding
milk. Cook over medium stirring frequently
until gravy is thick.

Per 1/4 C:
Calories: 90.5
Fat (gm): 6.0
Protein (gm): 2.8
Cholesterol (mg): 4.5
Sodium (mg): 39.4

Cheese Sauce

Preparation time: 20 minutes (includes
    cooking)
Yields: 1 C

*You can use up all the little tidbits of cheese
in your refrigerator in this sauce. Serve it over
steamed vegetables, toast or pasta. It's superb
over broccoli and cauliflower.*

2 T oil
2 T whole wheat pastry flour
1½ C milk
**1 to 1½ C grated cheese (more cheese
    makes a thicker sauce)**
1/2 t salt
1/4 t paprika
1/2 t thyme or 1/2 t mustard

Mix the oil and flour in a saucepan with a
wire whisk until smooth. Stir in milk and
bring to a boil. When smooth and boiling,

reduce heat to a simmer and stir in cheese
and seasonings.

Per 1/4 C:
Calories: 416
Fat (gm): 31.2
Protein (gm): 10.5
Cholesterol (mg): 99.0
Sodium (mg): 1432.5

NOTE: If the milk is too hot when the cheese
is added, the sauce may be stringy.

White Sauce
(Cream Sauce or Bechamel)

Preparation time: 20 minutes (includes
    cooking)
Yields: 1 C

2 T butter or oil
**2 T whole wheat pastry flour (for a truly
    white sauce, use white flour)**
**1 C milk or cream or half milk and half
    cream**
1/2 t salt
Optional seasonings:
    1/2 t CURRY POWDER (p.223)
    1/2 t celery salt
    2 T chopped parsley
    1/2 t thyme

Slowly melt butter. Add flour and stir until
well blended. Slowly stir in the milk, salt and
any desired seasonings. Simmer sauce while
stirring frequently with a wire whisk until it is
smooth.

Per 1 C:
Calories: 416
Fat (gm): 31.2
Protein (gm): 10.5
Cholesterol (mg): 99.0
Sodium (mg): 1432.5

VARIATIONS:

THIN SAUCE: Use 2 t flour and 2 t butter for
1 C milk.

THICK SAUCE: Use 3 T flour and 3 T butter
for 1 C milk.

Loaf and Burger Sauce

Preparation time: 15 minutes
Cooking time: 30 minutes
Yields: 3 C

4 T oil
2 T whole wheat pastry flour
2 T arrowroot dissolved in 1/4 C water
2³/₄ C water
2 T tomato paste
1/4 to 1/2 t salt

Brown flour in oil in a heavy skillet. Gradually add arrowroot paste, stirring until smooth. Continue stirring while adding the water, tomato paste and salt. Cook very slowly for at least 30 minutes.

Per 1/4 C:
Calories: 51.0
Fat (gm): 4.3
Protein (gm): .23
Cholesterol (mg): 0
Sodium (mg): 47.1

Easy Tomato Sauce

Preparation time: 20-30 minutes
Cooking time: 45-60 minutes
Yields: 1 quart

4 C chopped sauce tomatoes
  (approximately 4 pounds or 6 medium
  tomatoes)
1/2 C minced bell pepper
1 stalk celery, minced
1/4 t basil
1/4 t oregano
1/4 t salt
1 T flour

Simmer the tomatoes, bell pepper, celery, herbs and salt until the vegetables are soft. Put through a food mill to remove seeds and skin. Return the puree to the pan and stir in flour. Simmer until thick about 15 to 30 minutes. This may be used in any recipes calling for tomato sauce and can be canned in the same way as SPAGHETTI SAUCE (refer to CANNING AND PRESERVING, p. 225).

Calories: 309.2
Fat (gm): 13.8
Protein (gm): 5.6
Cholesterol (mg): 0
Sodium (mg): 1167.2

NOTE: If you aren't using a tomato grown specifically for saucing such as Italian Plum tomatoes or Roma, then quarter the tomatoes and bring them to a boil. Let them cool until "handleable." Place tomatoes in a colander and let all free running juice drain off. Puree through a food mill to remove skin and seeds. When using juicy tomatoes in the above recipe, remove the juice before measuring but do not puree until after measuring.

Tomato Paste

Preparation time: 30-40 minutes
Cooking time: several hours
Yields: about 1¹/₂ C

8 C very ripe sauce tomatoes, chopped
1/4 t salt (optional)

Simmer tomatoes and salt until very soft and thick. Remove from heat and cool slightly. Put through a food mill to remove seeds and skin. Simmer slowly until thick. This takes several hours depending on how juicy the tomatoes are. This recipe can be canned. Refer to CANNING AND PRESERVING, (p. 225).

1/4 C:
Calories: 48
Fat (gm): .3
Protein (gm): 1.3
Cholesterol (mg): 0
Sodium (mg): 21.3

Spaghetti Sauce

Preparation time: 25-30 minutes
Cooking time: 90 minutes-2 hours
Yields: 1 gallon

This is a very spicy sauce. For a mild sauce, adjust the seasonings.

4 large stalks celery, minced
3 bell peppers
1 large bunch parsley, finely minced
4 C eggplant, cubed or Chinese cabbage, finely shredded
12 to 16 chopped fresh tomatoes (9$\frac{1}{2}$ C) or 2 to 3 quarts canned
1/4 C oil
18 to 24 ounces tomato paste
1 T basil
1 T thyme
1/4 t tarragon
1/2 T sage
1 T oregano
1$\frac{1}{2}$ t salt
4 C BASIC SOYBURGER (p. 168) (optional)

Wash and cut up vegetables. Heat oil and saute bell pepper and celery. When limp and translucent, add the eggplant and parsley. Saute until eggplant is limp. Add tomatoes and tomato paste. Stir and cover to steam liquid out of tomatoes. If desired, add soyburger. Simmer until a homogenous mixture results. The longer it simmers, the better it is. Add herbs and salt and simmer another 45 to 60 minutes. Serve over spaghetti and garnish with grated parmesan cheese or alfalfa sprouts. Use in recipes calling for spaghetti sauce. It freezes and cans well, so it is worthwhile to make a large batch.

1/4 C:
Calories: 18.3
Fat (gm): .8
Protein (gm): .3
Cholesterol (mg): 0
Sodium (mg): 55.8

Buttered Almond Sauce

Preparation time: 10 minutes
Cooking time: 5-10 minutes
Yields: 2-4 servings

Delicious served over vegetables.

1/4 C butter
1/4 C blanched slivered almonds

Saute the butter and almonds over a low heat until the butter is lightly browned and the almonds lightly toasted.

4 servings:
Calories: 142.5
Fat (gm): 1.4
Protein (gm): 1.0
Cholesterol (mg): 33.0
Sodium (mg): 123.6

VARIATION: Substitute other nuts or seeds.

Lemon Herb Butter

Preparation time: 10 minutes
Cooking time: 5 minutes
Yields: 4-6 servings

1/2 C butter or oil
pinch of tarragon
1/4 t salt (optional)
1/2 t basil
1/2 t thyme
3 T lemon juice (juice of one lemon)

Warm butter. Add herbs and simmer a few minutes to release the flavor of the herbs into the butter. Remove from heat and stir in lemon juice. Serve on steamed artichokes, broccoli and other steamed vegetables. The herbs settle out, so stir just before serving.

6 servings:
Calories: 146.8
Fat (gm): 15.6
Protein (gm): trace
Cholesterol (mg): 44.0
Sodium (mg): 164.1

Desserts

DESSERTS

ABOUT HONEY

There are many sweeteners available in natural food markets today. However, honey is the least expensive, produces the most consistent results and is useful in more recipes. For these reasons the sweetener called for in this cookbook is usually honey. Crystallized honey can be melted over hot water or in a microwave oven on low.

The type of honey used depends on your preferences. Clover, alfalfa and orange honeys are the most mild-flavored. Wildflower has less pesticide residue than honeys made from commercially grown crops but the flavor is stronger. You may wish to avoid the very strong honeys such as Tarweed because they do flavor baked goods. The best quality baked goods are made with honey that has aged for at least a year.

If you have infants under a year of age, do not feed them honey as it can cause severe medical problems (botulism). Refer to your doctor or health department for more information.

COOKIES

About Cookies

Turn the oven on when you begin making the following recipes so it will be preheated. Unless noted, bake cookies on ungreased cookie sheets. Baking time will vary slightly according to your oven thermostat. Try cooling cookies on opened brown paper bags spread on the kitchen table. The bags absorb any extra oil and can still be recycled after use.

NOTE: Nutritional Analyses for cookies are per cookie.

Kate's Oatmeal Cookies

Preparation time: 20 minutes
Baking time: 8-10 minutes per batch
Yields: 2 dozen

1/2 C oil
1/2 C honey
3 T milk
1/4 t salt
1/2 t cinnamon
1 t baking soda
$1^1/_4$ C whole wheat pastry flour
$1^1/_4$ C oatmeal
1/2 C raisins

Mix oil, honey and milk. Mix in cinnamon and salt. Combine baking soda and flour and gradually add to oil and honey mixture. Stir in oatmeal and raisins. Drop by rounded tablespoon onto an ungreased cookie sheet and flatten with a fork dipped in cold water. Bake at 350° for 8-10 minutes.

Calories: 117.6
Fat (gm): 4.7
Protein (gm): 1.7
Cholesterol (mg): .1
Sodium (mg): 58.3

Barley Oat Cookies

Preparation time: 20 minutes
Baking time: 12-15 minutes per batch
Yields: 4 dozen

3/4 C oil
1 C honey
3/4 C milk or water
1 T vanilla
1 t nutmeg
2 C barley flour (whole wheat pastry
  flour may be substituted)
1 t baking powder
4 C oatmeal

Combine ingredients in the order listed. Drop by rounded tablespoon onto an ungreased cookie sheet. Bake at 350° for 12-15 minutes. If whole wheat pastry flour is substituted for the barley, bake 15-18 minutes.

Calories: 97.0
Fat (gm): 3.7
Protein (gm): 1.6
Cholesterol (mg): .3
Sodium (mg): 9.2

VARIATION: Substitute granola for all or part of the oatmeal. Add 1 C raisins.

Banana Oatmeal Cookies

Preparation time: 20 minutes
Baking time: 12-15 minutes per batch
Yields: 4 dozen

2/3 C oil
3/4 C honey
3 large ripe bananas, peeled and mashed
2 C whole wheat pastry flour
1 t mace or cinnamon or nutmeg or
  allspice
1/2 t salt
2 t baking soda
4 C oatmeal
1 C raisins (optional)

Beat banana, oil, and honey until smooth. Mix dry ingredients together (except oatmeal and raisins). Add dry ingredients gradually to the banana mixture. Stir in oatmeal and

raisins. Drop by rounded tablespoon onto an ungreased cookie sheet. Bake at 375° for 12-15 minutes.

Calories: 98.4
Fat (gm): 3.4
Protein (gm): 1.8
Cholesterol (mg): 0
Sodium (mg): 57.0

Ginger Cookies

Preparation time: 30 minutes
Baking time: 20 minutes per batch
Yields: 4 dozen

2/3 C oil
1/3 C soft butter
1/2 C honey
1 C molasses
2/3 C thick YOGURT (p.213) (or sour
  cream)
1 t cinnamon
1 t ginger
1 t nutmeg
1/2 t cloves
1/2 t salt
2 t baking soda
4 C whole wheat pastry flour

Cream together butter, oil, honey, molasses, and yogurt. Sift dry ingredients together and gradually add to butter mixture. Stir well. Drop by rounded tablespoonful onto an ungreased cookie sheet. Bake 20 minutes at 350°.

Calories: 116.3
Fat (gm): 4.4
Protein (gm): 1.7
Cholesterol (mg): 3.9
Sodium (mg): 76.0

Barley Gingersnaps

Preparation time: 30 minutes
Baking time: 15 minutes per batch
Yields: 4 dozen

1/2 C oil
1¹/₃ C molasses
**4 C barley flour (whole wheat pastry
flour may be substituted)**
2 t soda
1/2 t salt
1 T ginger
1 T cinnamon
1/2 t cloves
date sugar

Mix oil and molasses. Sift (or stir together
well) all dry ingredients except date sugar.
Add gradually to oil/molasses mixture,
beating well. Roll into one inch balls and roll
the balls in date sugar. Bake at 350° for
about 15 minutes. When made with barley
flour, these will still be soft when done. Do
not over-bake as they will get very hard.

Calories: 81.6
Fat (gm): 2.3
Protein (gm): 1.0
Cholesterol (mg): 0
Sodium (mg): 61.4

Vanilla Spice Cookies

Preparation time: 25 minutes
Baking time:10-12 minutes (if rolled, 30-40
minutes)
Yields: 2¹/₂ dozen

This is a versatile dough and can be rolled
and cut with intricate cookie cutters, stamped
with cookie stamps, or made into one inch
balls and flattened with a fork or dented with
a thumb for a natural food thumbprint
cookie.

1/4 C oil
3/4 C honey
1 t vanilla
1³/₄ to 2 C whole wheat pastry flour
1 t cinnamon
1/2 t cloves
1/2 nutmeg
1/2 allspice
1/4 t salt

Beat oil and honey. Add vanilla. Sift or stir
together all other ingredients and add
gradually to the oil honey mixture. Roll 1/4
inch thick and cut out with cookie cutters or
use in the recipes on the following pages.
Bake at 350° for 10 minutes.

Calories: 74.7
Fat (gm): 1.9
Protein (gm): 1.1
Cholesterol (mg): 0
Sodium (mg): 18.3

NOTE: The greater amount of flour makes
the dough easier to handle, but it tastes a
little dry. If using the smaller amount, chill
the dough for 30 to 60 minutes before rolling
out.

Painted Cookies

Preparation time: 90 minutes - 2 hours
Baking time: 10-12 minutes per batch
Yields: about 2½ dozen

1 recipe VANILLA SPICE COOKIE dough (p.183)
1 T beet powder
1 T grape juice concentrate
1 t turmeric
1/2 C evaporated milk

Roll out and cut out the cookies but do not bake. Place on cookie sheets (small sheets without edges are most manageable). Mix each color (the beet powder, grape juice concentrate and turmeric) separately with a little evaporated milk. Try using a clean paint dish with little depressions in it for mixing paints. Start with about 1/2 t of the color and add milk mixing until you have a smooth milk consistency paint. Then paint the cookies using new paint brushes or cotton swabs. Bake at 350° for 10 minutes. Do not overbake or the cookies will lose their color. Children love this activity, and the cookies make colorful holiday treats. Have fun!

NOTE: Exact nutritional analysis not possible; it would be similar to that of VANILLA SPICE COOKIES.

NOTE: Beet powder is available at or can be ordered through any natural foods store, herb shop or cooperative that carries herbs.

Filled Cookies

Preparation time: 90 minutes - 2 hours
Baking time: 12-15 minutes per batch
Yields: about 15 cookies

1 recipe VANILLA SPICE COOKIES (p.183)
1 recipe of the filling for the APRICOT DATE BARS (p. 188) or APRICOT FILLING (p. 207) or DRIED FRUIT FILLING (p. 207) or GREEN TOMATO MINCEMEAT (p. 231)

Roll VANILLA SPICE COOKIE dough 1/4 inch thick and cut out with a doughnut cutter without the hole. Make an even number of cookies and cut out a hole in half of them with the doughnut hole cutter or another small cutter (like a tiny star, heart or Christmas tree). Place 1 teaspoon of filling on each of the cookies without the center cut out. Do not get filling near the edges. Top each cookie and filling with one of the cookies with the center cut out. Press the edges of the cookies together with the tines of a fork or a pastry wheel. Bake at 350° for 15-18 minutes.

Calories: 186.0
Fat (gm): 3.8
Protein (gm): 2.6
Cholesterol (mg): 0
Sodium (mg): 92.1

Carob Cookies

Preparation time: 25 minutes
Baking time: 10 minutes per batch
Yields: about 2 dozen

1/2 C oil
1/2 C honey
1 t vanilla
1/4 t salt
1 t cinnamon
1/2 t allspice
1 t soda
3/4 C carob powder, sifted if lumpy
1¼ C whole wheat pastry flour

Mix together oil and honey. Add vanilla. Sift or stir together all other ingredients and add gradually to the oil honey mixture. Roll 1/4 inch thick and cut out with cookie cutters or follow a variation below. Bake at 350° for 10 minutes.

Calories: 105.2
Fat (gm): 4.4
Protein (gm): 1.1
Cholesterol (mg): 0
Sodium (mg): 57.2

Pinwheels

Preparation time: 35-40 minutes
Baking time: 10 minutes per batch
Yields: about 4^1/$_2$ dozen

Make 1 recipe of VANILLA SPICE COOKIES (p. 183) and 1 recipe of CAROB COOKIES (p. 184). Roll each cookie recipe 1/8 inch thick, into approximately the same size and shape sheet. Place the sheet of carob cookie dough on top of the vanilla cookie dough. Trim any overlapping edges. Roll up the dough, starting at the longest edge and rolling to the opposite side. Cover with waxed paper and freeze at least 1 hour. At this point, the dough can be frozen for up to 3 months. Remove from freezer and remove wax paper. Cut into 1/4 inch slices with a very sharp knife. Bake at 350° for 10 minutes.

Marbled Cookies

Preparation time: 30-35 minutes
Baking time: 10 minutes per batch
Yields: about 4^1/$_2$ dozen

Knead one recipe each of VANILLA SPICE COOKIES (p.183) and CAROB COOKIES (p.184) together. Roll into one inch balls and flatten on cookie sheets or roll 1/4 inch thick and cut out with cookie cutters.

NOTE: You can marble the scraps from PINWHEELS.

Almond Raisin Tea Cookies

Preparation time: 60 minutes
Baking time: 15-18 minutes per batch
Yields: about 3^1/$_2$ dozen

This is a very rich shortbread type cookie which is nice for Christmas and parties. These cookies are pretty stamped with ceramic or glass cookie stamps or baked in cast iron cookie molds.

1 C butter
1/4 C honey
1 t vanilla or almond extract
1/4 t salt
2 C whole wheat pastry flour
1 C currants or minced raisins
1/2 C finely chopped almonds

Cream butter and honey. Add vanilla, salt, currants and almonds. Stir in flour. Chill at least 1/2 hour. Form into one inch balls. Bake at 350° for 15 to 18 minutes.

Calories: 92.3
Fat (gm): 5.3
Protein (gm): 1.25
Cholesterol (mg): 12.6
Sodium (mg): 60.1

VARIATIONS: Raisins may be omitted and nuts increased to 1 C. Coconut may be substituted for raisins or nuts. Walnuts or pecans can be substituted for almonds (use vanilla instead of almond extract if not using almonds).

Spice Balls

Preparation time: 35 minutes
Baking time: 35 minutes
Yields: about 2 dozen

1/3 C oil
3 T orange juice
1 T honey
1/2 t nutmeg
1 t cinnamon
1/4 t salt
1/2 C chopped walnuts or almonds
1³/₄ C whole wheat pastry flour
1/2 C honey
1 T water

Mix until well blended the oil, orange juice, and 1 T honey. Add spices, salt, and flour, mixing well after each addition. Knead gently until it forms a smooth dough. Add nuts. Roll into one inch balls. Place on greased cookie sheet and bake 35 minutes at 375° until well browned. Make a syrup from the 1/2 C honey and water. Roll warm balls in the syrup. Coat well but don't get soggy. Cool.

Calories: 107.7
Fat (gm): 4.3
Protein (gm): 1.9
Cholesterol (mg): 0
Sodium (mg): 22.7

Sunseed Cookies

Preparation time: 25 minutes
Baking time: 15 minutes per batch
Yields: about 2¹/₂ dozen

3/4 C oil
1 C honey
1¹/₂ t vanilla
1/2 t salt
2 C sunflower seeds
2 C whole wheat pastry flour

Mix ingredients in order listed, mixing well after each addition. Drop by teaspoons on an ungreased cookie sheet. Bake at 350° until edges are brown, about 15 minutes.

Calories: 177
Fat (gm): 9.9
Protein (gm): 3.18
Cholesterol (mg): 0
Sodium (mg): 36.4

Joy's Raisin Nut Holders

Preparation time: 30 minutes
Baking time: 10-15 minutes per batch
Yields: about 4 dozen

These are hearty, filling cookies, good for kids' lunches and snacks. Joy's teenage daughter says they're great with orange juice when she doesn't take the time for a regular breakfast or before sports practice.

1¹/₂ C apple juice
1/4 C oil
1¹/₂ C date particles or chopped dates
1/2 t salt
2 C whole wheat pastry flour
2 t baking powder
3 C oatmeal
2 C walnuts, chopped
2 C raisins

Mix ingredients in order given, mixing well after each addition. Drop onto cookie sheets by tablespoons and bake at 350° for 10 to 15 minutes.

Calories: 123.3
Fat (gm): 4.1
Protein (gm): 2.9
Cholesterol (mg): 0
Sodium (mg): 37.0

VARIATIONS: Add 1 t cinnamon and 1 t vanilla. Substitute milk for apple juice. Substitute chopped dried apricots or other dried fruit for all or part of the raisins.

Carob Chip Cookies

Preparation time: 25 minutes
Baking time: 15 minutes per batch
Yields: $2^1/_2$ dozen

Follow the recipe for SUNSEED COOKIES,
increasing vanilla to 1 T and substituting 1 C
carob chips and 1 C chopped walnuts for the
sunflower seeds. Follow baking instructions.

Calories: 161.2
Fat (gm): 8.1
Protein (gm): 2.45
Cholesterol (mg): trace
Sodium (mg): 36.6

Grandma's Peanut Butter Cookies

Preparation time: 25 minutes (plus 30-45
   minutes chilling)
Baking time: 10-12 minutes per batch
Yields: 4 dozen

1/4 C oil
$1^1/_2$ C peanut butter, smooth or crunchy
1 C honey
$2^1/_2$ C whole wheat pastry flour
1 t baking powder
$1^1/_2$ t soda
1/2 t salt

Mix thoroughly the oil, peanut butter and
honey. Sift together the flour, baking
powder, soda and salt. Add the dry
ingredients to the peanut butter mix. Mix
thoroughly. Chill. Roll into balls the size of
unshelled walnuts. Place 3 inches apart on a
cookie sheet. Flatten with the tines of a fork
dipped in flour. Bake at 375° 10 to 12
minutes until brown but not hard.

Calories: 107.2
Fat (gm): 4.8
Protein (gm): 2.7
Cholesterol (mg): 0
Sodium (mg): 56.0

VARIATION: Substitute cashew or almond
butter for the peanut butter. Add 1/2 to 1 C
chopped nuts.

Macaroons

Preparation time: 25-30 minutes
Baking time: 10-12 minutes per batch
Yields: 5 dozen cookies

$1^1/_2$ C non-instant dry milk
2/3 C liquid milk
1/2 C honey
2 t vanilla or almond extract
6-8 C fine shred dried coconut

Blend the milks, honey and vanilla until
smooth. Stir in the coconut until mixture
holds together but is not runny. Let sit for
10-20 minutes so that the coconut will absorb
the moisture. Spoon by tablespoon onto a
lightly oiled cookie sheet. Squish cookies
together slightly on the cookie sheet or they
will be crumbly. Bake at 350° for 10 to 12
minutes but not until brown as they will be
dry if overdone.

Calories: 200.7
Fat (gm): 16.7
Protein (gm): 2.6
Cholesterol (mg): 3.3
Sodium (mg): 23.7

VARIATION: Substitute ground nuts for part
(up to half) of the coconut. Add 1 C raisins.

BAR COOKIES & CAKES

To tell whether a cake or bar cookie is done:

- A toothpick inserted in the middle comes
  out clean
- When pressed with a finger, the
  indentation bounces up rather than staying
  down
- The top of the cake or bar cookie is not
  glossy.

Apricot Date Bars

Preparation time: 30 minutes (plus 1 hour to
    soak apricots)
Baking time: 35 minutes
Yields: 32 bars

1 C date pieces
1³/₄ C dried chopped apricots, barely
    covered in hot water and soaked until
    plump
1/4 C honey
2 T lemon juice
1/3 C oil
1/3 C honey
1/2 C date sugar
1/2 C orange juice
1 t vanilla
2 C flour
1 t baking soda
2 C oatmeal

Make the filling first. In a saucepan, mix the
dates, apricots, honey, and lemon juice.
Simmer until thick. Make crumb mix from
other ingredients by mixing oil, honey, date
sugar, orange juice and vanilla. Then add the
flour and soda, mixing well. Stir in the
oatmeal last. Pat half of the crumb mix into a
9x12 inch pan. Bake 10 minutes at 350°.
Spread the filling on top. Pat on the rest of
the crumb mix. Bake 25 more minutes at the
same temperature. Cut into bars.

Calories: 127.0
Fat (gm): 2.6
Protein (gm): 2.2
Cholesterol (mg): 0
Sodium (mg): 27.3

Honey Spice Cake

Preparation time: 25 minutes
Baking time: 30 minutes
Yields: 9 servings

1/4 C oil
1/2 C honey
1/4 t salt
2/3 C milk
1 t vanilla
1 t cinnamon
2 C whole wheat pastry flour
1 t cream of tartar
1 t baking soda

Beat oil, honey and vanilla together well.
Add milk. Combine dry ingredients
(preferably sift them together) and gradually
add to wet ingredients, beating well. The
longer you beat this cake after each addition,
the lighter it will be. Pour into an oiled 9
inch square baking pan and bake at 325° for
30 minutes or until done. Adding the
BROILED TOPPING (p. 204) makes this one
of our family's favorite sweet treats.

Calories: 243.1
Fat (gm): 6.6
Protein (gm): 4.7
Cholesterol (mg): 1.3
Sodium (mg): 186.2

Carob Bars

Follow recipe for WHEAT GERM BARS
(p. 189). Substitute sifted carob powder for
non-instant powdered milk.

Calories: 211.1
Fat (gm): 8.4
Protein (gm): 5.7
Cholesterol (mg): 0
Sodium (mg): 137.4

Wheat Germ Bars

Preparation time: 20-30 minutes
Baking time: 30 minutes
Yields: 16 bars

1/4 C oil
1/2 C honey
1/3 C molasses
2 t vanilla
1/2 C water
1/4 t salt
1 C chopped walnuts
1 C non-instant dry milk
$1^1/_2$ t cream of tarter
$1^1/_2$ t baking soda
2 C lightly toasted wheat germ

Mix ingredients in the order listed, mixing well after each addition. Pour into an oiled 8x12 inch pan. Bake at 350° for 30 minutes. Cut into bars while still warm.

Calories: 210.9
Fat (gm): 8.4
Protein (gm): 8.3
Cholesterol (mg): 1.5
Sodium (mg): 176.9

VARIATION: Add 1 C raisins

Pineapple Upside Down Cake

Preparation time: 35 minutes
Baking time: 30 minutes
Yields: 9 servings

3 T butter
1/4 C honey
5 slices pineapple
HONEY SPICE CAKE (p. 188) batter, made
   without cinnamon

Melt butter on medium low. Stir in honey and simmer on low until well mixed and beginning to thicken. Do not brown. Pour into a well oiled 9 inch square pan. Arrange pineapple slices over the mixture. Make HONEY SPICE CAKE (p. 188), omitting the cinnamon. Pour the cake over the pineapple slices and follow the baking instructions for HONEY SPICE CAKE.

Calories: 327.5
Fat (gm): 10.5
Protein (gm): 4.8
Cholesterol (mg): 12.3
Sodium (mg): 228.2

Carob Honey Cake

Preparation time: 25-30 minutes
Baking time: 20 minutes
Yields: 9 servings

3 T oil
1/2 C honey
1 t vanilla
1 C milk
1/2 salt
6 T carob powder, sifted if lumpy
$1^1/_2$ C whole wheat pastry flour
1/2 t baking soda
1/2 t cream of tartar

Beat oil and honey together until almost frothy. Add vanilla. Sift dry ingredients together and add alternately with milk to oil and honey mixture. Beat well after each addition. The more the batter is beaten, the lighter the cake will be. Pour into an 8 inch square pan or an 8 inch or 9 inch round cake pan. Bake at 350° for 20 minutes until done.

Calories: 221.5
Fat (gm): 5.2
Protein (gm): 4.2
Cholesterol (mg): 2.0
Sodium (mg): 191.9

VARIATION: Add 1 t dried orange peel and 1/2 C raisins or nuts.

Carrot Cake

Preparation time: 40-45 minutes
Baking time: 45 minutes
Yields:12 servings

3/4 C oil
1/2 C almond or cashew butter
3/4 C honey
1/4 C lemon juice
2 T vanilla
1 C chopped walnuts
2 C finely grated carrots
$1^1/_2$ C raisins
$2^1/_2$ C whole wheat pastry flour
1/2 t baking soda
2 t baking powder
1/2 t salt
1 t cinnamon
1/2 t cloves
1/2 t nutmeg

Beat together oil, almond butter, honey, lemon juice and vanilla until thoroughly mixed. Add walnuts, carrots and raisins, stirring until thoroughly coated. Sift together dry ingredients and gradually add to wet mixture until thoroughly mixed. Bake in an oiled 9x12 inch baking pan at 350° for 45 minutes. Frost with CREAM CHEESE FROSTING (p. 204).

Calories: 505.6
Fat (gm): 24.4
Protein (gm): 7.9
Cholesterol (mg): 0
Sodium (mg): 187.6
(Does not include frosting.)

Aunt Agnes' Applesauce Cake

Preparation time: 25 minutes
Baking time: 60 minutes
Yields: 2 loaves (20 slices)

Joy says, "I remember as a child hearing my aunt telling my mother that my mom had ruined her cake by using an electric mixer and sifting the dry ingredients. My aunt just dumped all the ingredients in a bowl and stirred them together. Their versions were very different, but both were tasty. My aunt's was dense and moist and my mom's lighter and fluffier."

2 C applesauce
3/4 C honey
1/4 C oil
1 t cloves
1 t cinnamon
1 t nutmeg
1 t ginger
1 t dried lemon peel, ground
4 t baking soda
1/2 t salt
3 C whole wheat pastry flour
1/2 C chopped dates
$1^1/_2$ C raisins

Combine all ingredients (either dumping and stirring or sifting dry ingredients and adding alternately to wet ingredients) and bake in 2 oiled loaf pans at 350° for about an hour.

Calories: 206.2
Fat (gm): 3.1
Protein (gm): 3.2
Cholesterol (mg): 0
Sodium (mg): 220.5

VARIATIONS: Substitute 1 C mashed banana for 1 C of the applesauce.

PERSIMMON CAKE: Substitute 2 C mashed persimmon for the applesauce.

Brave Heron's Gingerbread

Preparation time: 25 minutes
Baking time: 40-60 minutes
Yields: 12 servings

3/4 C honey
3/4 C oil
1 C molasses
1²/₃ C sour milk, thin YOGURT (p. 213)
1/2 t salt
1 t ginger
1¹/₂ t cloves
1¹/₂ t cinnamon
1¹/₂ t baking soda
4 C whole wheat pastry flour

Beat together honey, oil and molasses. Add the sour milk. Sift the dry ingredients together and add gradually to honey mixture, beating well. Pour into an oiled 8x12 inch pan and bake at 350° for 40 to 60 minutes.

Calories: 282.9
Fat (gm): 13.3
Protein (gm): 1.5
Cholesterol (mg): 2.3
Sodium (mg): 230.7

Almond Yogurt Coffee Cake

Preparation time: 30 minutes
Baking time: 45-55 minutes
Yields:12 servings

1/2 C butter
2 C sifted whole wheat pastry flour
1 C date sugar
1/3 C sifted whole wheat pastry flour
1 t soda
1/3 t salt
1/2 t cinnamon
1/4 t cloves
1/4 t nutmeg
1/4 t lemon peel
1 C honey
1/4 C almond butter
1 t lemon juice
1 t vanilla
1 C yogurt
1/2 C chopped almonds
1/4 C whole almonds

Cut butter into the 2 C flour until it is like coarse cornmeal. Add the date sugar until just combined. Set aside 3/4 C of this mixture for the topping. To the rest, add the 1/3 C flour, soda, salt, cinnamon, cloves, nutmeg and lemon peel. Mix well. Combine thoroughly the almond butter, honey, lemon juice, vanilla, and yogurt and add to the flour mixture. Pour the batter into an oiled 9x12 inch pan. Add the chopped nuts to the mixture reserved for the topping and sprinkle over the batter in the pan. Decorate the top of the cake with the whole almonds arranged in circles with the points pointing toward the center. Bake at 350° for 45 to 55 minutes.

Calories: 448.8
Fat (gm): 16.3
Protein (gm): 7.2
Cholesterol (mg): 23.4
Sodium (mg): 227.6

 **DESSERTS**

Sweet Bo-pe

Preparation time: 60-75 minutes (filling must be made ahead)
Baking time: 20 or 30 minutes

1 recipe BO-PE dough (p. 159)
6 C filling (use APPLE TURNOVER filling (p. 197), APRICOT FILLING (p. 207), DRIED FRUIT FILLING (p. 207), GREEN TOMATO MINCEMEAT (p. 231) or a filling of your choice)

Make the dough for BO-PE as directed. While it rises, prepare the filling. Divide the dough into 24 small pieces. Roll out each piece until it is about 4 inches in diameter. Place 1/4 C filling on each piece. Draw up the edges, overlapping them as if wrapping a package. Place them seam side down about 4 inches apart on an lightly oiled baking sheet. Continue until all are stuffed. Let rise until double.

These can now be baked, deep fried or steamed (see note):

• Bake on cookie sheets at 400° for 20 minutes, or
• Deep fry in 2 inches of hot oil heated to 375° (be careful deep frying, the hot oil can cause very severe burns) or
• Steam on a steaming rack over boiling water 30 minutes.
• Do not overcook. Makes 24, serving 12.

NOTE: Baking is best for the sweet Bo-Pe as they are more healthy than fried, keep better than steamed, and pack very well in lunches.

Using APRICOT FILLING:
Calories: 108.2
Fat (gm): .05
Protein (gm): .6
Cholesterol (mg): 0
Sodium (mg): 7.1

VARIATIONS: These can be stuffed with basically anything. If you want to experiment, try filling them with BAKED CHEESECAKE (p. 200) (combining the two layers together before filling the BO-PE), or ricotta cheese sweetened with fruit and honey and spiced with cinnamon and lemon peel. Experiment and do have fun!

PUDDINGS

Vanilla Arrowroot Pudding

Preparation time: 15 minutes
Cooking time: 20 minutes
Yields: 4 servings

2 C milk
3 T arrowroot
1/4 C honey
1 t vanilla extract
1 t butter (optional)

Stir together all ingredients except vanilla. Heat in a heavy saucepan over medium heat, stirring constantly. When the mixture reaches a full boil, remove from heat and stir in vanilla. This is a simple pudding which is also excellent as a sauce over CARROT CAKE (p. 190), fresh fruit and BAKED APPLES (p. 55).

Calories: 149.2
Fat (gm): 2.2
Protein (gm): 4.4
Cholesterol (mg): 9.0
Sodium (mg): 62.0

Carob Pudding

Preparation time: 15 minutes
Cooking time: 25 minutes
Yields: 6 servings

4 C milk
1/3 C honey
1 t instant coffee substitute
1/2 t salt
1/4 C carob powder, sifted if lumpy
6 T arrowroot
1 t vanilla

Combine 3 C milk, honey, coffee substitute, salt, and carob in a heavy saucepan. Mix arrowroot thoroughly with 1 C milk. Slowly, while stirring frequently, bring mixture in pan to a slow boil. As pudding heats, stir in the arrowroot and milk mixture. Stir frequently to avoid lumps, making certain that you are getting the thick pudding off the bottom. Continue cooking at a slow boil for 20 minutes. Remove from heat and stir in vanilla. Let cool until firm.

Calories: 188.5
Fat (gm): 3.0
Protein (gm): 6.0
Cholesterol (mg): 12.0
Sodium (mg): 260.4

VARIATIONS:

CAROB CREAM PIE: Fill a GRAHAM CRACKER CRUST (p. 199) with CAROB PUDDING. Freeze until almost solid. Top with sweetened whipped cream.

FUDGESICLES: Pour CAROB PUDDING into popsicle molds and freeze.

Tapioca Pudding

Preparation time: 15 minutes
Cooking time: 20 minutes
Yields: 8 servings

This pudding is a great snack for children and teenagers. It is also an excellent addition to lunches (we pour it warm into washed yogurt containers for packing in lunches). Served with fruit, it also makes a nutritious breakfast.

2/3 C granulated tapioca
1/2 C honey
1/4 t salt
4 3/4 C milk
1 t vanilla extract

Combine all ingredients except vanilla in a heavy saucepan. Cook over medium heat, stirring frequently until the mixture begins to boil. Turn the heat down as low as possible and simmer 8-10 minutes. Remove from heat and stir in vanilla. This pudding will thicken as it cools.

Calories: 182.7
Fat (gm): 2.6

Protein (gm): 5.3
Cholesterol (mg): 10.7
Sodium (mg): 140.5

VARIATIONS: After removing from heat, stir in 1/2 t dried lemon or orange peel and 1/2 C coconut or slivered almonds, or 1 C chopped dates, or 1 banana crushed and 1 banana sliced.

ABOUT TAPIOCA: Tapioca is processed from cassava roots which are poisonous until boiled. The dried starch we know as tapioca is sold in several different forms, among them large pearl, small pearl and granulated. All forms of commercially available tapioca are virtually alike, having gone through the same processing. Due to the ease in cooking, the recipes in this cookbook call for granulated tapioca which does not need to be soaked before cooking.

NOTE: Pearl tapioca is used in the same proportions as in the previous recipe, but must be soaked in water for at least one hour, and preferably overnight, before cooking. Use twice as much water as tapioca for soaking. The water should be completely absorbed by the time you are ready to cook it. If not, the tapioca may be too old to soften.

Hasty Pudding

Preparation time: 25 minutes
Cooking time: 35-45 minutes
Yields: 8 servings

1/3 C molasses
1/3 C honey
1/3 C water
2 C whole wheat pastry flour
1 T baking powder
1/2 t salt
1/2 C honey
2/3 C milk
2 t vanilla
1/2 C oil
1/2 C raisins

Make a syrup by combining the molasses,
1/3 C honey and water in a pan and bringing
the mixture to a boil. Set this aside. Mix dry
ingredients together; mix unused wet
ingredients together and combine the two
mixtures, stirring only until smooth. Pour into
an oiled 8 inch square pan and sprinkle with
raisins. Pour boiling syrup over batter. Bake
at 350° for 35 to 40 minutes. Serve warm.

Calories: 594.8
Fat (gm): 18.4
Protein (gm): 7.4
Cholesterol (mg): 2.0
Sodium (mg): 360.3

Mom's Cranberry Pudding

Preparation time: 50 minutes
Cooking time: 3 hours
Yields: 8 servings

*Joy says, "When I was growing up, we had
this pudding every Thanksgiving and
Christmas. The cranberries must be sliced. It
doesn't come out with the same texture any
other way. I remember sitting at a card table
with other members of my family slicing
cranberries for this holiday treat."*

1/2 C molasses
1/2 C hot water
1½ C whole wheat pastry flour
1/2 t baking soda
2 C sliced cranberries (about 1/2 pound)

Rinse and sort the cranberries, removing any
with soft spots. Slice thinly from one end to
the other. Combine molasses and water. Sift
flour and soda and add to water mixture.
Gently stir in cranberries. Place in a steamed
pudding mold or a 2 pound coffee can with
aluminum foil securely covering the top and
tied on with string. Place mold on a rack a
few inches off the bottom of a large kettle.
Add 2 to 3 inches of boiling water. Cover
kettle tightly and steam 3 to 4 hours. Serve
with STEAMED PUDDING SAUCE (p. 206).

Calories: 172.0
Fat (gm): .6
Protein (gm): 3.5
Cholesterol (mg): 0
Sodium (mg): 62.0

PIES AND OTHER GOODIES

Grandmother's Pie Dough Revisited

Preparation time: 35 minutes (plus 30-45 minutes chilling)
Baking time: 40-60 minutes (varies with filling)
Yields: 6 servings

During the Depression, Joy's maternal grandmother supported her children by baking pies for a restaurant. She taught Joy how to make pies. This is her recipe, with butter substituted for the shortening and whole wheat flour instead of white.

2 C whole wheat pastry flour
1 t salt
1/2 to 3/4 C butter (the more butter, the richer the dough and the harder to handle)
2-4 T ice cold water (the amount will depend on the air temperature, altitude, amount of butter used, and the mood of the cook)

Have everything cold when you begin, including the bowl, the utensils and all the ingredients. Mix the flour and the salt in the bowl. Make a hole in the center and add the butter. Cut the butter into the flour with a pastry cutter, a fork, 2 knives or your hands (working fast) until the mixture is in pieces the size of peas. Add water 1 T at a time (you can make certain that it is cold by taking it tablespoonful by tablespoonful from a bowl of water with ice floating in it), mixing very lightly with a fork. Refrigerate until chilled, but not completely cold.

Divide the dough into two balls. Roll out between two opened plastic bags or 2 sheets of waxed paper. Peel off the plastic every now and then and replace it so that the dough doesn't stick to it too much. Rolling the dough between the sheets of plastic eliminates the need for additional flour, so the dough is softer. It also makes the crust easier to flip into the pan. Roll from the center outward so it doesn't get too thin on the edges.

When it is the right size, peel off one side of the plastic and flip the dough, plastic side up, into the pie pan. Push into corners and remove the second piece of plastic. Trim around the outside of the pan edge with a sharp knife. Put in the filling. Place the top crust on and make vent holes with a fork or sharp knife. Press the edges of the bottom and top crust together on the pan edge with a fork or pastry wheel and re-trim. Place the pie on a cookie sheet so that if any juice bubbles over it will not get on the bottom of your oven. Bake at 400° for 10 minutes and then lower the temperature to 350° and bake until done (40 minutes for soft fruit, 1 hour for apple). Test by inserting a fork to test for tenderness. If fruit is done before the crust is browned, broil pie for 2 to 3 minutes until brown. Watch very carefully as it will burn easily.

Per slice:
Calories: 360.4
Fat (gm): 20.3
Protein (gm): 6.05
Cholesterol (mg): 54.6
Sodium (mg): 558.9

Basic Pie Filling

Preparation time: 10-30 minutes
Cooking time: 50-60 minutes
Yields: 1 pie (6 servings)

4-6 C fruit, sliced (any fresh fruit can be used in a pie; however, some fruits such as strawberries are not as good cooked)
$1^1/_2$ to 3 T arrowroot or 3 to 6 T whole wheat pastry flour (the juicier the fruit the more thickener it will need)
1/2 to 3/4 C honey can be poured over the fruit (date sugar can be substituted for part or all of this)
1 to 2 T lemon juice
2 crust PIE DOUGH (p.195)

Mix the above ingredients and fill pie shell. The fruit should be piled high in the pie pan as it will shrink during cooking. Cover with top pie shell and bake as directed under PIE DOUGH RECIPE (p.195). Pie should be cooked immediately so that the bottom doesn't get soggy.

Apple Pie

Preparation time: 30 minutes (pie dough must be made ahead)
Baking time: 70 minutes
Yields: 6 servings

2 crust PIE DOUGH (p. 195)
6 to 8 apples, preferably tart green apples
1/3 C date sugar (optional)
1/2 C raisins (optional)
2 to 3 T flour
1 t cinnamon
1/4 C honey

Peel and thinly slice the apples. To determine how many you need, fill an empty pie shell with them until they are heaped 1 to $1^1/_2$ inches above the top of the pan. Place bottom pie dough in pan and trim edges. Cover the bottom of the pie pan with the date sugar. Mix the apples, raisins, flour, and the cinnamon and place in the pie pan. Pour honey over the apples. Top with the top crust. Seal the edges with the tines of a fork or a pastry wheel. Trim edges. Make an A (for apple) or other design in the top so that the steam can escape while it is baking. Place pie pan on a cookie sheet. Bake for 10 minutes at 400° to brown the crust. Then lower temperature to 350° and bake for 1 hour until the apples are tender and the crust is golden brown.

Calories: 502.9
Fat (gm): 20.6
Protein (gm): 23.3
Cholesterol (mg):54.6
Sodium (mg): 559.7

Apple Turnovers

Preparation time: 35-45 minutes (pie
  dough must be made ahead)
Baking time: 30 minutes
Yields: 8 turnovers

Turnovers are basically little pies that pack
much better in lunches and picnics.

3 C apples, peeled and diced
1 T lemon juice
2 t arrowroot
2 T water
3/4 C apple or pineapple juice
1/4 C honey
1/2 t dried lemon rind
1/2 t cinnamon
1 recipe of PIE DOUGH (p. 195) for a
  double crusted pie

Prepare the apples and mix with lemon juice.
In a small bowl, mix the 2 T water and the
arrowroot. In a heavy saucepan, combine
apples, juice, honey and spices. Cook over
medium heat for 5 minutes until apples begin
to turn transparent. Add arrowroot mixture
and cook 1 to 2 minutes until thick. Roll the
dough as for 2 pie crusts, cutting each round
into four equal wedge shaped sections. Place
filling on one half of triangle and fold over
the other half. Seal edges as for pie. Place on
a baking sheet and bake at 400° for 30
minutes or until golden brown.

Calories: 340.2
Fat (gm): 15.3
Protein (gm): 14.6
Cholesterol (mg): 40.9
Sodium (mg): 420.5

VARIATIONS: Other fillings that can be used
include the DRIED FRUIT FILLING (p. 207),
GREEN TOMATO MINCEMEAT (p. 231) or
APRICOT FILLING (p. 207). Fillings can also
be made as for a regular pie, remembering
the turnovers should not be soggy so they
can be eaten out of hand.

Banana Pies

Preparation time: 15-20 minutes (pie
  dough must be made ahead)
Baking time: 15-20 minutes
Yields: 4 servings

*This is an excellent beginner cooking recipe
for young children. Also makes great snacks
for all.*

2 bananas
1/3 C date sugar
1 t cinnamon
1 unbaked pie crust see PIE DOUGH
  (p.195)

Peel bananas and cut in half crosswise. Roll
them in date sugar and cinnamon. Wrap each
in one quarter of the pie dough. Bake 15-20
minutes at 400°. Delicious plain or with
lemon sauce.

Calories: 365.9
Fat (gm): 15.4
Protein (gm): 5.3
Cholesterol (mg): 40.9
Sodium (mg): 420.4

Tiny Tarts

Preparation time: 40 minutes (plus 45
  minutes chilling)
Baking time: 15 minutes
Yields: 24 tarts

*These are fun for parties and children really
have a good time making and filling them.*

**1 recipe PIE DOUGH for a double crust
  (p.195)**
Filling (See below)

Roll out pie dough and cut into pieces
slightly larger than the tart or muffin pans
being used. If you are using medium sized
muffin pans, this recipe will make 16 tarts. If
you are using tart pans or mini muffin pans,
this recipe will make 24 tarts.

For fresh fruit tarts, prick holes with the tines
of a fork in the bottom of each tart shell and
bake the tart shells at 400° degrees for 15
minutes.

The tart shells can then be filled with fresh
sliced strawberries or peaches topped with
LEMON SAUCE (p. 205) or VANILLA
PUDDING (p. 195). Other fillings for cooked
shells include FRUIT JELLS (p. 47) and
CAROB PUDDING (p. 192) swirled together,
or FREEZER CHEESECAKE (p. 199) topped
with fresh fruit or PINEAPPLE BERRY SAUCE
(p. 207). Use your imagination and have fun.
For fresh fruit, the smaller the tarts are the
better, so that they don't become soggy and
collapse.

For baked fillings, fill the unbaked tarts to
the top and then bake at the temperature in
the directions of the filling used. Adjust the
cooking time according to the size of the tart.
Suggestions for baked tart fillings include
BAKED CHEESECAKE (p. 200), GREEN
TOMATO MINCEMEAT (p. 231), or
PUMPKIN PIE (p. 199).

With CHEESECAKE filling:
Calories: 181.3
Fat (gm): 13.6
Protein (gm): 3.35

Cholesterol (mg): 39.6
Sodium (mg): 211.2

With PUMPKIN filling:
Calories: 81.2
Fat (gm): 1.23
Protein (gm): 1.9
Cholesterol (mg): 3.8
Sodium (mg): 76.3

Pumpkin Puree

Place your whole pumpkin on a cooking
sheet. Pierce the skin with a sharp knife so
that it won't explode as it bakes. Bake at
350° for an hour or until tender. This is the
preferred method for cooking a pumpkin as
the pumpkin doesn't dry out nor is more
moisture added to the pumpkin. After
baking, cool the pumpkin until "touchable",
peel, remove seeds and puree in a food
processor or food mill or mash with a potato
masher. Freeze unused pumpkin for future
pies. This is easiest if you freeze it in the
amounts which you will need later for pies.

If the pumpkin is too large to fit into your
oven, cut it into sections with a very strong
sharp knife (be careful) and bake in a
covered roasting pan or steam it. (Steaming
adds moisture which may make your pies
take longer to bake.) Cover the pumpkin
when baking it in pieces so that it does not
dry out. If you don't have a pumpkin, use
pureed cooked pumpkin—not pumpkin pie
filling—both of which come in similar
looking cans.

Pumpkin Pie

Preparation time: 20 minutes (pie dough
   must be made ahead)
Baking time: 90 minutes
Yields: 2 pies (12 servings)

**4¹/₂ C pumpkin, mashed or pureed
   smooth (see below)**
**2²/₃ C thick milk or canned evaporated
   milk**
2/3 C arrowroot
**1 C honey or 1/2 C honey and 1/2 C
   molasses**
1 t cinnamon
1 t ground dried lemon peel
3/4 t mace or nutmeg
3/4 t allspice
3/4 t ginger
1/2 t salt
1 T vanilla extract
**2 unbaked pie crust shells (see PIE
   DOUGH, p. 195)**

Combine all ingredients, beating until
smooth. Pour into 2 unbaked pie shells and
bake 15 minutes at 425°. Lower oven
temperature to 300° and bake 1 to 1¹/₂ hours.
You can tell when it is done by the way the
top will turn from shiny to dull all the way to
the center. As it bakes, it will crack. When it
is done, the cracks will circle to the center.
As a final test, a clean, room temperature dull
knife stuck into the center will come out
fairly clean but not perfectly clean. Do be
patient; this pie is worth waiting for.

Calories: 378.8
Fat (gm): 11.3
Protein (gm): 7.8
Cholesterol (mg): 31.9
Sodium (mg): 438.5

VARIATIONS: Substitute squash for pumpkin
or use 1 C cream cheese in place of 1 C milk
or use yogurt or sour cream in place of milk.
These last 2 variations will bake faster and
need only about 1 hour at 300°.

Graham Cracker Crust

Preparation time: 15-20 minutes
Yields: one 10 inch pie crust

**2 C finely crushed GRAHAM CRACKERS
   (p. 120) or dry cookies**
1/4 C butter, melted
1 T honey
1 T date sugar
1/2 t cinnamon

Graham crackers may be crushed in a food
processor or blender, or by placing in a
paper bag and rolling with a rolling pin. Mix
all ingredients together, adding a bit more
honey if it won't hold together. Press into a
pie tin.

Per slice:
Calories: 253.5
Fat (gm): 10.8
Protein (gm): 2.7
Cholesterol (mg): 22.0
Sodium (mg): 322.4

Freezer Cheesecake

Preparation time: 20-25 minutes
Freezing time: 30-45 minutes
Yields: 2 cheesecakes (8 servings each)

2¹/₂ C cream cheese, softened
1¹/₄ C YOGURT (p.213)
1/2 C honey
1 T vanilla extract
**2 8-inch GRAHAM CRACKER CRUSTS
   (See above.)**

Beat cream cheese and yogurt with an
electric mixer until light and airy. Add honey
and vanilla. Pour into graham cracker crust
and freeze until firm. Remove from freezer 30
to 45 minutes before serving. May be topped
with PINEAPPLE BERRY SAUCE (p. 207) or
fresh fruit.

Calories: 368.5
Fat (gm): 21.2
Protein (gm): 6.0
Cholesterol (mg): 60.3
Sodium (mg): 368.3

Baked Cheesecake

Preparation time: 25-30 minutes
Baking time: 25-30 minutes (plus several
   hours chilling)
Yields: 1 cheesecake (8 servings)

2 C cream cheese, softened
1/2 C honey
1 T arrowroot mixed with 1/4 C water
1 t vanilla
1 t orange juice
1 t lemon juice
1 T honey
1 C sour cream or thick yogurt
1 GRAHAM CRACKER CRUST (p. 199)

Beat together the cream cheese and 1/2 C
honey. Mix in the dissolved arrowroot and
the flavorings. Pour into the pie crust and
bake for 20 minutes at 350°. Meanwhile, mix
the 1 T honey with the sour cream. Pour this
over pie and bake an additional 5 to 7
minutes. Chill thoroughly, preferably
overnight. May be topped with PINEAPPLE
BERRY SAUCE (p. 207) or fresh fruit.

Calories: 528.7
Fat (gm): 33.6
Protein (gm): 7.6
Cholesterol (mg): 94.5
Sodium (mg): 457.2

Peach Cobbler

Preparation time: 30-40 minutes
Baking time: 45 minutes
Yields: 8-12 servings

This is a favorite in our family.

1/2 C oil
3 C whole wheat pastry flour
1 C milk
1/2 C honey
1/2 t salt
1/2 t cinnamon
1/2 t nutmeg
2 t baking powder
8 C sliced peeled peaches
2 T arrowroot

Mix oil and honey until smooth. Add milk
and mix. Add salt, spices, baking powder
and flour. Stir only until moistened (mixture
should still be lumpy). Mix peaches and
arrowroot and spread in the bottom of a
9x12 inch pan or 8 individual 4 inch pie
pans. Drop batter by spoonfuls on peaches.
Bake at 350° for 45 minutes. (Individual pie
pans take less time.) May be served with
yogurt or ice cream.

Calories: 398.8
Fat (gm): 11.5
Protein (gm): 7.1
Cholesterol (mg): 1.8
Sodium (mg): 182.9

VARIATIONS: Use other fruit. A favorite of
ours is blackberries.

NOTE: If you want a smoother top, use
$2\frac{1}{2}$ C flour instead of 3 C. If using canned
fruit, drain first.

Shortcut Cobbler

Preparation time: 15-20 minutes
Baking time: 30-40 minutes
Yields: 6 servings

1 quart fruit, drained
2 C purchased whole wheat biscuit mix
1/2 t cinnamon
1/2 t nutmeg

Spread fruit in the bottom of an 8x8 inch
pan. Add spices to biscuit mix and follow
instructions on mix for drop biscuits. Drop
biscuits on fruit and bake at 350° for 30 to 40
minutes.

With peaches:
Calories: 324.7
Fat (gm): 9.1
Protein (gm): 5.4
Cholesterol (mg): 4.3
Sodium (mg): 720.8

Strawberry Shortcake

Preparation time: 25-30 minutes
Baking time: 12-15 minutes
Yields: 6 servings

Joy says, "We use fresh biscuits for our strawberry shortcake. Some people prefer a cake-type shortcake in which case you can make large muffins out of the HONEY SPICE CAKE (p. 188) recipe. As a child, I remember that each summer, usually on an exceptionally hot day, my mother would serve only strawberry shortcake for dinner! She would make a huge double layer biscuit which filled an entire large cookie sheet and use boxes and boxes of berries. What a treat! We don't have them for dinner, but our family likes strawberry shortcake for breakfast during strawberry season."

1 recipe BISCUITS (P.124)
2 baskets strawberries
1/4 C honey

Make the biscuits, baking them 3 high with a larger biscuit on the bottom, then a small biscuit, and a tiny one inch biscuit on top (the inside of a doughnut cutter works well). Bake at the recommended temperature. Depending on how thin you roll them, they may take a little longer to bake. Using heart, star or flower shaped cookie cutters makes them festive. While the biscuits are baking, wash, stem and mash the berries, saving a few for garnishing. Mix well with the honey. When biscuits are done, split them open and spoon berries over the bottom 2 layers but not the top. Our favorite way is to have these plain, but they are good with yogurt, whipped cream or ice cream.

Calories: 224.2
Fat (gm): 1.5
Protein (gm): 6.8
Cholesterol (mg): 2.5
Sodium (mg): 352.3

Apple Crisp

Preparation time: 30-35 minutes
Baking time: 45 minutes
Yields: 12 servings

6 medium apples, grated (about 6 C)
1/4 C honey
1/2 T cinnamon
1/4 C lemon juice (if apples are tart, lemon juice may be omitted)
1 C raisins
$2^1/_2$ C oatmeal or granola
1/2 C whole wheat pastry flour
1 C date sugar
$1^1/_2$ C chopped walnuts
1 t vanilla
1/3 C oil
1 t cinnamon
1/4 t salt
1/4 C water

Mix grated apples, honey, 1/2 t cinnamon, lemon juice and raisins. Press into a 9x12 inch pan. Mix together the rest of the ingredients except the water and spread over the top of the apples. Sprinkle with water. Bake at 375° for about 45 minutes until the apples are tender. Good plain or served with VANILLA ARROWROOT PUDDING (p. 192), ice cream, or yogurt.

Calories: 381.7
Fat (gm): 14.7
Protein (gm): 7.2
Cholesterol (mg): 0
Sodium (mg): 49.5

VARIATIONS: Use other fresh fruits or drained canned fruits. The baking time may vary.

Milk 'n Honey Ice Cream

Preparation time: 45 minutes
Yields: 8 servings

1 quart cream or whole milk
2/3 C honey, warmed to thin
1 T slippery elm powder
2 t vanilla

Mix ingredients together thoroughly and freeze in a half gallon capacity ice cream freezer.

With whole milk:
Calories: 164.1
Fat (gm): 3.8
Protein (gm): 4.25
Cholesterol (mg): 16.5
Sodium (mg): 61.3

VARIATION: Nonfat milk or low fat milk can be substituted for the cream for a much more healthy treat. The texture is not as creamy, but still good.

Maple Moksha

Preparation time: 5-10 minutes
Yields: 2 servings

1 C vanilla ice cream or yogurt
2 T pure maple syrup
2 T slivered almonds or chopped walnuts
**   or pecans**

Serve the ice cream or yogurt in bowls. Top with syrup and then nuts. Enjoy.

Calories: 412.7
Fat (gm): 10.4
Protein (gm): 9.5
Cholesterol (mg): 33.0
Sodium (mg): 125.3

CANDIES AND NUT SNACKS

Ecstasy Nuts

Preparation time: 15 minutes
Roasting time: 45 minutes
Yields: 4 C (16 servings)

1 C whole almonds
1 C cashews, whole or large pieces
1 C walnut or pecan halves
1 C pumpkin or sunflower seeds
1 to 2 T soy sauce

Roast nuts on an ungreased baking sheet in an oven heated to 350°. Begin with the almonds, roasting them for about 15 minutes. Next add the cashews and roast another 10 minutes. Then add walnuts and roast 10 more minutes. Finally, add the seeds, roasting an additional 10 minutes. Remove nuts from oven and test. Cashews should have a brown tinge around the edges. Almonds should have a touch of brown at the very center (they roast from the inside out). The walnuts and seeds should be crisp. If nuts are not done, return to the oven for a few more minutes. Watch carefully as they will burn very quickly after becoming roasted. Remove from oven and add the soy sauce. Stir into the nuts and return to the oven for 5 more minutes. Remove, stir well, allow to cool and store in an airtight jar.

Calories: 207.5
Fat (gm):23.0
Protein (gm): 5.8
Cholesterol (mg): 0
Sodium (mg): 42.2

VARIATION: Any nut or seed combination will work. After being roasted and cooled, the nuts can be mixed with dried fruit or carob chips. The fruit and nut combinations do not last as well and must be eaten within a few days or the nuts will become soft.

Gooey Crispy Chewy Bars

Preparation time: 25-30 minutes (includes cooking)
Yields: 16 bars

Remember Rice Krispies® Bars? Here's a version that doesn't use marshmallows. I have included them in the candy section because they are very sweet and rich.

1 C Fruitsource® (this is made from grape juice and rice syrup and is available in most natural food stores)
1 C honey
1 t vanilla
8 C Brown Rice Crisps®

Mix all ingredients except cereal in a large heavy saucepan (mixture will foam). Cook, stirring constantly until it reaches the firm ball stage (forms a firm ball when dropped into water). Quickly pour over cereal, mix in and pack down into an oiled 8x8 inch pan. You can pack it most efficiently if you butter your hands. The butter keeps the mixture from sticking. Be careful, it is very hot and will easily burn you if it sticks. If you want to make more than this, make the recipe twice. Do not double.

Calories: 76.5
Fat (gm): .5
Protein (gm): 1.0
Cholesterol (mg): 0
Sodium (mg): 52.5

VARIATIONS: Substitute 2 C chopped nuts for 2 C of the cereal or make POPCORN BALLS by substituting popcorn for the cereal. Form into 4 to 6 popcorn balls. These can be wrapped in cellophane for parties.

NOTE: 1 C molasses can be substituted for Fruitsource®, resulting in a softer bar.

Carob Candy

Preparation time: 25-30 minutes (includes cooking)
Yields: 32 squares

1^1/$_3$ C honey
2/3 C peanut butter or other nut butter
2 C carob powder, sifted if lumpy
1 C shredded coconut
1 C mixed nuts (such as almonds, cashews, walnuts, etc.)
1 C seeds (such as sunflower, pumpkin and sesame)

Heat honey and peanut butter in a heavy sauce pan or double boiler until liquid. Watch this carefully as it burns easily. Add carob and mix well. Stir often to avoid sticking or burning. This will be difficult to stir. Add nuts and again mix well. Pat into a 9 inch square pan. This is incredibly good and habit forming.

With almonds and sunseeds:
Calories: 203.8
Fat (gm): 11.0
Protein (gm): 3.6
Cholesterol (mg): 0
Sodium (mg): 5.7

Honey Spice Nuts

Preparation time: 35-40 minutes (includes
    cooking)
Yields: about $1^1/_4$ pounds (32 pieces)

$1^1/_2$ C honey
3 T water
1 T cinnamon
1/2 t salt
1/2 t nutmeg
1/2 t vanilla
3 to $4^1/_2$ C nuts (whole or
    pieces)—walnuts, almonds, pecans,
    cashews

Combine all ingredients except vanilla and
nuts. Cook over medium heat, stirring
occasionally until it reaches the firm ball
stage, about 245°. (If you don't have a
thermometer, to test for firm ball stage, drop
a few drops from a spoon into cold water. If
it forms into a firm ball which holds its
shape, it is done.) Do not overcook. Remove
from heat, add vanilla and nuts. (The amount
of nuts depends upon how nutty you want
the finished candy.) Stir until mixture gets
creamy. Turn out on a greased glass or
ceramic plate or pan. Let cool and cut into
squares.

32 pieces:
Calories: 134.9
Fat (gm): 7.3
Protein (gm): 1.7
Cholesterol (mg): 0
Sodium (mg): 35.6

NOTE: For a firmer candy, cook until it
reaches the hard ball stage, about 250°.

FROSTINGS, FILLINGS, AND DESSERT SAUCES

Cream Cheese Frosting

Preparation time: 10-15 minutes
Yields: enough for one 2 layer cake or one
    9x12 inch loaf cake

1/2 pound cream cheese, softened to
    room temperature
1/4 C butter, softened
3/8 C honey
$1^1/_2$ t vanilla extract

Cream together the cream cheese and butter,
then add the honey and vanilla. (This is
easiest to make with an electric beater.) Mix
well.

12 servings:
Calories: 136.3
Fat (gm): 10.3
Protein (gm): 1.6
Cholesterol (mg): 32.4
Sodium (mg): 98.2

Broiled Topping (For Cakes)

Preparation time: 10 minutes
Yields: about 1 C

3 T butter, melted
2 T milk
1/2 C shredded coconut
1/3 C honey
1/4 C chopped nuts

Mix ingredients and spread over the top of a
warm cake. Make slashes in the top of the
cake for the mixture to seep into the cake.
Broil until it bubbles, about 3 minutes. Watch
carefully so that it doesn't burn.

1/9 recipe:
Calories: 180.0
Fat (gm): 13.2
Protein (gm): 1.7
Cholesterol (mg): 11.2
Sodium (mg): 48.2

Nona's Tangy Tastebud Tantalizing Carob Frosting

Preparation time: 10-15 minutes
Yields: enough for an 8 inch square cake

8 ounces cream cheese, softened
1/3 C honey
1/4 C carob powder, sifted

Blend cream cheese and honey together until creamed and smooth. Sift the carob. (It is very important to sift the carob or else the frosting will be lumpy.) Stir the carob into the cream cheese and honey mixture until fully mixed.

1/9 recipe:
Calories: 140.6
Fat (gm): .8
Protein (gm): 2.2
Cholesterol (mg): 28.6
Sodium (mg): 76.5

Carob Syrup

Preparation time: 10 minutes
Cooking time: 5-15 minutes
Yields: 3/4 C

1/3 C honey
3/4 C milk
3/4 C roasted carob powder, sifted
1 t vanilla or 1/2 t mint extract

Mix honey and milk in a heavy saucepan or double boiler. Add carob powder. Cook slowly until close to the desired thickness, stirring frequently (it will thicken more as it cools). For a syrup to flavor milk, cook about 5 minutes (use 3 to 4 t for a glass of milk). For a topping for ice cream, etc., cook about 15 minutes. Remove from heat and stir in the vanilla or mint. Store in a covered jar in the refrigerator.

1 Tablespoon:
Calories: 64.3
Fat (gm): .3
Protein (gm): .8
Cholesterol (mg): 1.1
Sodium (mg): 8.8

Honey Butter Sauce

Preparation time: 10 minutes
Yields: about 1 C

1/3 C butter
3/4 C honey
1 t lemon juice

Cream the butter and gradually beat in the honey. Add the lemon juice and chill. Serve on CAROB HONEY CAKE (p. 189), CRAN-BERRY PUDDING (p. 194), WAFFLES (p.140), FRENCH TOAST (p. 140), or pancakes.

1 Tablespoon:
Calories: 96.5
Fat (gm): 4.4
Protein (gm): trace
Cholesterol (mg): 4.1
Sodium (mg): 17.3

Lemon Sauce

Preparation time: 15 minutes
Cooking time: 5 minutes
Yields: about 1 C

This sauce will bring a dry cake back to life and is also good on pie.

1/2 C honey
1 T arrowroot
3/4 C water
1 T butter
1/4 t grated lemon rind
2 t lemon juice

Combine honey, arrowroot and water in a heavy saucepan. Heat on low, stirring constantly. When sauce is thick (approximately 5 minutes), remove from heat and add all other ingredients. Stir well. Serve on APPLE PIE (p. 196) or TURNOVERS (p. 197), GINGERBREAD (p. 191) or cake.

2 Tablespoons:
Calories: 82.4
Fat (gm): 1.5
Protein (gm): trace
Cholesterol (mg): 4.1
Sodium (mg): 17.3

Spiced Cream And Honey Sauce

Preparation time: 15-20 minutes (includes cooking)
Yields: 1$\frac{1}{3}$ C

2/3 C honey
2/3 C heavy cream
1/4 t cinnamon
1/8 t cloves
1/8 t allspice
1/8 t nutmeg

Heat honey in a deep saucepan (it will foam) and bring to a hard boil. Remove from the heat and stir in the cream and spices. Return to heat, stirring until the sauce just barely reaches the boiling point. Remove from heat immediately. Overcooking will cause the cream to curdle! (It tastes good anyway, but doesn't look as appetizing.) Serve on PANCAKES (p. 138), WAFFLES (p. 140), APPLE PIE (p. 196), or FRITTERS (p.126).

2 Tablespoons:
Calories: 114.4
Fat (gm): 5.1
Protein (gm): .3
Cholesterol (mg): 20.5
Sodium (mg): 6.9

Steamed Pudding Sauce

Preparation time: 15-20 minutes (includes cooking)
Yields: 1 C

1 C honey
1/2 C butter
1/2 C cream
1 t vanilla

Heat all ingredients except vanilla in a double boiler until very hot, stirring frequently. Remove from heat and stir in vanilla.

2 Tablespoons:
Calories: 145.5
Fat (gm): 8.4
Protein (gm): .1
Cholesterol (mg): 27.0
Sodium (mg): 65.5

Pineapple Berry Sauce

Preparation time: 20-25 minutes (includes cooking)
Yields: 3 C

1 C unsweetened pineapple juice
1/4 C honey
1 T arrowroot
2 to 3 C blackberries

Combine juice, honey, and arrowroot in a double boiler and cook, stirring frequently until sauce is thick. Remove from heat and add fruit. Use on HONEY CAKE (p. 188), CHEESECAKE (p. 200), yogurt, ice cream or pancakes.

1/4 C:
Calories: 50.3
Fat (gm): .1
Protein (gm): .3
Cholesterol (mg): 0
Sodium (mg): .6

VARIATION: Any unsweetened juice can be substituted for the pineapple juice (except straight lemon juice). Any berries, cherries, nectarines, plums, pineapples or peaches can be substituted for the blackberries. Fruit can be raw or cooked in the sauce.

Apricot Filling

Preparation time: 15 minutes
Cooking time: 30 minutes
Yields: about 2 C

1 C dried apricots, minced
1/2 C honey
2/3 C water

Mix ingredients and cook on low for 30 minutes until thick. Cool and blend until smooth. Use for filling in FILLED COOKIES (p. 184) or on CHEESECAKE (p. 200) or as a filling in muffins, cupcakes, or SWEET BO-PE (p.192).

1 Tablespoon:
Calories: 25.9
Fat (gm): 0
Protein (gm): .1
Cholesterol (mg): 0
Sodium (mg): .7

Dried Fruit Filling

Preparation time: 15 minutes (includes cooking)
Yields: 2³/₄ C

2 C ground or minced mixed dried fruit
1/2 C honey
2 T lemon juice
1/4 C water

Mix all ingredients and cook over low heat, stirring constantly until thick—about 15 minutes. Use for filling in FILLED COOKIES (p. 184) or on CHEESECAKE (p. 200) or as a filling in muffins, cupcakes, or SWEET BO-PE (p. 192).

1 Tablespoon:
Calories: 35.4
Fat (gm): trace
Protein (gm): .2
Cholesterol (mg): 0
Sodium (mg): 2.0

Milk Products

MILK PRODUCTS

ABOUT MILK PRODUCTS

LIQUID MILK is available in many different forms. This section will mention the kinds most frequently found in the United States and those called for in the recipes in this cookbook.

CERTIFIED RAW MILK is milk that is guaranteed to have been produced and distributed under conditions which conform to high standards. Raw milk can also be purchased directly from farmers. Although this is often the least expensive and best flavored milk, it may not be safe for human consumption due to bacterial contamination. Raw milks must be scalded before making yeast breads, yogurt or cheese.

PASTEURIZED MILK has been heated under controlled conditions to kill any bacteria which may be present in the milk. There are vitamin and enzyme losses when the milk is so heated.

HOMOGENIZED MILK is the most common form of milk sold in grocery stores. Through homogenization, the milk is mechanically treated to break up the fat into smaller globules which are permanently dispersed in a fine emulsion throughout the milk. After being so treated, the cream no longer separates from the milk.

Milks are FORTIFIED by adding nutrients not normally found in them. The most common nutrient added to milk is Vitamin D. Milk can also be found that is fortified with an additive that makes the milk digestible for those people who are lactose intolerant.

Milks are also found with varying amounts of FAT: whole milk (which has no fat removed); low fat (which has 2 % fat remaining);1% (with 1% of the fat still in the milk) and nonfat (with all the fat removed).

GOAT'S MILK is said to be more easily digestible than cow's milk, and doesn't usually cause the allergic reactions in young children so frequently encountered with cow's milk. The cream doesn't separate so mechanical homogenization is not necessary. Some goat's milk is quite mild in flavor and some quite strong. The flavor seems to depend on the breed of the goat, what they are fed, and whether the buck is near. The following is a comparison of the nutritional value of cow and goat milk.

Nutritional Comparison Between Cow and Goat Milk:

1 cup serving:	Cow	Goat
Calories	160.0	165.0
Fat (gm)	9.0	10.0
Protein (gm)	9.0	10.0
Calcium (mg)	288.0	315.0
Iron (mg)	0.1	0.2
Vit. A (units)	350.0	390.0
Vit. C (mg)	2.0	2.0

EVAPORATED MILK has had slightly more than half the water removed. It is sold in cans and requires no refrigeration until opened.

SWEETENED CONDENSED MILK has had water removed and sugar added. To make a natural substitute for this, refer to the recipes in this section.

All of the above milks except sweetened condensed milk can be used with success in the recipes in this cookbook. If a specific type of milk is needed, the recipe will indicate which type to use.

DRIED MILK comes in two forms: instant and non-instant. Although most dried milk is nonfat, some stores carry a dried whole milk which can be reconstituted into a full fat milk. The recipes in this cookbook call for nonfat dried milk. Non-instant dried milk can be purchased from natural and health food stores. It is dried at a lower heat without as much additional processing as instant dried milk. Besides the nutritional benefits from less heat and less processing, the milk has a better flavor. It is harder to reconstitute, which is why the special treatments to make instant milk were developed. When dried milk is purchased in a grocery store it will

most likely be the instant type. Unless a recipe specifies, the two types of dried milk are interchangeable in these recipes, but non-instant is preferable. Reconstituted dried milk can be used in any of the recipes in place of fresh milk, although there may be a loss of flavor in some recipes.

CULTURED MILK PRODUCTS such as buttermilk, yogurt, sour cream and kefir are made by adding a culture of healthful bacteria to milk and creating the right environment for the bacteria to grow. Included are recipes for some more frequently used cultured milk products. The term buttermilk also refers to what is left after butter is made from cream. Recipes calling for buttermilk in this cookbook need the cultured type.

BUTTER is available sweet (or unsalted) and salted. Sweet butter doesn't keep as well and should be frozen if not used immediately. Although butter has a taste that most people prefer over oil, butter is not nearly as healthful. For a spread that combines oil and butter, refer to BUTTER-OIL SPREAD (p.153). Ghee is a clarified butter which is used in East Indian cooking.

CHEESE is a coagulated milk product that may or may not be aged. Rennet is an extract from the stomach lining of calves used to coagulate milk into cheese or thicken milk into pudding. More and more cheeses are available without rennet, not so much as a service to vegetarians but because the vegetable coagulants are cheaper than rennet. Imported cheeses still usually contain rennet. Recipes for simple types of fresh (not aged) cheese are included in this book. In general, stay away from processed cheeses; for example, American process cheese contains many chemicals and not much real cheese.

Cheeses should be refrigerated in airtight containers. If your cheese molds, in most cases the mold can be cut off and the remainder of the cheese will still be edible. After removing the mold, place the cheese in a clean plastic bag or container.

RECIPES

Sour Milk

Preparation time: 5 minutes
Yields: 1 C

1 C milk
1 to 2 t lemon juice or vinegar

Stir lemon juice into the milk. Wait for a few minutes and use in recipes calling for sour milk.

Calories: 122.5
Fat (gm): 4.4
Protein (gm): 8.8
Cholesterol (mg): 18.0
Sodium (mg): 123.5

Sweetened Condensed Milk Substitute

Preparation time: 10-15 minutes
Yields: $1^1/_3$ C

$1^1/_2$ C non-instant dry milk or
   $1^2/_3$ C instant powdered milk
2/3 C fresh milk
1/3 C honey

Mix the above ingredients until smooth. Use this in the same amounts as called for in the recipes you are adapting to natural foods cookery.

Calories: 837.4
Fat (gm): 2.8
Protein (gm): 57.6
Cholesterol (mg): 37.0
Sodium (mg): 810.1

Ghee

Preparation time: 20-30 minutes

Ghee is a clarified butter which is used in East Indian cooking.

2 pounds sweet butter

To prepare, bring butter to a boil over medium heat. Remove from heat and let sit for one to two minutes. Skim off the solids on the top. Bring to a boil again and repeat the process two more times. Finally, let the ghee sit for 10 minutes and then pour slowly through cheesecloth, letting the sediment in the bottom remain in the pan. Ghee does not need to be refrigerated.

NOTE: Because of what is lost in sedimenting and skimming, nutritional analysis is not possible.

NOTE: Salted butter can be used but will have more sediment as the salt is also removed in the process.

Yogurt

Preparation time: 20-30 minutes
Cooking time: 6-8 hours (incubation)
Yields: about 2 quarts

2 quarts milk
1½ C powdered milk
2 T yogurt
1 16 ounce can evaporated milk
(optional)

The yogurt in the above recipe is a "starter". The culture will grow and turn your milk into yogurt. Use an unprocessed plain yogurt with no additives for your starter. It is not necessary to buy a special culture; any fresh active unpasteurized yogurt will work. The yogurt you make can be used as the culture for your next batch as long as it doesn't smell yeasty or moldy and is used within 5 to 7 days.

Blend the milks until smooth. Heat slowly, stirring frequently until the milk scalds (tiny bubbles begin to rise to the surface around the edge of the pan). Remove from heat and allow to cool until you can hold your finger in it for a slow count to 10. (Cooler milk makes sweeter yogurt; hotter milk makes it more sour.) When the milk is lukewarm, add a little of it to the starter. Stir until smooth and then add back to the pot of milk. Stir it in thoroughly, stirring only in one direction. (Stirring in only one direction may be only superstition but supposedly has an effect on the structure of the yogurt.) Place a clean absorbent towel over the top of the pan (or several layers of paper towels), being careful to not touch the yogurt. Wrap the pan up in a heavy blanket and set it in a warm place in your kitchen. If you do not have a warm spot, use a cooler which insulates to warm as well as cold, or the milk yogurt mixture can be poured into clean mason jars and kept in a warm water bath. DO NOT DISTURB OR MOVE it for 6 to 8 hours. Remove wrapping and refrigerate.

Calories: 134.5
Fat (gm): 3.9
Protein (gm): 10.6
Cholesterol (mg): 18.4
Sodium (mg): 156.4

NOTE:
- If the yogurt has separated, it has over "cooked." Add less starter or incubate for a shorter period of time.
- If the yogurt doesn't "set up" it may be that the milk was too cold or too hot when culture was added, or it wasn't kept warm enough, or the culture was not good.
- Sometimes a yogurt culture will go bad by picking up a yeast or bacteria from the air. If this happens, begin with a new culture.
- Don't make bread on the same day or even the day before as the yogurt will pick up the yeast from the air and smell and taste like yeast.

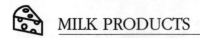

TIPS ON COOKING WITH YOGURT

- Fold it into other foods, do not beat it or it may separate.
- Cook yogurt at low temperatures so that it doesn't separate.
- Beating in a little flour will help it smooth out before adding it to a recipe.
- Yogurt can be substituted for sour cream in most recipes.
- Always use a clean spoon when removing yogurt from a container and level out the yogurt remaining in the container. This keeps the yogurt from seeping.

Yogurt Cheese

Preparation time: 15 minutes
Draining time: 1-2 hours
Yields: varies

This is similar to cream cheese and can be substituted for cream cheese in the recipes in this cookbook.

1/2 batch of YOGURT
cheesecloth

Make a square of cheesecloth that is about 3 layers thick. Place the yogurt on the cheese cloth and pull up the corners. Tie securely and let drain into a bowl or the sink. If the whey that drains at first is thick, it may be used instead of buttermilk or sour milk for baking.

NOTE: Yield varies, making nutritional analysis not possible.

Farmer's (Cottage) Cheese

Preparation time: 20-25 minutes
Draining time: 60 minutes
Yields: about 3/4 C

There are as many recipes for farmer's cheese as there are farmers. This one works reasonably consistently.

1 quart milk
3 T lemon juice
salt to taste (optional)

Heat the milk and add lemon juice. Stir well. Turn off heat and let milk sit a few minutes while it curdles. Heat slowly again to separate the curds and the whey. When lukewarm, put it in a muslin bag or several layers of cheesecloth. Hang the bag up and let it drip. Squeeze for a dry cheese. This cheese is very perishable and should be eaten within 2 to 3 days.

NOTE: nutritional analysis not possible due to whey nutrient loss.

NOTE: This cheese can be used in any recipe in this cookbook calling for cottage or ricotta cheese or it can be eaten as is. The texture of this cheese will vary depending on how hot the milk was heated. If raw, unprocessed milk is used (instead of pasteurized), it can be left at room temperature in an open bowl (covered with a clean cloth). The milk will clabber (turn solid) in 24 to 48 hours; then it can be gently heated as above. You will not need to add the lemon juice because the milk has already coagulated. Do not try this method with pasteurized or homogenized milk because toxic bacteria will develop.

Nuts & Seeds

NUTS & SEEDS

This section does not contain recipes, but
does contain nutritional information on nuts
and seeds and also ways of processing nuts
to obtain the form called for in the recipes in
this book (for example, blanching almonds).

COMPARISON OF PROTEIN VALUES

Source of Protein	Grams of Protein per 100 grams edible portion (% protein)	Approximate percent of protein which is completely utilizable (NPU)	Grams of complete protein per 100 gram portion (% protein x NPU)
Almonds	19	30%	5.7
Black Walnuts	20.5	50%	10.3
Brazils	14.3	50%	7.2
Cashews	17.2	60%	10.2
English Walnuts	15.2	36%	5.5
Peanuts	26	36%	8.4
Sunflower Seeds	24	60%	14.4
Tofu (soybean curd)	8	60%	4.8
Cottage Cheese	17	75%	12.8

Nuts become rancid very easily and must be stored carefully. Storing them in their shells is preferable, as the shell protects them from light and exposure to air. However, this takes much more room and time as the nuts need to be shelled before use. We keep our nuts under refrigeration, and in the freezer for long-term storage. After defrosting, do not refreeze as the flavor will suffer. Freezing not only prolongs the nutritional life of the nuts but it prevents any insect development.

When sorting nuts, discard any that are moldy or shriveled as the taste and nutritional content may be adversely affected.

ALMONDS are nutritionally some of the best nuts. They are a good source of thiamin (B1), niacin, iron, phosphorus, potassium and protein. They have more riboflavin and calcium than other nuts.

Blanching almonds:
Pour boiling water over shelled almonds and let them sit for no more than a minute. You do not want to cook them. Drain the nuts. Rinse in cold water and rub off the skins. The result will be a white skinned almond which has a better taste and consistency for some recipes such as SPICED HOT MILK (p. 33) or NUTMILK (p. 30).

BRAZIL NUTS are well supplied with unsaturated fatty acids but low in carbohydrates. They contain enough extra tryptophan and methionine (essential amino acids) to make them a valuable complement for bean protein. Brazil nuts can be more easily shelled by pouring boiling water over the nuts and letting them steep in it for 15 to 20 minutes.

CASHEWS are only sold in their shelled state because the shell is poisonous. They are higher in carbohydrates and lower in fats than other nuts. Cashews are more easily digestible than many other nuts.

CHESTNUTS are starchy rather than oily and lower in protein, fat and calories than other nuts. They are usually available only in the winter and should not be confused with water chestnuts. Chestnuts are perishable at room temperature but will keep several months in the refrigerator in ventilated plastic bags. Shelled, blanched chestnuts can be frozen for longer storage. Chestnuts can be blanched by first removing the shell and then following the directions for blanching almonds.

Roasting chestnuts:
With a sharp knife on a cutting board, slash the shells on the flat side. Then place the nuts, cut sides up, on a baking sheet. Roast at 400° until tender (about 20 minutes). Insert a fork through the cut to test for tenderness. When tender, remove both the outer shell and the inner skin, which is bitter.

COCONUTS are lower in protein than other nuts. They are higher in calories and saturated fats. When picking out a coconut, choose one that has no cracks and when shaken, the milk sloshes around inside. Coconuts with cracks or no milk are apt to be dry, moldy, or rancid.

To shell a ripe coconut, puncture the depressions in the end (there will be 3 of them) with a large nail and a hammer. Drain off the liquid through the holes and drink it or use it in cooking. The nut can either be cracked open with a hammer and the inside pried out, or the nut can be placed in a pan and baked at 350° for 12 to 15 minutes to loosen the nutmeat from the sides. Scoop out the nutmeat and if desired, peel off the outer skin with a vegetable peeler. Grate the coconut or process in a food processor.

Fresh coconuts in the shell retain a good quality up to a month in the refrigerator. Fresh coconut meat and coconut milk can be kept up to a week in airtight containers in the refrigerator.

Toasting coconut:
Spread grated coconut on a baking sheet and place in a 350° oven for about 10 minutes. Stir frequently.
Reconstituting dried coconut:
Cover dried coconut with milk and refrigerate for 6 to 8 hours. Drain before using.

Coconut milk:
Combine the grated meat of a coconut with its natural milk. Place in a 325° oven and let it heat thoroughly. Remove and cool, strain and put solids in cheese cloth to squeeze out all the remaining liquid. Refrigerate the coconut milk as soon as it is made, as it spoils easily. The coconut cream will rise to the top and form a hard cake within 24 hours (be sure to refrigerate).

FILBERTS OR HAZELNUTS are a good source of minerals. The skin of the filbert can be removed by roasting for 10 to 15 minutes at 300°, stirring occasionally. Cool slightly and slip skins off.

MACADAMIA NUTS are usually sold shelled in the continental United States. They contain a high percentage of fat but are a good source of calcium, phosphorus and iron.

PEANUTS are considered nuts but are actually members of the legume family (same family as beans and peas). Peanuts are lower in iron than other nuts and seeds. They can be blanched as in BLANCHING ALMONDS (p. 217) or roasted.

Roasting peanuts (and other nuts):
Spread in a single layer on a cookie sheet. Roast at 350° for 15 to 20 minutes, stirring occasionally.

PECANS are high in unsaturated fats and therefore calories.

PINE NUTS (PIGÑOLIAS OR PIÑON NUTS) are small, rich-tasting nuts which are excellent additions to many dishes including RICE PILAF (p. 111), YOGI RICE (p. 111), SPICED HOT MILK (p. 33), CURRIED VEGETABLES (p. 95), and CHINCH BHAT (p. 112).

PISTACHIOS are members of the cashew family. They are higher in potassium and iron than most nuts and contain high amounts of protein.

PUMPKIN SEEDS or **SQUASH SEEDS** can be processed from the squash or pumpkins which you use for other dishes (or "jack 'o

lanterns"). Remove the membranes and wash seeds. Seeds can then be dried (thoroughly to prevent mold) or roasted. To roast, spread in a single layer on a cookie sheet and roast, stirring frequently, at 300° for 15 to 20 minutes. Watch carefully so that they do not scorch as they will continue to cook after they are out of the oven. After cooling, the seeds can be shelled.

SESAME SEEDS have a high oil content (45 to 63%) and are 16 to 32% protein. Sesame seeds are available in two forms, hulled and unhulled. Although we are not proponents of hulled foods, sesame seeds are more easily digestible and easier to use in the hulled form.

SUNFLOWER SEEDS are probably the most nutritious nuts, containing more protein, phosphorus, iron, sodium, potassium, thiamin and riboflavin than most nuts or seeds.

WALNUTS (Black) are not usually available commercially. If harvested from trees, remove the hulls immediately and dry well. The shells are hard to crack, but the taste of the nuts is worth the effort. Soaking in hot water (see BRAZIL NUTS) may help in the cracking. Black walnuts can be substituted for walnuts in any of the recipes in the cookbook. They do have a stronger taste, so you may want to reduce the amount used.

WALNUTS (English) contain about 15% protein and 16% carbohydrate. They have a milder flavor than black walnuts and are easier to shell. They should also be removed from the hull right after harvesting and dried. The hulls contain a dye so your hands may turn brown if the nuts are fresh.

Toasting walnuts:
Drop the nutmeats into rapidly boiling water and boil for 3 minutes. Drain well. (This removes an acid which some people find objectionable). Spread nuts evenly in a shallow pan and bake at 350° for 12-15 minutes until golden brown.

Herbs & Spices

HERBS & SPICES

Herbs and spices are the seeds, roots, leaves, flowers, and barks of plants that are used for flavorings, teas, beverages and herbal curatives. Natural flavorings (such as vanilla extract) are derivatives of herbs or of other plants and fruits.

Equivalents

1/4 t dry herbs = 1 t fresh herbs

Releasing Flavors

Herbs usually need to be heated (especially dry ones) before they will release much of their flavor into the food. Be careful that you do not add too much, because the heat brings out the flavor of the herbs in the dish you are seasoning. If a dish containing herbs is going to be cooked more than an hour, add the herbs for only the last 30 to 45 minutes, as the flavors will be lost somewhat with more cooking. Freshly ground spices are more potent than those which have been sitting around for a while.

Most of the flavors in herbs and spices come from their oils. Rubbing a leaf herb between your fingers before adding it to a dish or grinding whole herbs in a mortar will help release the flavors. Certain kinds of dishes (such as curries) will direct you to put the seeds and whole spices in hot oil for a few minutes to release the flavor. This is a good technique for any recipe that is stir-fried, sauteed or braised.

Storage

Spices and herbs deteriorate when exposed to light, air and heat, so they need to be stored in airtight containers and be kept in a dark, cool place such as a closed cupboard. Spice racks near the stove may be pretty and convenient, but herbs and spices quickly deteriorate near the heat.

Drying

Herbs can be dried by tying them in bunches and hanging them upside down or spreading them on screens. To retain the oils and flavors, dry them inside in a room that is dry and dark.

Buying Herbs And Spices

The least expensive way to buy herbs and spices is in bulk from a natural food store or herb store. (Bulk does not mean "lots", it means without the jars and other packaging.) If possible, don't buy more than you can use in a month or two and buy them from a store that has a good turnover so the herbs and spices you purchase are fresh. Whole seeds and spices last much longer than ground ones, and therefore can be purchased in larger containers.

In this section we have included some favorite herb and spice blends which are called for in the recipes in this cookbook.

If you are unsure what herb to use in a particular dish you are cooking, rub a little of the herb between your fingers and smell it. The smell will help you decide if the flavors will blend.

HERB AND SPICE BLENDS

Italian Seasoning

1/3 t thyme
1/3 t basil
1/2 t oregano
pinch tarragon
pinch cumin (optional)

Mix thoroughly and use as directed in recipes. Store what you don't use in a tightly covered jar in a dark, cool place.

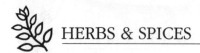

Simple Salad Herbs

Equal parts of:
   oregano
   basil
   thyme
Optional : Add 1/4 to 1/2 part
   ground cumin
   savory
   dill weed
   parsley

Mix thoroughly and use in salad dressings or sprinkle on green salads. Store what you don't use in a tightly covered jar in a dark, cool place.

Salad Herbs

1 part each:
   lemon thyme (or regular thyme)
   summer savory
4 parts each:
   marjoram
   basil
   tarragon
   parsley
   dried celery tops
   chervil
1 part each:
   oregano
   thyme
optional: 1/4 to 1/2 part
   ground cumin
   dill weed

Mix thoroughly and use in salad dressings or sprinkle on green salads. Store what you don't use in a tightly covered jar in a dark, cool place.

Vegetable Herbs

1 part each:
   marjoram
   basil
   chervil
   parsley
Pinch of:
   savory
   thyme

Mix thoroughly and use as directed in recipes. Store what you don't use in a tightly covered jar in a dark, cool place.

Soup Herbs

2 parts each:
   parsley
   chervil
   basil
   marjoram
   dried celery tops
1 part each:
   thyme
   summer savory
   sage
   rosemary
   dried lemon peel

Mix thoroughly and use in steamed vegetables or rice, or as directed in the recipes. Store what you don't use in a tightly covered jar in a dark, cool place.

Garam Masala (Used in East Indian Cooking)

seeds of 2 cardamom pods
1/2 t whole peppercorns
1 two inch piece of cinnamon stick
1 t whole cloves
2 t whole cumin seed

Grind as finely as possible with mortar and pestle, blender or spice grinder. Use as directed in recipes. Store what you don't use in a tightly covered jar in a dark, cool place.

Curry Powder

5 cloves
6 cardamom seeds
1 one inch piece of cinnamon stick
1/2 t black mustard seed
1/2 t cumin seed
1 t turmeric
1 t ground coriander
1 T finely minced fresh ginger or 1/2 t
**   ground ginger**

Grind as finely as possible with mortar and pestle, blender or spice grinder. Use 1 to $1^1/_2$ t to one quart vegetables or fruit or as directed in recipes. Store what you don't use in a tightly covered jar in a dark, cool place. The blend made with fresh ginger will not keep unless refrigerated, and then only for a week or so.

Gomasio

This is a tasty seasoned salt which will help cut down the salt you use to flavor your meal and which will add calcium and other nutrients to your meal.

5 parts sesame seeds
1 part sea salt

Wash seeds to remove any dirt. Do this by placing seeds in a bowl and pouring cold water over the seeds. Agitate and pour into a strainer. Repeat several times. On the last washing, pour the water and seeds out slowly so any sediment remains in the bowl.

Toast the salt by placing it in a heavy frying pan over a high flame. Move salt around with a wooden spoon or paddle for 5 minutes or so. Then place salt in a suribachi (a serrated or grooved grinding bowl). A mortar and pestle or bowl and spoon can also be used, but not a blender as the oils are not properly released due to the speed.

Toast the seeds in the frying pan on high heat, moving them around quickly for 10 to 15 minutes. They are done when they can be easily crushed between two fingers. Place the seeds in the suribachi with the salt.

Grind the seeds and salt until about 80% of the seeds have been reduced to a fine powder. Store in a tightly covered jar, refrigerated. Use as salt.

Dried Grated Orange or Lemon Peel

Keep the unblemished parts of the peels of organically grown lemons or oranges. Cut the rinds into long strips and dry in a warm dry spot. These can be dried in a food dehydrator, but it is not necessary. When the peels are dry enough that they snap when bent, grind them into a powder in a spice grinder or blender. Use as dried lemon or orange peel.

Vegie Herb Bouillon

This is a very concentrated browned soup stock which can be used to flavor soups and casseroles. It can be used in any recipe calling for bouillon cubes.

1 C grated carrots
$1^1/_2$ C grated sweet potatoes
1 C grated parsnips
1 C finely minced bell pepper
3 T honey
water
1/4 t each:
**   basil**
**   thyme**
**   oregano**
3 bay leaves
1 T salt

Mix the vegetables. Spread one third of them on the bottom of an unoiled covered baking pan. Drizzle with 1 T honey. Repeat with vegetables and honey twice again. Cover and bake at 350°, stirring occasionally until the mixture becomes dark brown. This takes $1^1/_2$ to 2 hours. If the vegetables begin to dry out, sprinkle with water and stir. Transfer mixture to a saucepan. Add 1 to $1^1/_2$ C water, herbs and salt. Simmer covered, stirring occasionally, until the mixture forms a rich, brown, thick syrup. Strain. Freeze in an ice cube tray until solid. Remove from tray and

store in a freezer container or zip lock plastic
bag. Use cubes as needed.

NOTE: If the mixture is very dry or thick, add
a little more water. This is easier to make in a
mini crockpot than on the stove. Bake
vegetables as directed and then transfer them
to the crockpot for simmering. Simmer
overnight.

VARIATION: Substitute for the oregano:
thyme, and basil, 1/4 t each of ground
cloves, allspice, and cinnamon. This will
have a Greek flavor.

Canning & Preserving

CANNING & PRESERVING

This section contains some basic information about the long-term storage of food. Step-by-step instructions for canning fruit and making jams and jellies are included, along with briefer discussions of pressure canning, freezing food, storing fresh produce, and drying fruits and vegetables. More information about food storage can be found in KITCHEN WAYS (p 17).

Canning

Canning (or perhaps it should be called "jarring," since that is what home canners use) is a method by which food and its container are sterilized. The high temperatures involved in the process kill microorganisms which might cause spoilage or disease, and also de-activate all enzymes in the food, thereby arresting the natural processes of decay.

Canned food may be kept at room temperature (preferably in a dark, cool cupboard), allowing for easy storage throughout the year and eliminating the cost of constant refrigeration which would otherwise be necessary. Canned foods are easy to transport. The quality of the food is reduced by canning; since all the enzymes are killed, it is, in a sense, lifeless food. Fresh food has much more life-energy, but it is, of course, not always available or affordable. Canning is one way to preserve summer's surplus for winter use.

There are two basic ways to can food. The WATER BATH method involves a lower temperature process suitable for fruits (including tomatoes) and certain other foods which have a high acid content. Water bath canning doesn't require a lot of fancy equipment or jars and good results can be realized even by those with little or no experience. PRESSURE CANNING is a high temperature process which can be used to preserve vegetables and some other foods. Low acid foods require processing at very high temperatures to kill the enzymes and microorganisms in them, so canning jars and a pressure canner are used. Since certain of these microorganisms can be very poisonous

to human beings, it is necessary that great care be taken in canning low acid foods. Before they are eaten, foods that are pressure canned at home must be brought to a boil and cooked for 20 minutes or used in a dish that requires cooking at a high temperature for 30 minutes or more (e.g., casseroles).

When deciding to get involved in canning, it is important to understand the expenditure of time, energy and resources that it requires. All produce must be of good quality, and a fair amount of preparation of the produce is required before it can be canned. The canning process itself requires a great deal of energy. It is important not to overwork yourself or try to take shortcuts. If you over-extend yourself, it will show in the results. In hot weather it is best to work in the early morning or late in the evening to avoid overheating yourself.

Canning Equipment

The most readily available JARS are mason jars with a lid (seal) and band. Check even new ones for cracks or flaws in the jars or chipped or cracked lips. The band should be flawless, rustless and without dents or deformations. Lids should have no imperfections in the rubber or dents around the sides. DO NOT REUSE LIDS. Look at the inside of a used one and you will see the mark made by the jar's lip when sealed. If you tried to reseal it the lip would be in a different place and the warping generally caused by opening would keep it from sealing. Discard all jars, lids and bands which are not perfect, as they will most likely cause the jar to not seal. It isn't worth the danger and wasted food to try to make inadequate equipment do the job.

Jars do not need to be sterilized; the water bath or pressure canner does that during the course of canning. When hot packing food, it is wise to have the jar warm. Never pour boiling hot food into a jar on a cold metal or tile surface, as it will probably crack. Set the jars on a towel or a rack when filling with hot food, and preheat them with warm water first.

When choosing news jars, think about what you are going to can, and for whom. Do you eat a lot of fruit at one time or just a little (half-gallon versus pint jars)? If you think you might be using the jars for freezing at some time, get tapered jars that give the frozen food room to expand without breaking the jar. Wide mouth jars are more convenient for cold packing large pieces of fruit, as you can reach further down into the jar, but the lids are more expensive.

If you are using used jars, choose those with lips that screw into a wide or regular mouth band. Be aware that non-mason jars crack more readily and cannot withstand being placed in a boiling water bath. If using them, place them into a lukewarm bath. Use only mason canning jars for pressure canning because of the greater stress involved.

There are a couple different kinds of LIDS on the market. The ones with enamel inside are less apt to corrode or discolor from the action of acid of the food inside the jar. This is particularly important with tomatoes.

A WATER BATH CANNER or a pot must be large enough to allow jars on a rack to be covered with 1 inch of water, while still leaving room for the water to boil.

A PRESSURE CANNER is needed for canning vegetables and other low-acid foods. Pressure saucepans can be used for canning pint jars, if they are set to maintain 10 pounds pressure. Check the pan carefully to make sure it is functioning properly before investing time and energy in preparing food. Authorities recommend that when you are using a saucepan type pressure cooker you lengthen the processing time to $1^1/_2$ times the recommended amount of time. If you use a pressure canner that is old, take it in and have it checked to make sure it maintains 10 pounds pressure and all seals and rubber parts are in good shape. A hardware dealer can tell you where this can be done. Always follow the manufacturer's instructions carefully.

The kettle or canner should have a RACK on the bottom so the jars don't touch the area where the heat is entering the pan. Theoretically, the jars should not touch the sides or each other, but usually if they slide together nothing disastrous will happen.

Other utensils you will most likely need are:

- SHARP PARING KNIFE for peeling and cutting out bad spots
- BOWL OF WATER for rinsing hands during preparation so you don't drip sticky stuff all across the room
- CONTAINER FOR COMPOST (all the skins, scraps, etc.)
- LADLE or CUP for putting syrup or fruit in jars
- MEASURING CUPS
- PAN FOR SYRUP
- TABLE KNIFE with which to remove air bubbles (see below)
- HOT PADS (mitts are best)

Optional utensils include:

- FUNNEL to control spillage when putting food into jars
- TONGS for lifting jars out of hot water if the hot pack method is used
- JAR LIFTERS for lifting jars out of boiling water

(These are especially handy if your rack doesn't have handles; if you have neither you will have to ladle or suck the water out with a baster until there is enough room to easily and securely grasp jars.)

CANNING FRUIT: THE BOILING WATER BATH METHOD

It is a common fallacy that fruit not good enough for eating fresh is good enough to be preserved. Preserving can maintain flavor and texture but not improve it, so unless the fruit is excellent, don't bother canning it. Another common fallacy is that fruit to be canned should be slightly green. Slightly green fruit will maintain its shape better so it is prettier. However, it does not have full flavor, it may be tough and you will have to use more sweetener.

There are two basic methods for packing fruit for canning: hot pack and cold or raw pack. First we will describe the steps in each of the two methods. Following that will be a chart that shows which method is best to use for different types of fruit.

Hot Packing Fruit

1) Prepare a canning syrup of 2 parts liquid (water and/or juice) to 1 part honey, or all juice.

2) Cover fruit with syrup and bring to a boil.

3) Using a slotted spoon (one with holes in it), pack fruit into the jars hot.

Many authorities say that pricking whole, unpeeled fruit will prevent the fruit from bursting inside the jar, but we haven't found this always to be so. Follow processing instructions for hot or cold packed fruit. Processing times are given on the quick reference chart.

Cold Packing Fruit

1) Prepare syrup (directions follow) and keep warm.

2) Peel fruit if necessary (chart will give guidelines). Some fruits will need to be blanched in order to be peeled. To blanch fruit, bring a pan of water to a boil. Dip fruit in for 30 to 60 seconds; remove, and place in cold water. The fruit can be placed on a fork or in a basket or strainer for easy dipping. The skin will peel easily after the fruit has been blanched. Cut fruit in half and remove pit or core. Some fruits should be cut in smaller pieces (see chart).

3) Fill the jar with fruit, putting half of a piece of fruit, cut side down, in the middle of the bottom and then spiraling fruit around and up, overlapping, cut side down, putting as much fruit as possible into the jar, stopping 3/4 inch from the top.

Processing Instructions for Hot and Cold Packed Fruit

1) Fill with syrup to 1/4 inch from the top for pint jars, 1/2 inch from the top for quart jars, and 3/4 inch from the top for half gallon jars. (This is called "headspace.")

2) Take a wide blade table knife and insert through the middle of the fruit to the bottom of the jar. Twist slightly and tap jar gently. This expels air bubbles. Then put knife down between the jar and the fruit to any air bubbles so they are released up the knife.

3) Add more syrup if necessary to be the correct distance from the top.

4) With a moist, clean wash rag or paper towel, clean the lips of the jars. Any food remaining on the lip will prevent the jar from sealing.

5) Put on a new clean lid and screw band on firmly.

6) Put jars on a rack in a canning kettle 2/3 full of water. If you are using jars that are not mason canning jars, start out with warm water at this stage so the quick change in temperature will not break the jars. Otherwise use very hot water. If necessary, add water until it covers the jars by 1 inch. Heat water to boiling and then continue boiling for the time listed in the following chart. Start timing from the point when the water reaches a rolling boil, and the whole top is in bubbles.

7) After food has been processed, remove from the water bath. Let cool on a rack, away from drafts. Don't touch jars or lids until they have cooled or they may not seal.

Testing for Seal

When cold, test for seal. You can hear the seal by tapping it with a spoon when the jar is cold. A clear, ringing sound means a seal. You can also see the seal. If the lid is curved inward, the jar is sealed. You can feel the seal by pressing the center of the lid. If it is down and will not move, it is sealed. The bands can be removed after 24 hours. It is very important to determine whether the seal has been made. Unsealed jars will result in spoiled, perhaps dangerously contaminated food. If you do not have a seal, either use the food within a few days (store in refrigerator until used) or reprocess with a new lid. Reprocessing does cause the food to be overcooked and the quality is poorer.

CANNING SYRUPS

A syrup composed of liquid and sweetener is used on fruits that are canned. The liquid is needed for the jar to seal and the sweetening keeps the liquid from leeching out the flavor as plain water does.

One part honey to three parts water makes a nice, light canning syrup sweet enough, yet not too sweet for most fruits. For fruits that pack more densely in jars (such as peaches), a sweeter syrup can be used, as sweet as equal parts water and honey.

Syrups used can also be spiced with orange or lemon peel chunks, cinnamon or other sweet spices. Use about 1 t ground spice per quart of canning syrup. Whole spices may be used by placing them in each jar with the fruit or simmering them in the syrup and removing them before using it. The flavor will be fuller if the spice is in the jar with the fruit. A small stick of cinnamon or 2 or 3 cloves is about right for a quart jar.

Any sweetener can be used. Honey is mentioned most here, but sorghum, molasses, etc., can be used, with each resulting in a different flavor.

The water in a canning syrup can be replaced with fruit juice either from the fruit being canned (e.g., blackberries canned in blackberry juice) or some other fruit (peaches canned in plum juice, cherries canned in apple juice). The syrup is made the same way as with water. Fruit can be canned without sweetener, if you use fruit juice.

Don't throw away leftover canning syrup. It can be refrigerated until you can again or canned with your last batch for the day, and saved until it is needed.

Procedure for Making Syrup

Combine liquid, honey and spices in a pan large enough for the honey to foam up some. Bring to a simmer and keep hot all the time you are canning with it.

INSTRUCTIONS FOR INDIVIDUAL FRUITS

It is generally advisable (especially with the cost of canning jars and lids) to get as much food into a jar as possible. Therefore, in the instructions for canning fruit that follow, some fruits are recommended for hot packing and some for raw or cold packing because these are the ways we have found most effective in packing large amounts of that particular fruit in the containers.

Tomato Juice

Preparation time: 45-60 minutes
Processing time: 10-15 minutes
Yields: 6 pints

9 pounds tomatoes or 20 C chopped tomatoes
1 T lemon juice
1/4 t salt per pint

Cook tomatoes until soft, stirring frequently to prevent them from sticking. Put through food mill. Return 12 C tomatoes to kettle and bring to a boil. Add 1 T lemon juice. Pour into jars, leaving 1/2 inch headspace. Add 1/4 t salt to pints, 1/2 t to quarts.

Process pints 10 minutes, quarts 15 minutes in boiling water bath.

NOTE: 1/2 t lemon juice per pint helps insure that the low-acid tomatoes which are popular these days will be acid enough to be safe.

Green Tomato Mincemeat

Preparation time: about 2¹/₂ hous
Processing time: 10 minutes
Yields: about 6 pints

**3 pounds green tomatoes (may be firm
    tomatoes)**
1 lime, peeled
1 orange, peeled
2 C (packed) date sugar
1¹/₂ C raisins
1/2 t salt
1 t cinnamon
1/2 t cloves
1/4 t allspice
1/4 t ginger
1/2 t nutmeg

Grind tomatoes, lime and orange with
medium blade of food grinder. Pour mixture
into a 4 quart pan. Stir remaining ingredients
in and heat mixture to boiling. Reduce heat.
Simmer uncovered over low heat, stirring
occasionally, for 1¹/₂ hours. Fill jars, leaving
1 inch at top. Process 10 minutes.

Sweet Pickled Figs

Preparation time: 1 hour, over a period of 4
    days
Processing time: 10 minutes
Yields: about 6 half pints

fresh figs (about 70)
1 gallon water
small handful salt
2 C vinegar
4 C water
12 C honey
**spice bag containing 2 small boxes
    broken stick cinnamon and 2/3 C
    whole cloves**
sterile jars

Wash figs and leave stems on. Make a brine
of one gallon water and the salt. Put as many
figs in as will still be covered. Let stand
overnight and wash next morning. Boil
together 2 C vinegar, 4 C water, 12 C honey
and the spice bag. Put figs in and boil 15
minutes. Set aside and repeat boiling for 3

mornings. Move the spice bag around each
morning. On the 4th morning, bring to a boil
and can in hot sterile jars. If you don't have
enough syrup to cover figs, add some boiling
water to last few jars.

PRESSURE CANNING

Here are the basic instructions for canning a
few recipes from this book. (Be sure to
become familiar with the procedures for
water bath canning, because that knowledge
is assumed here.)

Canning is not usually the best way to
preserve vegetables. Better tasting results can
be obtained when the vegetables are dried or
frozen (instructions later in this section).
Detailed information about canning
vegetables can be found in several of the
books and pamphlets listed in the
bibliography of this section.

Spaghetti Sauce

Follow recipe in this cookbook. Fill pint
canning jars 1/2 inch from the top with the
hot mixture. Clean lips, put on lids and
bands. Set in the pressure canner on the
rack. Fill with water 3/4 of the way up the
sides of the jars. When pressure builds up to
10 pounds, maintain the pressure and
process for 45 minutes. Let the pressure go
down slowly and remove jars when it is
down. Check for seal when cool. Cook for 20
minutes or more at a boil or 30 minutes or
more in the oven before using, in case of
contamination resulting from poor canning
procedures, or a lack of a good seal. Be sure
to read the information on CANNING
EQUIPMENT in this section.

Boston Brown Bread

Fill pint jars 1/2 full with raw batter. Process
1 hour at 10 pounds. Use wide-mouthed,
tapered jars.

JAMS AND JELLIES

(See also: QUICK REFERENCE CHART FOR
WATER BATH CANNING, p.237)

Honey

When using honey in jams and jellies: (1) use
a large kettle because honey tends to foam;
(2) cook slightly longer than called for in
sugar recipes to compensate for the extra
moisture in honey, if you want the same
consistency.

Pectin

Pectin is what causes the jelly or jam to jell.
There is relatively more pectin in unripe fruit
than in ripe fruit. It is concentrated right
under the peel. You can test fruit juice to see
how much pectin it contains by adding 1 t of
cooked fruit juice to 1 T of rubbing alcohol
(70% alcohol). Stir slightly to mix, but don't
taste! Juice rich in pectin will form a jelly-like
mass that can be picked out. Juices low in
pectin will form only a few pieces of this
material. If the juice is low in pectin, add
commercial pectin or mix with another juice
high in pectin (see, for example, the use of
apple peels in GRAPE APPLE JELLY.) If you
want to guess how much commercial pectin
is needed, measure pectin into 1 C fruit and
mix well until your alcohol test is positive,
then add corresponding amounts to the rest
of the juice or fruit.

Canning Jam

Use half pint jars or other small jars which
have a rim the size of a mason lid and ring.
Boil your jars and lids for 5 minutes. Remove
them from the boiling water when your jam
or jelly is bubbling hot and completely
cooked. As you remove each jar, immediately
ladle the boiling jam into it, filling it to 1/4
inch from the top with the hot jam (be
careful that you don't burn yourself). Slide a
butter knife between the jar and jam to help
any air bubbles escape. Wipe rim clean,
place hot lid on top and screw on band.

Place filled jars on a rack in a canning kettle
half filled with hot water. Add boiling water
to cover jars with an inch of water. Cover
kettle. For half pints and pints, process 10
minutes after water boils. Remove jars and
cool in a draft free place without moving.

Paraffin Sealing (Jams)

If you do not have small canning jars to use,
jam can be sealed with paraffin. Follow the
procedure outlined above to the point where
the canning lid is put on the jar. At this point,
pour on a thin layer of melted but not too
hot paraffin. When cool and starting to turn
hard, add another thin layer. Make certain
both layers go from edge to edge and cover
the entire top of the jam. Do not move them
until they are very cool. Store the jars in a
cool, dark, dry place. If the jars have to travel
a lot, for example in the mail for presents or
if you move, do not use this method. This
method works very well for small amounts of
jam which will be used within a year. If only
a spot of mold appears on the top of a jar of
jam, it can be removed and the jam eaten.
However if the wax has completely broken
and the jam is covered in mold, it should be
discarded.

Testing For Jell Point

You can test for the jell point by dipping a
spoon in the jelly and watching how the
liquid runs off. As the liquid reaches the
jelling point it will first slide off in two drops,
then as it gets just right, the drops will run
together and run off in a flake or sheet from
the side of the spoon. Remove the jelly from
the heat at once. Another way is to put a
little of the jelly on a plate and put it in the
refrigerator. If it jells in a few minutes it is
done. You must remove the jelly from the
heat while doing this so you don't overcook
it. If it doesn't jell, reheat the jelly until a test
is positive.

Grape Apple Jelly

Preparation time: 3 to 8 hours
Processing time: 10 minutes
Yields: varies

apple peels and cores
grape juice
honey

Fill a pan with apple peelings and cores, preferably from cooking apples (green transparents or not-very-ripe apples). Add grape juice until you can barely see it through the apples. Cook slowly until apples are very soft. Place in a pillow case or muslin bag and let the juice drip out. Squeeze out the last juice (the more you get out, the higher the jelling ability of the mixture, but it causes cloudiness in the jelly). Measure the juice and add 1 C honey for every 4 C juice. Cook very slowly until it slakes off the spoon (see TESTING FOR JELL POINT). This may take all day. When cooked, pour into sterilized jars to within 1/4 inch from the top. Put on lids, screw bands firmly tight, and process in boiling water bath for 10 minutes.

Pear Apple Jam

Preparation time: 3 hours plus overnight
Processing time: 10 minutes
Yields: 6 half pints

4 C peeled diced pears
4 C peeled diced apples
4 C honey
5 t lemon juice
grated rind of one lemon

Mix all ingredients thoroughly and bring to a boil. Boil, stirring often, for 30 minutes. Remove from heat and let stand a couple hours or overnight to plump fruit. Bring back to a boil, turn down heat to simmer. Simmer until thick—about 1 hour. Pour into hot sterilized jars to 1/4 inch from the top. Wipe rims clean. Put on lids and screw bands firmly tight. Process in boiling water bath for 10 minutes.

Cherry Jam

Preparation time: 45 to 60 minutes
Processing time: 10 minutes
Yields: 5 half pints

$3^1/_2$ pounds Royal Anne cherries, pitted
($7^1/_3$ C pitted cherries)
$1^1/_2$ C honey

Grind the cherries and juice in a food mill with a large or medium blade. Add honey (the amount could vary according to sweetness of cherries). Cook at low boil or simmer until thick, stirring occasionally to prevent sticking. Remember it will appear less thick when hot than when cool. Try setting a little saucer of it in the freezer or refrigerator to test (see TESTING FOR JELL POINT). When cooked enough, remove from heat and let the foam form. Skim it off. Pour into jars, to within 1/4 inch from the top. Clean rims. Put on lids and screw bands firmly tight. Process in boiling water bath for 10 minutes.

Orange Marmalade

Preparation time: 3 hours plus overnight
Processing time: 10 minutes
Yields: about 6 to 8 pints

4 C orange peel, sliced thinly
4 C orange pulp, cut in chunks
1 C lemon, sliced thinly, seeds removed
$4^3/_4$ C water
1/4 t salt
honey (3/4 C for each C fruit mixture)

Add water to fruit. Bring to a boil and simmer for 5 minutes. Cover and let stand 12 to 16 hours. Bring to a boil and cook rapidly until peel is tender (about 1 hour). Measure fruit mixture and add salt and 3/4 C honey for each cup fruit mixture. Cook rapidly until the jelling point is reached (221° F). Stir frequently to prevent sticking. Pour into hot sterilized jars to within 1/4 inch of the top. Clean rims. Put on lids and screw bands firmly tight. Process in boiling water bath for 10 minutes.

Pear Conserve

Preparation time: about 1½ hours
Processing time: 10 minutes
Yields: about 6 pints

15 chunked, peeled and cored pears (5-10 pounds whole)
4 to 5 C honey (depends on sweetness of pears and how sweet you like your jam)
2 to 2½ C raisins
1/4 C dried orange rind or about 1/2 C fresh, cut fine
1/2 C orange juice
1/4 C lemon juice

Mix all ingredients. Bring to a boil. Lower heat and simmer until thick and pears are cooked, but not completely mushy. Stir frequently as raisins stick to bottom. Pour into hot sterilized jars to within 1/4 inch of the top. Wipe off rim and place on lids and screw bands firmly tight. Process in boiling water bath 10 minutes.

Blackberry Jam

Preparation time: about 1 hour
Processing time: 10 minutes
Yields: about 6 pints

8 C blackberries, cooked and smashed
4 C honey
1/4 C pectin

Bring to boil (which won't stir down) and boil for 4 minutes. Pour into hot sterilized jars. Process in a boiling water bath for 10 minutes.

Spiced Apple Butter

Preparation time: about 2 hours
Processing time: 10 minutes
Yields: 4 pints

Follow the recipe for SPICED PEAR BUTTER, using 6 pounds (about 12 apples) and add 1/2 C orange or apple juice.

Spiced Pear Butter

Preparation time: about 2 hours
Processing time: 10 minutes
Yields: 4 pints

6 pounds firm ripe d'Anjou or Bosc pears (about 12 large pears)
1/4 C lemon juice
1½ t ground cinnamon
1/4 t ground cloves
3½ C honey

Wash, quarter, and core, but do not peel pears. In a 6 quart or larger pan combine pears, water, and lemon juice; cover and simmer until fruit is soft, 20 to 30 minutes. Whirl mixture in a blender (a small portion at a time) or puree in a food mill. Return to pan and add the cinnamon, cloves, and honey. Simmer, uncovered, stirring more frequently as the mixture thickens, until mixture is very thick and reduced to about 8 C—it takes about 1½ hours. When cooked, pour into sterilized jars to within 1/4 inch of the tops. Clean rims. Put on lids and screw bands firmly tight. Process in a boiling water bath for 10 minutes.

Cranberry Conserve

Preparation time: about 1 hour
Processing time: 10 minutes
Yields: 3½ pints

1 quart cranberries
1 orange
1 C raisins
1 C honey
1 C chopped nuts
1 t cinnamon
1/2 t cloves
1/2 t allspice

Wash cranberries. Cover with water and cook until tender. Then press through a sieve. Peel orange and put peel through food chopper. Dice peeled orange. Mix cranberries, chopped raisins, orange, orange peel and spices together and cook slowly for 10 minutes. Add honey and simmer very gently until thick. Add nuts to mixture a few minutes before cooking is complete. Pour into sterilized jars to within 1/4 inch of the tops. Put on screw bands firmly tight. Process in boiling water bath for 10 minutes.

QUICK REFERENCE CHART: WATER BATH CANNING

Food	Amt. which fits in qt. jar	Method	Processing Time (mins.)		Recommended Procedures
Apples	2¹/₂-3 pounds	hot pack in apple juice	pints: qts.	15 15	Peel, cut into fourths, core, bring to boil in apple juice for 3 mins., add cinnamon and other spices, if desired.
Applesauce	4 C	hot pack	both	10	
Apricots	2¹/₂ pounds	raw (cold) pack	pints: qts:	25 30	Pack unpeeled, but pitted.
Berries (not strawberries)	2-4 pints	raw pack	pints: qts:	10 15	
Cherries	2-3 pounds	hot pack	both	15	NOTE: Royal Anne cherries are best for canning. Bing cherries tend to have a tough skin when cooked.
Nectarines and Peaches	2-3 pounds	raw pack	Cling, pints: qts: Freestone, pints: qts:	25 30 20 25	Blanch, remove peel, pit: orange peel chunks and cinnamon may be added.
Pears	2-3¹/₂ pounds	raw pack	pints: qts:	20 25	Peel and core. 1¹/₂ t ginger per quart of canning liquid or very strong peppermint tea can be used.
Plums	2-2¹/₂ pounds	hot pack	both	15	
Prunes	2-2¹/₂ pounds	hot pack	both	15	
Rhubarb	1-2 pounds	hot pack	both	10	Cut in 1/2 inch lengths, add 1/2 C honey to each quart. Let stand 3-4 hours to draw out the juice. Bring to boil. The best rhubarb is picked in the spring.
Tomatoes	2¹/₂-3¹/₂ pounds	hot pack	both	15	Blanch, peel, bring to a boil. No syrup. To each quart add 1 t salt and 2 t lemon juice (lemon juice and hot packing are important to prevent botulism).
Tomato sauce	Use pint jars	hot pack		15	Prepare according to recipes in this book. Add 1 t salt and 2 t lemon juice per quart.
Tomato paste	Use half pints and pints only	hot pack		30	

FREEZING

Frozen fruits and vegetables taste better and are more nutritious than canned food. However, one needs to be aware of the cost of freezing food. First, there is the initial investment in the freezer, and secondly, there is the cost of running it all year round. The food can easily be ruined if the electrical power goes out for any period of time. A small refrigerator-freezer is practical only for freezing small amounts of things for a short time. It is handy to use for prepared casseroles, baked goodies, etc.

General Tips

• Freeze in amounts that are easy to use. Smaller portions defrost faster, and waste is reduced by thawing only the amount you can use right away.

• Freeze food immediately: don't store in refrigerator first.

• Package food in airtight, moisture-proof packages to prevent flavor and moisture loss and the transference of flavors, but leave room for expansion of food during freezing.

• Date packages and label: freezing will disguise the contents.

• Don't refreeze food, since you will lose nutrients and there is a chance of bacterial infection.

• Plastic bags inside washed milk cartons make good freezing containers if the bags are tightly sealed. Jars must flare towards the top or they will crack when the food expands during freezing.

• COOKIES and BREADS can be frozen in plastic bags after they have cooled. Don't keep baked goods over 6 months in the freezer. All prepared foods (except pies) should be thawed at room temperature in their airtight containers to prevent drying out.

• CORN can be frozen on the cob by either husking and putting in sealed plastic bags, or leaving the husk on and freezing.

• There are 4 steps in freezing vegetables: (1) blanching, (2) cooling, (3) drying and packaging, (4) excluding air from the package and freezing.

• To BLANCH, prepare the fruit or vegetable (cleaning and cutting), place in a colander or strainer and dip into a pan of rapidly boiling water for 1 to 2 minutes to kill the enzymes and bacteria. Remove from water and dip into cold water to cool it off quickly. DRAIN or DRY on cloth, or in a colander. Package into plastic bags or containers. Some people with very cold freezers like to spread the food out on cookie sheets to freeze (so that each piece of vegetable freezes individually), and then package them the next day. When packaging, get rid of as much air as possible, and SEAL TIGHTLY.

Frozen Foods

HERBS can be frozen to be used in cooking later. Examples are parsley and chopped green pepper. Try small amounts of others and see how they freeze for you. Use within 6 months.

PREPARED FOODS can be cooked in larger amounts than needed and then frozen for a quick meal or snack later. It is recommended that prepared foods be used in 2 to 4 months after freezing. After cooking or baking, let food cool to room temperature. Package in airtight container, leaving headspace for expansion.

PIES are best frozen raw. Bake without thawing for 15 to 20 minutes in a pre-heated 450° oven and then at 375° until done. Pack pizzas on cardboard covered with wax paper and place in a tightly sealed plastic bag.

CASSEROLES such as EGGPLANT PARMESAN and LASAGNA are best frozen in the container they were baked in and reheated in that container.

DRYING FOODS

There are several methods for drying fruits and vegetables which apply best to certain kinds of produce and give varying products afterwards. We will quickly go through different ways to dry foods. You can adjust these to your own produce, climate and needs. More information is available in other resources (books, pamphlets and magazines) which will be of help to you if you want to pursue drying foods.

Fruits and vegetables which are to be dried should be in good condition. The blemishes need to be cut out. Fruit should be ripe, but not overripe. Wash and dry the produce. Figs, grapes, prunes, plums and very small vegetables can be dried whole; others should be pitted (if applicable) and cut into pieces. Very juicy fruits need to be cut into small pieces; apples, pears and peaches need to be quartered or sliced. The fruit or vegetables can be layered one layer deep, with the cut side up, not touching, on a double screened drying tray to let air in and keep insects out. Take trays indoors at night. Solar dryers are available and can speed up the process. Make a simple one by elevating a piece of glass over the drying food at an angle to catch the sun.

Food can be dried in the oven if it is set at the lowest possible temperature. Turn the oven off occasionally so it cools some, and shift racks around. Temperature should be less than 110°.

Certain foods dry better when hung on a string. One example is peppers, which can be cut into circlets and strung up. "Leather britches" are green beans which have been strung up with a needle and thread, looking like a clothesline of britches when you are done. Herbs are best dried by hanging bunches of leaves and stalks upside down (so the flavor doesn't concentrate in the stems, but goes into the leaves). Apples can be cored and sliced in circles and strung up through the hole left when the core was removed.

Foods like honey, sugar, salt and vinegar have long been used as preservatives, since bacteria do not grow well in them. The DRIED HONEYED FIG and FRUIT GLACE' recipes included in this section can be used with other foods also.

Fruit Leather

Preparation time: 6-8 hours
Processing time: 2½ -24 hours
Yields: 5-6 pounds

4 C very ripe fruit (apricots are great)
1/4 C lemon juice
1/4 to 1/2 C honey (amount needed
   depends on the sweetness of the fruit)

Mix the fruit with the lemon juice and honey and puree in a blender, food processor, or food grinder. Cover dehydrator trays with cut open plastic bags or plastic wrap. Pour 3/4 C of the puree on each tray and spread out until equally thick throughout the tray. Repeat for the other trays. Dehydrate on high until almost crisp. It will be crisp around the edges. The length of time depends upon the moisture content of the fruit and the heat of the dehydrator. Cut each tray of fruit leather into 4 equal pieces and roll up. Makes 24 pieces of fruit leather.

NOTE: If you don't have a dehydrator, small cookie sheets can be used. Cover them with plastic and proceed as in the recipe. Set the sheets on a level surface in the sun, covered with a screen to keep out insects, or dry in an oven heated to 150°. If using an oven, leave the oven door slightly ajar to let out moisture.

Dried Honeyed Figs

Preparation time:12 to 14 hours
Yields: 10 pounds

10 pounds firm, ripe figs
water
1/4 C salt
7 C honey

Soak figs in water 4 hours with salt. Wash
and drain. Lay greenest on bottom of large
pan, cover pan and simmer on lowest heat 1
hour or until figs are half covered in their
own juice. Add honey and simmer until
dissolved. Turn off heat, cool to lukewarm,
bring back to simmer about 5 times, cooling
in between. Cook at low temperature with a
cover until translucent and skin is tender.
Drain and put on 2 or 3 large pans (such as
cookie sheets) and dry in oven set at lowest
possible temperature or dehydration. Dry
until dry on outside (about $2^1/_4$ hours). The
oven door should be left ajar. Do not leave
too moist or they will mold later. Put in jars
with lids.

VARIATIONS: use other fruits. Bring to
simmer only a couple of times.

Fruit Glacé
(Candied or Glazed Fruit)

Preparation time: 1 hour
Processing time: 10 minutes
Yields: 4-5 C

1 C honey
1/2 C water
4-5 C citrus peel, dried apricots or other
    dried fruit

Combine honey and water in a saucepan and
bring to a boil. Add fruit and cook in syrup,
turning frequently until tender and
translucent. Remove fruit and drain. The fruit
can be used immediately or processed in a
boiling water bath for 10 minutes.

The fruit may be cherries, pineapple chunks,
orange and lemon peel, or apple chunks.
Fruit is used in the same way as commercial
candied fruit (example: in fruitcake).

Canning and Preserving
References

Ball Blue Book. Ball Corporation, Dept.
PK2A Box 2995, Muncie, Indiana 47302.

Kerr Home Canning and Freezing Book.
Kerr Glass Mfg. Corp. Consumer Products
Division, Sand Springs, OK 74063.

Stocking Up. Edited by Carol Stoner, Rodale
Press (Organic Gardening and Farming staff).
The recipes don't use sugar. This is by far the
best book we've run across on canning. It
does, unfortunately, include information on
meat.

CONVERSIONS AND EQUIVALENTS

VOLUME EQUIVALENTS

1 Tablespoon = 3 teaspoons
48 teaspoons = 16 Tablespoons = 1 cup=
  8 fluid ounces
2 cups = 1 pint
2 pints = 1 quart
16 cups = 4 quarts = 1 gallon

WEIGHT EQUIVALENTS

16 avoirdupois (av.) ounces = 1 pound
1 avoirdupois ounce = 28 grams

WATER MEASUREMENT EQUIVALENTS

8 fluid ounces = 8 av. ounces
1 pint = 1 pound

TEMPERATURE EQUIVALENTS

Water boils at 212°F, 100°C
Water freezes at 32°F, 0°C

MEASUREMENT ABBREVIATIONS

t = teaspoon
T = tablespoon
C = cup
Pt. = pint
Qt. = quart
Gal. = gallon
fl. oz. = fluid ounce
av. oz. = avoirdupois ounce (1/16 pound)
gm. = grams
mg. = milligrams

INGREDIENT EQUIVALENTS

$3^1/_2$ pounds ALMONDS in shell = 1 pound
  shelled

1 pound unpared APPLES = 3 cups pared

$5^1/_2$ pounds fresh APRICOTS = 1 pound dried

3 cups DRIED APRICOTS = 1 pound

2 t ARROWROOT = 1 T cornstarch or 4 t flour

1 t BAKING POWDER = 1/4 t BAKING SODA
  plus 5/8 t cream of tartar

3-4 medium sized BANANAS = 1 pound or $1^3/_4$ C
  mashed

1 stick BUTTER = 1/4 pound = 4 ounces = 1/2 C

1 C BUTTERMILK = 1 C YOGURT

3 T CAROB POWDER plus 3 T liquid =
  1 ounce CHOCOLATE

1 C HONEY = $1^1/_4$ C sugar plus 1/4 C liquid

juice of 1 LEMON = about 3 T

grated peel of 1 LEMON = 1 t

1 pound fresh RHUBARB = 2 C cooked

1 pound (6 cups) RAW ROLLED OATS = 8 C
  cooked

1 C SUGAR = 1 C honey with 1/4 C less liquid
  in recipe

2 C TOMATO SAUCE = 3/4 C TOMATO PASTE
  plus 1 C water

1 pound WALNUTS in the shell = $1^1/_2$ C shelled

1 cake compressed BAKING YEAST = 2 T
(packages) dry yeast

1 pound or $2^1/_4$ C LENTILS = 5 C cooked

1/2 C MAPLE SUGAR = 1 C maple syrup

1 C whole MILK = 1/2 C evaporated plus
  1/2 C water = 1 C NUT MILK = 1 C other liquid
  when called for in baking

1 large GREEN PEPPER (about 6 ounces) =
  1 C diced

3 medium sized POTATOES (about 1 pound) =
  $2^1/_4$ C cooked or $1^2/_3$ C mashed potatoes

ABOUT THE AUTHORS

Joy McClure

Joy has two teenaged children, Josh and Wynona. Besides being a mother, she is a licensed clinical social worker with a Masters degree in Social Work. She works full time as a school social worker in two elementary schools. In addition, she has a part time private psychotherapy practice, she teaches foster parenting classes and frequently does training. She works as a volunteer in child abuse prevention community organizations and events. In her free time she is an avid reader and enjoys needlework, pottery, other crafts and gardening.

Joy lives on five acres near the little town of Mariposa in the Sierra Nevadas outside Yosemite National Park in California. She enjoys the peaceful quietness of the mountains and doubts she will ever again live in a city or town. Joy's mom taught her how to bake and follow a recipe. Many summers they canned fruit in tin cans at a do-it-yourself cannery. They froze peas and corn each summer and baked their own bread and most other baked goods. Joy began cooking meals her senior year of high school after her mother died and she and her father lived alone.

Joy became a vegetarian at 19 and began writing her recipes down when people started asking her how she had made the dishes she took to potluck dinners. Her interest and knowledge of natural foods grew in the years she spent working in the retail natural foods business. Now she enjoys cooking and trying new foods and recipes when she has the time.

Kendall Layne

Kendall Layne was born in Palo Alto, California and first became involved in natural foods retailing and cooking there in 1970. He worked with Joy McClure and others over the years in non-profit natural foods stores and wholesale operations in the Santa Cruz area. Frustration with local government regulation of those businesses and a little prodding from his parents led him to Stanford School of Law, where he graduated in 1981. Since then, he has been a practicing civil trial attorney in the San Francisco Bay area. Whenever circumstances permit, he can be found skiing the steep and deep slopes at Squaw Valley and other Lake Tahoe resorts. A private pilot, roller-blader, neophyte scuba diver, amateur photographer and musician, he is also the proud father of two sons, Joshua and Tyler.

Sons Josh and Ty share Kendall's fascination with computers to some extent, but he is (by his own admission) the member of the family most immersed in computer technology. He is in the process of learning how to manage a local area network of computers at work, and now that the work on the new revised edition of *Cooking for Consciousness* is complete, he hopes to continue work on a semi-fictional account of life in the San Francisco Bay area, titled *Vista del Diablo*. He lives in Concord, California with his second wife Susan Elwood, their son Tyler, and Tyler's golden retriever, Ginger.

INDEX

A

THE VEGETARIAN LUNCHBASKET

225 easy, nutritious recipes for the quality-conscious family on the go

by Linda Haynes $12.00

Linda Haynes, an experienced cook and mother of three vegetarian kids, writes with warmth and humor. Her recipes are easy to follow, fun to make, and beautiful to behold! Whether you are a vegetarian or not, these recipes can add zest and sparkle to your everyday fare. Try new ways of packing lunches, using leftovers, and combining foods. Use alternatives to meat and eggs, thus lowering fats and cholesterol without robbing yourself of taste and variety. Best of all, these healthy alternatives are delicious!

FOOD FOR THOUGHT

The Vegetarian Philosophy

by Ananda Mitra $7.00

This is an excellent resource for beginning and established vegetarians. It shows where to find the nutrients that compose a balanced, healthy vegetarian diet. It covers proteins, vitamins and minerals one by one, and points out which foods are good sources of each. There are chapters on protein combining, dietary suggestions for specific ailments, and fasting. Includes extensive tables of the nutritional composition of all the basic foods.

SOME STILL WANT THE MOON

A Woman's Introduction to Tantra Yoga

by Vimala McClure $9.95

A gentle introduction for women to a path in which all life is spiritualized. Included are chapters on yoga practices and the philosophy on which they are based. The author simply and clearly explains the universal outlook of Tantra Yoga, and shows the relationship between body, mind, and spirit. Covered are topics such as kundalini, the cakras, yoga's creation theory, karma, psychic development, yoga postures, beauty secrets of the yogis, meditation, mental outlook, ethics, and family life. Beautifully illustrated with a complete set of exercises.

THE ETHICS OF LOVE

Using Yoga's Timeless Wisdom to Heal Yourself, Others and the Earth

by Vimala McClure $9.00

The Ethics of Love gives you a unique blend of Eastern wisdom and up-to-date Western psychology. The author examines yoga's age-old ethical precepts concerning: Kindness, Honesty, Responsibility, Simplicity, Unity, Clarity, Acceptance, Sacrifice, Broad-mindedness, and Spirituality. As in *The Tao of Motherhood, Some Still Want the Moon*, and *Infant Massage*, the author has used her gift for expressing complex issues in simple, human terms to help people heal themselves.

  "The best part of this book is the feeling of great kindness and good humor that radiates from the pages. There is no pretension here. This is a lovely book about making peace with yourself and your family."—Pat Wagner,The Bloomsbury Review

THE TAO OF MOTHERHOOD

by Vimala McClure $10.95

Chinese philosopher Lao Tzu's timeless *Tao te Ching* is adapted to inspire parents . A long-awaited follow-up to her classic *Infant Massage: a Handbook for Loving Parents, The Tao of Motherhood* takes the idea of parenting-as-art much further. The book's short passages make it accessible; its elegance makes it the perfect gift book for any parent—at any age.

"A quick fix of deep wisdom!"—Peggy O'Mara, Editor, *Mothering Magazine*